Responding to Populist Parties in Europe

Responding to Populist Parties in Europe

The 'Other People' vs the 'Populist People'

Angela K. Bourne

Great Clarendon Street, Oxford, OX2 6DP,
United Kingdom

Oxford University Press is a department of the University of Oxford.
It furthers the University's objective of excellence in research, scholarship,
and education by publishing worldwide. Oxford is a registered trade mark of
Oxford University Press in the UK and in certain other countries

© Angela K. Bourne 2023

The moral rights of the author have been asserted

All rights reserved. No part of this publication may be reproduced, stored in
a retrieval system, or transmitted, in any form or by any means, without the
prior permission in writing of Oxford University Press, or as expressly permitted
by law, by licence or under terms agreed with the appropriate reprographics
rights organization. Enquiries concerning reproduction outside the scope of the
above should be sent to the Rights Department, Oxford University Press, at the
address above

You must not circulate this work in any other form
and you must impose this same condition on any acquirer

Published in the United States of America by Oxford University Press
198 Madison Avenue, New York, NY 10016, United States of America

British Library Cataloguing in Publication Data

Data available

Library of Congress Control Number: 2023945525

ISBN 9780198892588

DOI: 10.1093/oso/9780198892588.001.0001

Printed and bound by
CPI Group (UK) Ltd, Croydon, CR0 4YY

Links to third party websites are provided by Oxford in good faith and
for information only. Oxford disclaims any responsibility for the materials
contained in any third party website referenced in this work.

To my son, Samuel

Acknowledgements

I was able to write this book thanks to the Carlsberg Foundation, which awarded me a one-year Monograph Fellowship (CF19-0258). This gave me the space to think through many of the ideas I explore in the book, a much more challenging task when combined with the usual daily routines of academic life.

I am indebted to many people who have helped me with ideas, inspiration, and fact-finding. These include Francesco Campo and Mathias Holst Nicolaisen, PhD fellows at Roskilde University, with whom I worked almost daily collecting information about opposition to populist parties and thinking through many of the concepts and categories used in this book. My colleagues from the Carlsberg Foundation's *Challenge for Europe* project (CF20-008) have sharpened my thinking, agreed, and disagreed with me on many points in this book and I am grateful to them for their engagement. These include Aleksandra Moroska-Bonkiewicz, Bénédicte Laumond, Franciszek Tyszka, Katarzyna Domagała, Tore Vincents Olsen, Anthoula Malkopoulou, Juha Tuovinen, and others. I have had invaluable help collecting data from Christof Schaefer, Filippo Faraotti, Iacopo Taddia, and Guillermo Arranz Sánchez.

Contents

List of Figures	xiii
List of Tables	xv
Abbreviations	xvii

Introduction: Opposing Populist Parties in Europe — 1
- The 'other people' vs the 'populist people' — 1
- Beyond 'militant democracy' — 5
- Democratic defence as 'normal politics' — 10
  - Who opposes populist parties and how do they do it? — 11
  - What does opposition to populist parties achieve? — 11
  - Tools for achieving goals — 15
  - Working out what works — 18

1. Muddy Waters: Populism and Democratic Defence — 21
- What Is Populism? — 22
- The Power of Populist Appeals — 25
- Populism and Democracy: Threat or Corrective? — 32
- Populism, 'Democratic Backsliding', and Competitive Authoritarianism — 35

2. Mapping Initiatives Opposing Populist Parties in Europe — 43
- Populist Opponents: Public Authorities, Parties, and Civil Society — 47
- Tolerant and Intolerant Modes of Engagement with Populists — 49
- Intolerant Initiatives Opposing Populist Parties — 52
  - Rights restrictions by public authorities — 53
  - Ostracism by other political parties — 55
  - Coercive confrontation by civil society actors — 56
- Tolerant Initiatives Opposing Populist Parties — 58
  - 'Ordinary' legal controls and pedagogy by public authorities — 58
  - Forbearance by political parties — 60
  - Adversarialism by civil society actors — 62
- Initiatives and National Patterns of Opposition to Populist Parties — 64

3. Manipulation of Voter and Party Choice — 69
- How IoPPs Work by Manipulating Strategic Incentives — 70
  - Winning and losing votes — 70
  - Moderation and radicalization — 72
  - Boosting and diminishing party resources — 75
- The Mixed Blessings of Ostracism — 76
- Policy Cooptation and the 'Original' versus the 'Copy' — 82
- Populists in Government as the 'New Normal' — 85

4. Enforcement through the Constitution, Courts, and Coercion — 99
    How IoPPs Work through Coercion and Institutional Constraint — 100
        Political opportunity structures and constrained democracy — 100
        Repression and its effect on resources, votes, and moderation — 104
        Compliance with international and supranational law — 108
    Checking Populists in the Executive — 112
    Repressive IoPPs: Rights Restrictions and Trouble in the Courts — 115
    European Supranational Courts and the Empowerment of Domestic Oppositions — 124

5. Leverage, International Sanctions, and Disruption — 137
    How IoPPs Work through Leverage — 138
        International sanctions and political conditionality — 138
        Political disruption as social leverage — 144
    EU Voting and Financial Sanctions — 146
    Upheaval and Tumult in the Public Sphere — 159

6. Persuasion, Talk, and New Ideas — 165
    How IoPPs Work through Persuasion — 166
        Framing and stigmatization — 166
        Shaming and negotiations abroad — 172
    Defending Democracy, the Anti-Populist Frame, and Demonization — 177
    EU Dialogue on the Rule of Law — 186

Conclusion: A 'Bottom-Up' Theory of Effective Opposition to Populist Parties — 195
    What is an 'Effective' Initiative Opposing Populist Parties? — 196
    From Initiatives to Goals — 198
        Curb implementation of anti-democratic or illiberal policies by populists in government — 199
        Reduce support for populist parties — 200
        Diminish populist party resources — 202
        Induce moderation — 203
    From Initiatives to Perverse Effects — 204
        Increase support for populist parties — 204
        Boost populist party resources — 205
        Induce radicalization — 206
    Effective Opposition as Achieving Goals without Perverse Effects — 207
    Practical Applications and Future Research — 211

APPENDICES

Appendix I: Quality of Democracy Scores (V-Dem) for Governments Led by Populist Parties in Europe (2000–2020)   *217*

Appendix II: Moderation and Radicalization of Populist Party Ideological Positions   *221*

Appendix III: Selected European Court of Human Rights Rulings against Fidesz (2010–2021) and Law and Justice (2015–2021)   *223*

Appendix IV: Selected EU Infringement Rulings on Values-Related Cases against Poland and Hungary (2012–2021)   *227*

References	231
Books and Articles	231
Official Documents	248
List of Cases	249
Newspaper Articles and Internet Publications	250
Index	253

List of Figures

0.1.	Effective opposition to populist parties.	19
1.1.	'Degrees of populism' for major European populist parties in 2018 (POPPA dataset).	31
1.2.	Electoral democracy and liberalism scores for EU states (V-Dem).	38
1.3.	Quality of democracy for governments led by populist parties in Europe (2000–2020).	39
2.1.	Typology of initiatives opposing populist parties (IoPPs).	47
2.2.	Actors opposing populist parties: overlapping fields.	49
2.3.	Tolerant and intolerant modes of engagement with populist parties.	52
3.1.	Vote share for established populist parties subject to long-term policies of ostracism (represented in national parliaments in 2020).	79
C.1.	Interaction of goals pursued by the opponents of populist parties.	208

List of Tables

1.1.	Populist parties with representation in European national parliaments 2020 (% vote share)	26
1.2.	Liberal democracies, electoral democracies, and electoral autocracies in the EU (2020)	37
3.1.	Populist parties represented in national parliaments in 2020 subject to electoral, parliamentary, and governmental ostracism	78
3.2.	Moderation and radicalization of ostracized parties' ideological positions (1999–2019)	81
3.3.	Governing status of populist parties and change in percentage vote share after incumbency 1999–2021	86
3.4.	Moderation and radicalization of ideological positions when populist parties become junior governing parties	93
3.5.	Moderation and radicalization of ideological positions for populist parties with senior governing status	94
A.1.	V-Dem data on quality of democracy scores for governments led by populist parties in Europe (2000–2020)	218

Abbreviations

5SM	*Movimiento 5 Stelle* (Five Stars Movement)
ADR	*Alternativ Demokratesch Reformpartei* (Alternative Democratic Reform)
AfD	*Alternative für Deutschland* (Alternative for Germany)
ANO	*Akce nespokojených obcanu* (Action of Dissatisfied Citizens)
BP	Brexit Party
BfV	*Bundesamt für Verfassungsschutz*, Office for the Protection of the Constitution
CH	*Chega!* (Enough!)
CJEU	Court of Justice of the European Union
DF	*Dansk Folkeparti* (Danish People's Party)
DLF	*Debout la France* (France Arise)
DP	*Darbo Partija* (Labour Party)
DP (Italy)	*Partito Democratico* (Democratic Party)
ECHR	European Convention of Human Rights
ECtHR	European Court of Human Rights
EDU-UDF	*Eidgenössisch-Demokratische Union* (Federal Democratic Union of Switzerland)
EKRE	*Eesti Konservatiivne Rahvaerakond* (Conservative People's Party)
EL	*Elliniki Lisi* (Greek Solution)
F	*Flokkur fólksins* (People's Party)
FdI	*Fratelli d'Italia* (Brothers of Italy)
FI	*Forza Italia* (Let's Go Italy/Forward Italy)
Fidesz	*Fidesz – Magyar Polgári Szövetség* (Hungarian Civic Alliance)
FPÖ	*Freiheitliche Partei Österreichs* (Freedom Party of Austria)
FrP	*Fremskrittspartiet* (Progress Party)
FvD	*Forum voor Democratie* (Forum for Democracy)
GERB	*Grazhdani za Evropeysko Razvitie na Balgariya* (Citizens for European Development of Bulgaria)
HDSSB	*Hrvatski demokratski savez Slavonije i Baranje* (Croatian Democratic Alliance of Slavonia and Baranja)
IoPPs	Initiatives Opposing Populist Parties
Jobbik	*Jobbik Magyarországért Mozgalom* (Movement for Better Hungary)
KPV-LV	*Par cilvēcīgu Latviju* (Who Owns the State?)
LdT	*Lega dei Ticinesi* (Ticino League)
Lega	*Lega per Salvini Permier* (League for Salvini Premier)
LeU	*Liberi e Uguali* (Free and Equal)
LFI	*La France Insoumise* (Unbowed France)
LMŠ	*Lista Marjana Šarca* (The List of Marjan Šarec)

M	*Miðflokkurinn* (Centre Party)
MeRa25	*Metopo Evropaikis Realistikis Anypakois* (European Realistic Disobedience Front)
NB	*Nye Borgerlige* (The New Right)
OĽaNO	*Obyčajní Ľudia a nezávislé osobnosti* (Ordinary People & Independent Personalities)
OP	*Obedineni Patrioti* (United Patriots)
P	*Podemos* (Together We Can)
PiS	*Prawo i Sprawiedliwość* (Law and Justice)
PM	Prime Minister
PS	*Perussuomalaiset* (Finns Party)
PVV	*Partij voor de Vrijheid* (Party for Freedom)
REP	*Die Republikaner* (The Republicans)
RUK	Reform UK
SD	*Sverigedemokraterna* (Sweden Democrats)
SDS	*Slovenska demokratska stranka* (Slovenian Democratic Party)
SF	*Sinn Féin* ([We] Ourselves)
SMER-SD	*Smer – sociálna demokracia* (Slovakian Direction – Social Democracy)
SNS	*Slovenská Národná Strana* (Slovakian National Party)
SP	*Socialistische Partij* (Socialist Party)
SPD	*Svoboda a přímá demokracie* (Freedom and Direct Democracy)
SR	*SME Rodina* (We Are Family)
SVP	*Schweizerische Volkspartei* (Swiss People's Party)
SYM	*Symmachía Politón* (Citizens Alliance)
SYRIZA	*Sinaspismós Rizospastikís Aristerás – Proodeftikí Simachía* (Coalition of the Radical Left)
RN	*Rassemblement national* (National Rally)
TEU	Treaty on European Union
TFEU	Treaty on the Functioning of the European Union
UKIP	United Kingdom Independence Party
V	*Venstre* (Liberals)
VB	*Vlaams Belang* (Flemish Interest)

Introduction

Opposing Populist Parties in Europe

The 'other people' vs the 'populist people'

Over the last decade or so, populist parties have been increasingly successful, both in Europe and beyond. Populist parties win significant numbers of votes in many countries. They have helped win epoch-defining referenda, such as the Brexit referendum in the United Kingdom. They win power at home and govern alongside others in the European Union's complex machinery of shared sovereignty. There are not many major populist parties in Europe that have not had some role in governing as either support parties, coalition partners, or running single-party governments. Victor Orbán, Marine Le Pen, and Matteo Salvini are household names. We already know a lot about what drives populist success but have only scattered knowledge about opposition to populist parties. Taking up this challenging topic, this book looks at what people do when they oppose populist parties and what kinds of opposition might work. In so doing, it contributes to important but complex debates about the relationship between populism and democracy.

While there is debate about how best to define populism, most scholars agree that populists invoke a vision of society sharply divided between the 'people' and the 'elites' (Mudde 2004; Laclau 2005; Mudde and Rovira Kaltwasser 2017; Hawkins and Rovira Kaltwasser 2017; Mouffe 2018). The people—in a democracy the carriers of popular sovereignty—are variously presented as the 'pure', 'genuine', or 'hardworking' citizens whose interests are undermined by a 'corrupt' elite hoarding political, economic, and cultural power for themselves. Populism has a chameleon-like quality, reflecting salient identities and political issues in different contexts (Taggart 2002). It is often described as a 'thin' ideology, supplementing other more comprehensive political ideologies of the left, right, centre, or otherwise (Mudde 2004). Populists may thus imagine the people and elite rather differently. Right-wing populists, for example, are typically 'nativist', mobilizing against cultural 'threats' by outsider groups such as immigrants or religious minorities.

Responding to Populist Parties in Europe. Angela K. Bourne, Oxford University Press. © Angela K. Bourne (2023).
DOI: 10.1093/oso/9780198892588.003.0001

Left-wing populists tend to focus on socio-economic inequalities, downplaying insider–outsider differences.

Some populist parties are treated as pariahs, remaining parties of permanent opposition. This includes parties such as Alternative for Germany and National Rally (formerly National Front) in France. Others are integrated into the political mainstream through governmental collaboration. The Danish People's Party, Podemos in Spain, Austrian Freedom Party, and League and the Five Star Movement in Italy are important examples of this kind of mainstreaming. Some populist parties are so successful they have been able to run their countries for long periods, including Victor Orbán's Fidesz in Hungary, Jarosław Kaczyński's Law and Justice Party in Poland, or Boyko Borissov's Citizens for European Development of Bulgaria.

Opposing populist parties is far from straightforward. Opposition to populists is often pitched in the language of 'democratic defence'. The memory of the Nazi's rise to power, the subsequent slide into World War Two, followed by the communist takeover in Central and Eastern Europe is still alive in the public imagination. Contemporary European identity is built on a shared desire to avoid a replay of the moral catastrophe, personal tragedies, and hardships that accompanied these events. Yet populist appeals to popular sovereignty, to put ordinary people first, and their very success with voting publics, shakes confidence in opposition to populism framed as democracy protection.

There is uncertainty in scholarly and public debates about what populism amounts to and this muddies the waters for those who oppose populists. Some see populism as the path to 'real democracy', others see it as the royal road to dictatorship, or at best a hybrid form of 'illiberal democracy' (e.g., Mudde 2004; Mudde and Rovira Kaltwasser 2012; Stavrakakis 2014; Müller 2016a; Mouffe 2018; Pappas 2019). The success of populist parties is built on deep—and sometimes reasonable—dissatisfaction with the working of liberal democracy. Grievances are easy to recognize: The lack of real choice between mainstream parties, increasing inequalities and feelings of insecurity. There is something in the claims: 'They do not represent us', 'the Courts are packed', 'the media is biased', 'Brussels has taken over'. Some populist leaders effectively mobilize this 'democratic malaise' to build autocratic and or semi-autocratic regimes, but many do not, or cannot.

Where populists are powerful, as they are in many European countries, opposition to populist parties is largely a struggle about who the people are and what can be done in their name. Populism, and opposition to it, is partly a struggle about policies and constitutions, but it is also a struggle about identity. As the subtitle of this book signals, opposition to populism is often resistance to a populist vision of the 'people' by those who could be called 'the other people'. Populists claim to represent the common, ordinary, and authentic people, against a distant, self-serving, and at worst, a corrupt elite. It relies on a fictional, homogenizing vision of what unites people, sometimes in a way that enhances the status of the excluded, at other times building political barriers against those defined as outsiders. The 'other people' include those who reject the populist way of picking teams in the political game and those excluded from the populist conception of the people. They include those who feel alienated from the populist vision of how politics should work. They can be people fighting to retain their power and dignity as political subjects, when populists say they don't belong. The 'other people' may or may not have the democratic high ground. They include elites demonized in populist discourses; both those pitching themselves as the 'good democrats' taking a stand in defence of what they see as an ethically superior status quo, and 'anti-populists', taking a polarizing stand and refusing to acknowledge even the most reasonable claims of populist parties. The 'other people' include populists opposing other populists in a contest about who the 'real' people are.

The success of populist parties in Europe, coupled with deep uncertainty about what this means in democratic terms not only shakes confidence in opposition to populism framed as democracy protection. It raises questions about the relevance of knowledge built up over the post-World War Two period about how to deal with democracy's challengers. Most of what we know deals with more clearly anti-democratic, anti-system, and extremist challengers.

How then, in this new, muddy political conjuncture, ought we to respond? In this book I contribute to debate on this important question by providing new concepts and theories to study *how* those who disagree with populist parties go about opposing them, and the *effects* of this opposition on populist parties themselves. The book does not present a normative theory of how best to respond to populist parties from a democratic point of view, although it provides knowledge likely to inform such theories. It provides a theoretical toolkit, illustrated with numerous empirical examples from across Europe, showing the range of contemporary responses to populist parties, what opposition might achieve, unintended outcomes, and the underlying mechanisms producing change.

The book is structured around a discussion of first: *who* opposes populist parties and *how* they oppose populist parties. It then develops a new theory to evaluate *what works* and *to what ends*. The *who* opposing populist parties includes public authorities, political parties, and civil society actors undertaking initiatives within the state, transnationally, and in the international sphere. The *how* of populist opposition includes repressive, rights-denying, 'exceptional' measures and more frequently, opposition deploying the kinds of 'normal' strategies used against all types of parties in liberal democracies. On the challenging issue of *what works* and *to what ends* I argue that responses to populist parties are effective if they achieve at least one of four goals: Reducing support for a populist party, diminishing their resources, inducing ideological moderation, or curbing their ability to implement illiberal or anti-democratic policies. These should be achieved without producing unwanted or perverse effects of increasing support for populist parties, boosting their resources, or inducing radicalization. Goals are typically achieved using one or more of four mechanisms: The manipulation of strategic incentives of voters and parties in the context of democratic competition; enforcement of national and international law; exploitation of interdependence to leverage change; and persuasion (see Figure 0.1 below).

The book focuses on populist *political parties* because despite limitations they remain important agents of change in liberal democracies. Parties participating in government have control of many instruments to implement their policies, even if they are rarely free to do exactly what they want. This includes the possibility that populist parties in government will undermine liberal democratic institutions, although this is not inevitable. In addition, successful populist parties have the added democratic legitimacy of obtaining power through substantial voter support. The book focuses on populist parties in *Europe* because it provides a setting for observing a wide range of opposition forms undertaken in relation to a wide range of populist party types. Europe is a region of the world—although not the only one—where populist parties have been particularly successful in the last decade or so. While right-wing parties predominate, there are salient examples of leftist, centrist, minority nationalist, and 'valence' populists (see Table 1.1). Populist parties in Europe have different kinds of governing statuses, as indicated above. Those opposing populist parties have used a wide range of opposition strategies. More than any other region in the world, Europe's populist parties operate within a multilevel system of governance which constrains and enables actions of member governments and citizens. It thus provides a setting well suited for observing and theorizing opposition by international and transnational actors.

Beyond 'militant democracy'

Opposition to populist parties is incredibly diverse. The coercive authority of the state may be deployed, but opposition can also be orchestrated by political parties and civil society actors. Public authorities have powers to punish populists, usually when they are in opposition, with party bans, surveillance, and criminalization of offensive speech. Populists in government may be constrained by authorities with countervailing powers, such as the courts or other regulatory bodies. Political parties can respond to their populist competitors by addressing grievances underpinning populist support or stealing their policies; reduce incentives to vote for populists by systematically excluding them from government; or, alternatively, incentivize moderation by inviting them into government. Civil society actors may organize a demonstration, riot, run media and online campaigns, perform a play, or hack a website. Networks of transnational organizations monitor, report on, and critique the actions of populists to influence national and international debates. International bodies and foreign governments, upon whom a populist-run government may depend economically or strategically, may pressure and persuade populist governments to change their ways. The European Union has the power to sanction populist (or other) governments flouting EU values by denying voting rights or EU funds, or to challenge infringements of EU law. Opposition can also be individualized, including voting, sending a tweet, ridiculing a racist neighbour, or talking around a family member. Existing studies don't fully acknowledge this wide range of responses.

'Militant democracy', usually traced from Karl Loewenstein's (1937) work on responses to interwar fascism, is a classic concept in the field. Militant democracy is a set of policy tools and political theories justifying the restriction of political rights of extremist groups in liberal democracies. The policy tools include party bans, criminalization of hate speech and holocaust denial, and bans on public displays of politically controversial symbols, such as the Nazi swastika. These measures are typically set out in constitutions or legislation and authorize, as an exception to the rule, restrictions on basic political rights mostly linked to free expression and association. Their goal is to pre-emptively marginalize those who otherwise act within the law from undermining liberal democratic institutions (Müller 2012: 1253; Tyulkina 2015a: 14; Invernizzi, Accetti, and Zuckerman 2017: 183; Malkopoulou 2019: 12). During the Cold War, militant democracy typically targeted neo-fascist or orthodox communist parties which more or less openly declared the goal of replacing liberal democracy but did so by contesting elections rather than through violent regime change (Müller 2012: 1255, 2016a: 250). In other words, militant democracy sought to counteract those who might take advantage of the rights and privileges liberal democracies gave citizens to compete for political power. The postwar Federal Republic of Germany, which banned both neo-fascist and communist parties in the 1950s, is the paradigmatic example of militant democracy (Kommers 1997; Backes 2006).

At the end of the Cold War, questions naturally emerged about the contemporary relevance of militant democracy. Liberal democracy's post-Cold War challengers—such as religious fundamentalists or groups using terrorist tactics—were less likely to work within existing institutions. Some scholars, and even the European Court of Human Rights, reconceptualized 'militant democracy' to capture some of these new challenges, including new ways of thinking about supranational and transnational militant democracy (Rosenblum 2008; Macklem 2012; Tyulkina 2015a). Similarly, a new generation of political theorists distanced themselves from the more repressive measures of Loewenstein's postwar militant democracy, seeking instead to 'rehabilitate it by identifying liberal grounds for militant policies' (Malkopoulou 2019: 3). These neo-militant democracy theorists argued that 'decisions to exclude should be guided by strict normative criteria' including 'the protection of core values', 'the right to participate', or 'the ability to revise past decisions' (ibid.).

As populist parties became increasingly successful, an obvious question was whether militant democracy would be an appropriate conceptual framework. Jan-Werner Müller (2012), for example, argued that populism was a form of extremism against which initiatives of militant democracy should be applied. Populists, Müller argued, 'speak in the name of the people as a whole, systematically denying the fractures and divisions of society (in particular those associated with the contest of political parties) and systematically seek to do away with the checks and balances which have come to be associated with *all* European democracies created after 1945' (ibid.: 1267–1268).

Müller's argument that populism is necessarily anti-pluralist and detrimental for liberal democratic politics is questionable, as **Chapter 1** 'Muddy Waters: Populism and Democratic Defence' discusses in more detail. Indeed, a long list of political scientists have been at pains to count the differences between populism and political extremism of the kind traditionally targeted by militant democracy (Betz 1994: 108; Kitschelt and McGann 1997: 31; Mudde 2004; Weyland 2017; Eatwell and Goodwin 2018: 278; Fieschi 2019; for counterarguments see Rummens and Abts 2010). Some of the repressive tools used against extremists, such as party bans, are very controversial in any case, not least because they are at odds with liberal democratic commitments to pluralism and tolerance (Bourne 2018). They seem even harder to justify when a party is willing to compete for power in elections, wins many votes, and represents at least some genuine popular grievances. In fact, rights-restricting initiatives typical of militant democracy are rarely used against populist parties. Another limitation is that militant democracy approaches focus predominantly on initiatives undertaken by public authorities such as governments, courts, and security services, with much less to say about the role of political parties and civil society actors.

More promising is the work of scholars which can be grouped under the rubric of 'defending democracy' (e.g., Capoccia 2001; Pedahzur 2004; Capoccia 2005; Rummens and Abts 2010; Akkerman and de Lange 2012; Downs 2012; Capoccia 2013; van Spanje 2018, Albertazzi and Vampa 2021). Much of this work deals with responses to West European radical right populist parties emerging in Europe in the 1980s and 1990s and, as such, it is more useful for analysing responses to contemporary populist parties. This work addresses responses that are almost routine compared to the rights-restricting initiatives of public authorities in militant democracy. Scholars in this tradition have asked: What happens if a party is treated as an outcast, or if another party steals its policies? Or alternatively, what happens if it is invited into government? Importantly, it is the body of work which tells us most about effects of party opposition to populist parties, especially how party strategies of inclusion and exclusion may affect votes, party resources, and stylistic and ideological moderation of party positions (see for example: Akkerman, de Lange, and Roodouijn 2016; van Spanje 2018).

This work must be incorporated into an analysis of responses to populism, which is reflected in the name I give to my approach (see below). There is still a lot it leaves out. While we might criticize the literature on militant democracy for its exclusive focus on responses by public authorities—especially courts and security services—the 'democratic defence' approach can be criticized for being heavily focused on political parties. Once a party is big enough to govern alone, responses like ostracism or 'moderation through inclusion' in government are off the cards. This is the situation in many parts of Europe. It is widely known that Victor Orbán's Fidesz has been in power in Hungary since 2010 and the Polish Law and Justice Party since 2015. It is less well known that populists have dominated governments, or currently do so, in Bulgaria, Czechia, Greece, Italy, Slovakia, Slovenia, and Switzerland (see Table A.1). Opposing populists dominating government is fundamentally different from constraining or marginalizing populists in opposition. When populists are in power, the focus of attention must turn to the acts of opposition parties in parliament, institutional checks and balances on government power, the mobilization of civil society, and the reactions of international organizations and other states. Where ruling populist parties weaken liberal checks on government power and make life hard for those who oppose them—which is the stark reality in Hungary and Poland, and to a lesser extent elsewhere (see Table A1.1)—opposition to populist parties is an entirely different game from the orderly competition for votes, office, and acheiving policy goals in consolidated democracies. Existing literatures on militant democracy and democratic defence provide limited guidance for studying these developments (one interesting exception is Rovira Kaltwasser and Taggart 2016).

A careful reading of the literature on populism points to an additional 'grievance model' of democratic defence. This model draws on knowledge about causes of populist successes to deduce policy responses that might undercut support for populist parties deemed problematic in democratic terms. Accounts of populist success and failure often focus on the interaction of new societal grievances or 'demands' and the ability of populist parties to 'supply' attractive solutions (Kitschelt and McGann 1997; Mudde 2007; Akkerman, de Lange, and Roodouijn 2016: 17–20). New demands typically come from broader, longer-term economic, cultural, and political changes shaking up the distribution of 'winners' and 'losers' in society. There is widespread agreement that populist successes have something to do with the longer-term evolution of capitalism. That is, market globalization and the ascendency of neo-liberal policies weaken commitments to publicly funded universal welfare programmes, sometimes prompting popular indignation about growing economic inequality and material insecurity (Betz 1994; Kitschelt and McGann 1997; Swank and Betz 2003; Kriesi et al. 2005; Kriesi and Pappas 2015; Mouffe 2018; Rodrik 2018). Changing patterns of migration have generated new cultural demands as relatively homogeneous European societies came into closer contact with people with fundamentally different religious backgrounds and ways of living (Ignazi 2003; Minkenberg 2003; Eatwell and Goodwin 2018; Zielonka 2018; Norris and Inglehart 2019). Intergenerational change pitched a defence of traditional communitarian values against postmaterialist, socially liberal, and cosmopolitan values of younger generations (Ignazi 2003; Norris and Inglehart 2019). Meanwhile, the political mainstream failed to adequately respond to these new economic and cultural demands, producing 'democratic malaise' and widespread feelings of powerlessness, lack of trust in political leaders, and ultimately dissatisfaction with the functioning of liberal democracy (Betz 1994; Kitschelt and McGann 1997; Mair 2002; Mény and Surel 2002a; Taggart 2002; Eatwell and Goodwin 2018; Zielonka 2018). Add to this mix political polarization, resentment or indignation, the redemptive promise of taking back control, the 'mediatization' of politics and access to more unfiltered forms of communication in the social media age, and we find promising conditions for populist successes (Canovan 2002; Zúquete 2007; Sunstein 2017; Gerbaudo 2018; Fieschi 2019).

Public and scholarly debates often air proposals calling for responses addressing these underlying grievances or long-term 'demand-side' explanations for populist successes. A key plank of this 'grievance model' of democratic defence are calls for new policies addressing economic inequalities and economic insecurity (Swank and Betz 2003; Mounk 2018: 186; Zielonka 2018: 68–69; Galston 2018: 16–17; Norris and Inglehart 2019: 463). In this direction, we have seen calls for more inclusive labour market policies; welfare reforms to offset costs of globalization for workers; raising tax rates for the highest earners and most profitable corporations; policies to fix housing crises; and the abandonment of neo-liberal economic policies. A second plank of the grievance model addresses challenges posed by increasingly multicultural societies, immigration and cultural anxieties (Eatwell and Goodwin 2018: 281–282; Galston 2018: 16–17; Mounk 2018: 214–215; Norris and Inglehart 2019: 465). This has generated appeals to open up public debates about immigration and national sovereignty; search for new compromises and new ways to address concerns about immigration; repatriation of EU powers to nation states; and redesigning EU structures to better channel local and citizen interests. The third plank, focusing on political causes of populism, has included calls for institutional reforms addressing failures of democratic governance, such as corruption and poor policy performance, and calls for parties to offer voters a clearer choice among competing political options (Abedi 2002: 571; Mudde and Rovira Kaltwasser, 2017, 110; Hawkins 2018: 243, 257; Mounk 2018: 242–244). There have been many calls for reforms giving citizens more say in political life, with ideas ranging from an increased use of referenda, the creation of citizens' assemblies, and use of digital technologies for deliberation and monitoring government activity (Eatwell and Goodwin 2018: 126; Mény and Surel 2002a: 16; Zielonka 2018: 118–128; Sunstein 2017: 216–233). They also include proposals to reinvigorate liberal democratic political culture through a 'reinvention' or 'fresh, radical beginning' for liberalism or civic education (Mudde and Rovira Kaltwasser 2017: 112; Zielonka 2018; Pappas 2019: 262).

The strength of this grievance model is that it shifts discussion from the elitist, punitive, and adversarial register of responses to populism. It picks up on what has long been something of a minority position in the literature, which focuses on responses to those challenging the status quo in the form of persuasion, deliberation in the public sphere, routine practices of political opposition, civil society engagement, and a search for solutions addressing causes rather than symptoms of dissatisfaction with the status quo (see for example Pedahzur 2004; Rummens and Abts 2010; Malkopoulou and Norman 2018). On the other hand, it can be difficult to work out whether a new policy—for example, reform of immigration policy, labour markets or the welfare state—is actually a response to populism, given that such policies pursue multiple, general political goals. In practice, implementation of new policy and legislative initiatives of the kind often proposed in the grievance model are few and far between. Without dismissing the relevance of this approach, the book focuses on the larger set of more common responses pursuing short- to medium-term goals. These are familiar to approaches falling under the rubrics of 'militant democracy' and 'democratic defence'.

In sum, there is a lot to build on but many gaps in our knowledge. We need a new conceptual language to talk about responses to parties that are more ambiguous in their orientation towards liberal democracy than many of those discussed in the existing literature. We need to understand the effectiveness of responses that go beyond an exclusive focus on exceptional rights-restrictions and coercion, and also to examine initiatives channelled through routine institutional procedures and practices of normal politics. We need to look beyond the role of public authorities within the state, and the strategies of political parties, to understand the role of civil society in opposition to populist parties. Interaction of populists and their opponents in the international arena requires that we also find ways to integrate transnational and international politics into our theoretical constructs. I now turn to outline the model of 'Democratic defence as "normal politics"', which aims to achieve these objectives.

Democratic defence as 'normal politics'

The model of democratic defence as normal politics is built in three steps. The first is a classification of initiatives opposing populist parties (IoPPs), which builds a new conceptual map charting the main types of initiatives deployed against populist parties in contemporary Europe. The second and most challenging step is to work out how different types of IoPPs affect populist parties and identify the processes producing these effects. The final step is to bring what was learned in steps one and two together into a theory of effective opposition to populist parties. I now turn to discuss each of these steps in turn, simultaneously introducing the book's structure and arguments.

Who opposes populist parties and how do they do it?

Chapter 2, 'Mapping Initiatives Opposing Populist Parties in Europe' presents one of the main novelties of the book. It lays out a comprehensive, up-to-date typology, which can be used to chart the contours of opposition to populist parties. It has been tested, adjusted, and improved thanks to the work of a cross-Europe team of researchers in the *Populism and Democratic Defence in Europe* project (CF20-008) financed by the Carlsberg Foundation's 'Challenges for Europe' programme. The conceptual map has two dimensions. The first distinguishes between different types of populist opponent, namely *public authorities*, such as courts and governments, *political parties*, and *civil society actors*, such as social movements, NGOs, the media, and local protest groups. These categories include international actors such as the European Union, individual European states, and transnational civil society groups. The conceptual map's second dimension distinguishes between *tolerant and intolerant modes of engagement* with populist parties. The two dimensions produce six types of opposition initiatives (and various subtypes): Intolerant IoPPs are 'rights restrictions' by public authorities, 'ostracism' by political parties, and 'coercive confrontation' by civil society. Tolerant IoPPs are called 'ordinary legal controls and pedagogy' by public authorities, 'forbearance' by political parties, and 'adversarialism' by civil society (see Figure 2.1). In this typology, we can still plot the rather rare, highly controversial, exclusionary, and intolerant initiatives opposing populist parties, such as banning a party or international sanctions, or principled ostracism of 'pariah' parties. But we can also place the less spectacular, and sometimes routine, operation of constitutional checks and balances, or the outcome of a corruption or racism trial. There is also scope for multitudinous protests outside party HQ, systematic monitoring of 'democratic backsliding', and a ruling by the Court of Justice of the European Union. In the remaining chapters I turn to the second and most complex theoretical challenge, that is, *working out what works*.

What does opposition to populist parties achieve?

Do initiatives opposing populist parties make a difference? Does it matter if the courts ban a party or cut its access to public money, or the government declares a populist party a threat to liberal democracy and subjects it to surveillance? Does it matter if other parties refuse to ever form a government with it? Or alternatively, does it matter if parties choose to cooperate with it in parliament or government? Does it matter if almost every hotel owner in town refuses to hire out meeting spaces, or if protestors throw eggs and tomatoes at populist leaders? What if populist parties always get a bad press, or opposition parties and people on the street demonize populists as 'fascists', 'Nazis', or 'racists'? Does it matter if party leaders end up in jail for corruption, or for racist or hate speech? What if the courts strike down the laws of governing populist parties, or a populist leader is impeached, or opposition parties use parliamentary procedure to thwart illiberal or anti-democratic laws, or mount a counter-offensive from local government strongholds? Does it matter if the European Union threatens to cancel financial aid, or the European Court of Human Rights identifies a human rights violation? These are real examples of initiatives opposing populist parties. But are they effective?

Curiously, an earlier generation of scholars were rather sceptical about populist parties' longer-term prospects. While big on challenging the status quo, populists were often seen as limited by an inability to define attractive alternatives (Mény and Surel 2002a: 28; see also Zielonka 2019: 15). The allure of charismatic leaders could wane in the long term, it was argued, and a reliance on relatively unorganized, movement parties could become a liability (ibid.). Populist parties in government would struggle to square government responsibility with anti-establishment appeals (Taggart 2002: 69–70; Heinisch 2003: 91). In 2002, Mény and Surel argued that populist parties 'are by nature neither durable nor sustainable parties of government' and that their 'fate is to be integrated into the mainstream, to disappear, or to remain permanently in opposition' (2002a: 28). In that same year, Taggart (2002) argued that populism had a 'self-limiting quality' tied to the centrality of crisis in their appeals. Yet, despite expectations, populist parties have not only become more numerous in Europe, collectively winning more and more votes, but many have become institutionalized, creating enduring organizational structures, surviving leadership changes, finding loyal supporters, and repeatedly participating in, or winning control over, government in consecutive elections.

Scholarly prognosis now tends to lean towards Canovan's (2002) argument that populism is a more permanent, or at least episodic phenomenon. Canovan argued that inherent tensions at the very heart of modern democracy will persistently generate populist movements. On the one hand, she argued, the 'ideology of democracy' emphasizes the sovereignty of a unified people expressed by a majority. On the other hand, modern democracy does not directly implement what 'the people' want. It is a 'political maze', a 'tangle' of public debate, pressure groups, and citizen mobilization, elections, and political deal-making, court decisions and global governance. This generates a 'standing invitation to raise the cry of democracy betrayed and to mobilise the discontented behind the banner of restoring politics of the people' (ibid.: 26). Other scholars point in a similar direction. Peter Mair argued that globalization and the all-too-similar policies of mainstream parties might make populist democracy more pervasive than twentieth-century 'party democracy'. Cas Mudde's (2004) seminal article on populism was titled 'The Populist Zeitgeist' hinting at the mainstreaming of populist discourses in Western democracies. Pappas saw in populism the potential for a 'new democratic canon', that 'seeks to institute a novel—indeed, innovative—form of modern democratic politics that is antagonistic towards liberal democracy' (2019: 1, 9). Eatwell and Goodwin predict a scenario of 'post-populism', where 'in future "success" might come more in the shape of national-populist-lite parties and politicians … willing to adopt a broad swathe of national-populist policies' (2018: 292). Albertazzi and Vampa argue that many populist parties 'have been so resilient and successful' that they are 'the new mainstream' (2021: 13).

The scale of populist successes over the last few decades and a reasonable expectation that populism will remain entrenched in European party systems for the medium term means their opponents cannot reasonably expect to 'defeat populism'. It is therefore more useful to look at whether initiatives opposing populist parties achieve a series of less ambitious, but still consequential, goals and whether efforts to achieve these goals generate unanticipated perverse effects. This approach is also more normatively attractive. European populist parties often articulate widely held and sometimes reasonable grievances with the status quo and pursue a variety of objectives, which do not necessarily undermine the quality of democratic politics in a country. Aiming to 'defeat' populism in this context could only with great difficulty overcome foundational liberal democratic commitments to pluralism and tolerance.

The four goals of opposition to populist parties

Taken together, initiatives opposing populist parties aim to delimit the participation of populist parties in the public sphere and/or the impact of at least some of their ideas and actions on public policy. These ambitions can be broken down into four main goals, which I spell out below. These goals approximate what those who oppose populist parties set out to achieve in practice, *for better or worse*. In other words, I build an empirical argument about what those opposing populist parties pursue rather than a normative theory of legitimate goals. The long tradition of philosophical debate on the virtues and perils of 'tolerating the intolerant' shows the need for deep normative reflection over the appropriateness of, and best modalities for, achieving these goals (Locke 1689; Popper 1966; Rawls 1971; Rummens and Abts 2010; Müller 2016b; Rijpkema 2018; Malkopoulou 2019). This important discussion is beyond the scope of this book.

Populist opponents often aim to *curb the ability of populist parties in government to implement illiberal or anti-democratic policies*. Even the most powerful populist parties in Europe are subject to constraints. They need to be re-elected. They are sensitive to protests that may swing public opinion against them. They rarely control all political institutions. Some regulatory bodies or courts, or opposition parties successful in local government, may check the power of populist parties controlling government at the centre. States and international organizations may create problems at home for populist parties pursuing policies unpopular abroad.

Second, populist opponents often aim to *reduce support for populist parties*. They want to reduce the number of people who vote for populist parties at elections, which can be measured in swings of support from election to election. Knowing parties usually need more than a good argument to do well in elections, opponents may seek to diminish *populist party resources*. Material resources cover unavoidable costs of advertising, office space, salaries, and campaign materials. Competent and skilful individuals are invaluable human resources. Organizational resources, especially internal cohesion, are vital, as are moral resources, which give the general sense, among supporters at least, that the party pursues appropriate objectives.

If people keep voting for populist parties regardless, their opponents might try *inducing ideological or behavioural 'moderation'*. Populists could be pressured to pursue less-radical agendas. For example, they may come to accept the basic institutions of the political system more-or-less as they are. They may oppose minorities or international organizations less trenchantly. Their language may be less provocative, and populists may increasingly adopt the 'manners' of the political mainstream. It is worth pointing out that strategies aiming to induce moderation are normatively complex. Many studies on moderation position (usually right-wing) populist parties as 'pariahs' threatening an unproblematic liberal democratic status quo populated by worthy mainstream parties of the centre-left and centre-right (e.g., Downs 2012; Akkerman, de Lange, and Roodouijn 2016; Van Spanje 2018). This position is probably too harsh in characterizing all populist parties as 'pariahs' (Mudde 2004), outdated in its conception of populists as somehow separate from the political mainstream (Albertazzi and Vampa 2021); and too generous in its evaluation of the virtues of the political mainstream (Mouffe 2018). Critical reflections on the delegitimizing, discrediting, and stigmatizing effects of 'anti-populist' discourses and the extent to which they may be used to maintain a problematic status quo should be taken seriously (Stavrakakis 2014, 2018).

Bad reactions and perverse effects

Opposition to populist parties often falls short of achieving these goals. It can even be counterproductive. Voters and populist party supporters may react badly. Populists can fight back using many of the same tools as their opponents. International sanctions, harsh jail terms for populist leaders, permanent exclusion of their party from power, or dismissive comments about supporters might *increase support for populist parties*. Voters may sympathize with populist parties seemingly under attack by already unpopular political elites. Mobilizing the protest vote is a classic move. So are attempts to increase voter support by 'rallying around the flag' in the face of repressive measures from abroad. Mobilizing these kinds of responses often rely on a persuasive framing of opposition as the machinations of an out-of-touch elite or as attacks on national sovereignty.

Members of a party under siege may deepen their commitment, thereby *boosting party resources*. Adversity can inspire unity and support for the leader. New members may join. Instead of ideological moderation, opposition to populists *might induce ideological or behavioural 'radicalization'*. Where channels into the mainstream are blocked off, a populist party might opt out of institutional politics. Moderates might lose their sway, opening parties up to extremists. A party that does not have to compromise with others is freer to pursue more radical policy ideas.

Of course, initiatives opposing populist parties may do more than produce perverse effects. They may ultimately fail. A populist party may win enough support, and possess sufficient resources, to capture and fully undermine liberal democratic institutions. Opponents may not have been able to prevent this slide into authoritarianism. Something short of authoritarianism is also on the cards. Or, on the contrary, populist mobilization may improve democratic politics. This uncertainty is another reason why we need a theory that aims to understand effective opposition short of an all-out struggle to defend the state against authoritarianism. Analysing the goals of populist opposition and tools for realizing them, and identifying possible perverse effects, helps us better understand effective opposition under these complex conditions.

Tools for achieving goals

Answering questions about the effects of political actions is always tricky in the social sciences. It is truly difficult to separate the effects of individual acts in the sea of initiatives and counter-initiatives that influence political outcomes. There are usually more potentially significant factors that should be accounted for than cases (and research time) available to study them in. These challenges are especially significant when taking a comprehensive view as I do here. I hope to demonstrate that while difficult, it is not impossible to find ways to evaluate the effectiveness of initiatives opposing populist parties. The task is to ask the question in the right way and look for answers in the right place. In fact, social scientists ask questions about political effectiveness all the time. Scholars specializing in the study of political parties, social movements, national and international law, the European Union, and International Relations, have theories to explain the impact of political interventions in their field. This work tells us that political interventions can work through the manipulation of strategic choice, enforcement of the law, leverage, and persuasion. I discuss each of these processes, or 'mechanisms' as they are often called in the social sciences, in detail in chapters three to six of the second part of the book.

Chapter 3 looks at how initiatives opposing populist parties may achieve goals through the 'Manipulation of Voter and Party Choice'. Opposition initiatives may manipulate incentives for voters and supporters of populist parties, making it less attractive to vote for, or to join, populist parties. For example, it may not be the most rational decision to vote for an ostracized party that will never get into government, especially if another party has coopted or 'stolen' its core ideas (van Spanje 2018). Populist parties that want to win back voters may have incentives to moderate, or at least change the policies provoking ostracism. Similarly, the chance of entering government may provide incentives for office-seeking parties to make themselves more agreeable to potential partners by softening their rhetoric or their most radical policy ideas. Or populist parties entering government may alienate voters won over by their anti-establishment appeals, and, like other parties, face 'costs of incumbency'. The opposite might occur if, for example, polarizing opposition tactics like ostracism or international sanctions increase support for populist parties by reinforcing anti-establishment critiques or boost the resource of a unified and highly committed membership.

Chapter 4 looks at how initiatives opposing populist parties may achieve their goals with 'Enforcement through the Constitution, Courts, and Coercion'. Constitutions, institutional and procedural rules structure the political environment in which populist parties operate both nationally and within Europe's common institutions. When enforced, these rules give teeth to exceptional, rights-restricting initiatives like party bans, or ordinary legal controls punishing offensive speech such as holocaust denial or racism, and other crimes like corruption or incitement to violence. Constitutional rules, and international human rights and other treaties, allow opponents to check abuses of power, and sometimes curb the ability of populist parties to implement illiberal or undemocratic policies. Sometimes enforcement relies directly on the coercive power of the state. Othertimes coercion lurks in the background. Even where there is 'democratic backsliding', at least some law-enforcement bodies may retain sufficient autonomy to block the policies of populist governments. Initiatives relying on law as political constraint may have secondary effects. Legal strife can taint a party, reducing its support. To avoid trouble, a party may be forced to moderate, or at least fix its 'front stage' image. Working out what to do may disturb internal party peace. Or, trouble with the law may attract sympathy for 'martyred' leaders. Coercion or the threat of it may be seen as 'proof' that 'corrupt elites' will do anything to protect their corner. The 'oxygen of publicity' may be invaluable and solidarity in the face of trouble may both unify and radicalize core members.

Chapter 5 looks at how initiatives opposing populist parties may achieve their goals through 'Leverage, International Sanctions, and Disruption'. Leverage exploits mutual interdependence to gain concessions in bargaining situations. It relies on those making demands being credible and clear about what they want. Those making concessions need to have something important at stake to give way. Leverage is what can, if conditions are right, give force to international rights restricting initiatives. These include EU voting sanctions for states violating liberal democratic values, or new rules withholding EU funds for states subverting the rule of law. Leverage can, if conditions are right, make international ostracism work. Civil society groups can create power by mustering mass support for widespread, disruptive protest. Exploiting dependence of all kinds of governments on consent and political stability, disruptive protesters may be able to block populist government's illiberal or anti-democratic policies or even force them from power. On the other hand, leverage entails a degree of mutual dependence and populist parties can sometimes resist pressures by exploiting this. Their concessions may be superficial, evading meaningful change. International interventions provide opportunities to 'rally around the flag', perhaps increasing support for governing populist parties. Or they may convince voters against re-electing a populist government when its actions incite international partners to impose punishing sanctions that threaten livelihoods.

Chapter 6 looks at how initiatives opposing populist parties may achieve their goals through 'Persuasion, Talk, and New Ideas'. Political protests, media campaigns, public critique, or denigration may 'reframe' the terms of public debate, stigmatizing or shaming populist party leaders and their supporters.

It might even win them over with the better argument. Eye-catching protests can offer a fresh, critical perspective on what populist parties are up to. Supporters may change their minds if they hear of corruption scandals, or if many of their fellow citizens or foreign leaders condemn 'democratic backsliding'. Populist promises to 'clean up' politics, to be the 'true democrats' or to defend ordinary people against 'unscrupulous elites' may not stand up to scrutiny. Demonization of populist parties as fascists, Nazis, communists, racists, or anti-Semites may 'contaminate' party identities. If they invoke fear or aversion from potential supporters, stigmatization may undermine the party's moral resources, and make supporting or cooperating with it unattractive. Many parties have responded to these challenges with 'de-demonization strategies'. Likewise, national, and international initiatives monitoring, publicizing, and entering into dialogue with populist parties about inconsistencies in what they 'say' and 'do' may 'shame' them into changing their ways. On the other hand, persuasion is precarious. We seem to live in a 'post-truth' era, often believe what we want to hear in online 'echo chambers', and the populist style is often anti-intellectual. Talk and new ideas can fall flat or be dismissed as 'fake news'. Lies and corruption can be overlooked. If it deepens suspicion of fellow citizens or foreign detractors, denigration or critique may simply increase support for populist parties or boost internal solidarity.

A last point to note is that most of these processes work by altering the incentives of populist parties, their supporters, and allies. They assume a consequentialist logic of rational choice. That is, populist parties have good reasons to change their behaviour if it means better access to resources, a better chance at achieving electoral goals, avoiding the costs and uncertainty of disruptive opposition, avoiding international sanctions, and maintaining the fruits of international competition. Persuasion works differently. It follows norm-driven, identity-affirming logics of appropriateness. It relies on the value we place on the good opinion of the people we identify with. It mobilizes methods of social control, such as stigmatization and shaming. It can also rely on convincing people that their understanding of how the world works needs adjustment.

Working out what works

The final step for developing a model of democratic defence as 'normal politics' is to knit together what we know about initiatives, processes of change, goals, and perverse effects into a theory of effective opposition to populist parties (see Figure 0.1 below). The Conclusion chapter spells out 'A 'Bottom

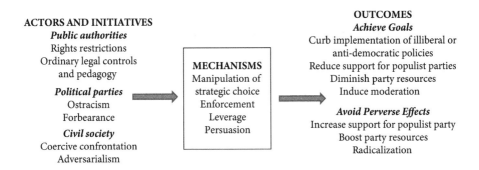

Figure 0.1 Effective opposition to populist parties

Up' Theory of Effective Opposition to Populist Parties' in more detail, but the basic idea can be summarized with reference to the simple formula: Effective initiatives opposing populist parties achieve at least one goal of opposition, without producing perverse effects.

The theory is 'bottom up' because it starts with specific actions—initiatives—and then theorizes the broader consequences of these initiatives for the achievement of goals. The advantage of this approach is its flexibility. We already know that some kinds of initiatives are used in some countries, but not others. Some initiatives make more sense depending on a party's governing status. The theory provides a menu of theoretical constructs and propositions that can be tailored to the reality of opposition in different contexts. The bottom-up approach also allows us to study the effects of individual initiatives, perhaps across different countries. We can look at combinations of initiatives within the same country, how the effects of separate initiatives interact, or how effectiveness might change over time. Researchers can then use the approach to compare effectiveness across many countries, even though traditions of opposition vary. It also allows us to observe what social scientists call 'equifinality'. That is, we can observe whether the same outcomes—say the achievement of a specific goal or occurrence of a combination of perverse effects—may come about through different combinations of factors—such as different combinations of initiatives.

In the main body of the book I spell out the model of democratic defence as normal politics in more detail, discussing both its theoretical and conceptual foundations and illustrating their plausibility in light of empirical examples. This theoretical framework merges the insights of several types of scholarship. The first was the small literature examining the effects of principally party-based strategies of opposition targeting radical-right populists in Western Europe (e.g., Downs 2012; Akkerman et al. 2016; van Spanje 2018; Albertazzi et al. 2021). Many of the insights of these studies could be applied to relatively new left-wing populist parties and parties further to the East in Europe. I also use data from political party databases (such as the Chapel Hill Expert Survey, Parties and Elections in Europe, and ParlGov) to supplement and update findings of existing studies. A second strand of literature provided insights on opposition by a broader range of actors, including public authorities, civil society, and international actors (e.g., Capoccia 2005; Rovira Kaltwasser and Taggart 2016; Scheppele et al. 2020), as did a careful reading of the large comparative and single-case study literature on populist parties. Data collected with colleagues on the *Carlsberg Challenges for Europe* project on *Populism and Democratic Defence in Europe* CF20-008) provided additional insights into the range of opposition initiatives (see Bourne 2022; Bourne, 2023). This second strand of literature lacked clear hypotheses on mechanisms and effects of opposition. However, these were available from a third strand; namely, broader theoretical literatures on the effectiveness of social movement mobilization and political opportunity structures (Benford and Snow 2000; Guigni 2004; Tarrow 2011); new institutionalism in political science (March and Olsen 1996; Pierson 2000; Schmidt 2008); political conditionality in the context of complex interdependence (Keohane and Nye 1987; Schimmelfennig and Sedelmeier 2004 and 2020); the role of international actors in democratization processes (Levistly and Way 2010); and compliance with international and supranational European law (Keohane 1997; Helfer and Slaughter 1997; Guzman 2008; Simmons 2009; Alter 2012; Kosař et al. 2020).

There are many questions that this book does not address. As hinted above, one issue which naturally arises is whether, and in what ways, opposition to populist parties in the name of democratic defence is legitimate. By better understanding the range of responses used by many different types of political actors in practice and learning something about potentially desirable and not so desirable consequences of that opposition, this book provides insights about when and whether people should oppose populist parties—if at all—and what kinds of responses might be most appropriate. A next step is to subject the theories I develop here to empirical research and to reflect on the ability of theories designed with Europe in mind to 'travel' to other world regions. Further research may discover new types of initiatives opposing populist parties or other goals not covered here. Opponents may achieve their goals in ways other than the mechanisms I have identified here, or we may discover some initiatives may work better in some contexts than in others. My goal here is to start a conversation, building on what we already know, and identifying possible pathways to better understand how people who oppose populist parties may do so effectively.

1
Muddy Waters

Populism and Democratic Defence

This book was written because for many people, populism seems to profoundly challenge liberal democratic politics. Behind this seemingly straightforward proposition lies a mass of difficult issues. First, there is the basic question: What is populism? There is sufficient consensus on this topic to define populism as something to do with political appeals favouring the ordinary or common people against a corrupt or self-interested elite. This still leaves the questions: What distinguishes populist from other kinds of parties? How do we work out whether a specific party is a populist party? How powerful are populists? Even more complex is the question of whether populism is a problem for liberal democracy. Perhaps populism is an unavoidable consequence of a system of rule based on the legitimizing idea that the people are sovereign, as Canovan (1999, 2002) argued. Maybe liberal democracy in its current form needs to be challenged, as Mouffe (2018) contends. Or perhaps populist denigration of political pluralism makes it necessarily undemocratic, as Müller (2016b) has argued. Uncertainty and debate about what populism amounts to makes muddy waters for those who oppose populists. Populist calls for 'real democracy', and their very success with voting publics, shakes confidence in the effectiveness and legitimacy of opposition framed as 'democratic defence'.

In this chapter 1 try to paint a picture of the challenges facing those who oppose populism. I begin with debates about what populism is and who the most important populist parties in Europe are. This section shows that populism comes in many shapes and sizes and that it has in many ways entered the political mainstream, including routine participation in government. I then turn to discuss populist orientations to democracy. Images of the Nazis' rise to power and Stalinist party dictatorship are not that helpful for understanding contemporary European populism. Many of today's populists appear to be illiberal democrats, still favouring elections but less happy with checks on government power. However, populist projects vary, with some more inclined to authoritarianism, and others pursuing emancipatory and progressive agendas. The third part of this chapter explores links between

Responding to Populist Parties in Europe. Angela K. Bourne, Oxford University Press. © Angela K. Bourne (2023).
DOI: 10.1093/oso/9780198892588.003.0002

populism and what is frequently called 'democratic backsliding'. Populist parties have dominated governments in a significant number of European states, and parties like Fidesz in Hungary and Law and Justice in Poland have overseen important illiberal reforms. But there does not appear to be a direct relationship between the strength of populist parties and democratic backsliding. Hybrid democracies evolving in these states stop short of outright dictatorship and still leave some scope for opposition, at least for now.

What Is Populism?

Most scholars agree that populism involves a vision of society sharply divided between two groups, 'the people' and the 'elite'. Many stress the strong moralistic undercurrent of this belief. The people are 'pure' and the elite 'corrupt' as Mudde (2004) put it in his seminal piece. The people are seen as somehow intrinsically good, the elites as intrinsically evil. The struggle between 'the people' and 'the elites' looks to many like a Manichean, or antagonistic battle, in which there are only friends and enemies and few points of compromise (Mudde 2004: 545; Laclau 2005; Hawkins and Rovira Kaltwasser 2017: 515; Mouffe 2018). At best, the elite are seen as working against the best interests of the people.

'The people' glorified by populists and 'the elites' they denigrate have many faces. For populists, 'the people' are often the common or ordinary people, such as hardworking taxpayers or those producing the real wealth of the country. They are the genuine citizens. Especially for right-wing populists, the people are 'the natives', the people from *here*. Paul Taggart memorably described 'the people' in populist thinking as the populace of the 'heartland'. This is a romanticized, fictional community of the past, seemingly bound together by 'a tried and tested "good life"'(Taggart 2002: 67).

For populists, the true, good, and authentic people are at odds with either 'the elites' or 'outsiders' and sometimes both. The elites hoard political, economic, and cultural power for their own interests. These are typically the people running the government and mainstream parties. They can be judges or bureaucrats, business leaders or corporations, intellectuals, and journalists. In Europe, populists are typically Eurosceptics, seeing the EU as the tool of a corrupting, foreign elite. International elites may also include international financiers, transnational corporations, or especially for left-wing populists, the ideology of neo-liberalism or capitalism (Hawkins 2010: 252–253).

The other group at odds with 'the people' in the populist imagination are 'outsiders'. This way of differentiating the true, good, and authentic people is particularly strong for right-wing populists. For this group 'outsiders' tend to be ethnic or religious minorities or those who are 'not from here', such as immigrants. Outsiders may also be those who don't produce anything valued economically, such as those dependent on welfare. They may be cultural antagonists, such as liberal, city-dwelling cosmopolitans, 'the woke' and the 'politically correct', or in strongly religious societies, LGBTQ+ people (Mudde 2004: 561; Heinisch and Mazzoleni 2017: 108). For many right-wing populists the elite are in cahoots with the outsiders against the people.

There are many scholarly disputes beyond basic agreement that populism involves a vision of politics as a struggle between a sharply divided true, good, and authentic 'people' and a corrupt, self-serving 'elite'. A full discussion of this debate would need to consider many important technical differences between ideologies, frames, discourses, logics, imaginations, ontic and ontological approaches. This is beyond the scope of this book but can be found elsewhere (Moffitt 2016; Kaltwasser Rovira et al. 2017; de la Torre 2019). What is relevant to note is that one of the major dividing lines is between those who see populism as a set of ideas or discourse, and those who think populists should be set apart because of their actions. Mudde's (2004) definition of populism as a 'thin-centred' ideology is perhaps the most influential definition of populism as a set of ideas (for counterarguments see: Freeden 2017). By describing populism as a thin-centred ideology, Mudde wants to make the point that populism has a narrow range of core ideas—its vision of politics as struggle between 'the people' and 'elites'—and that it is typically filled out by the worldviews of other more comprehensive ideologies. This way of thinking helps capture the difference that we can see between right-wing and left-wing populism, although some populists defy classification in these terms. As hinted above, right-wing and left-wing populists typically define the people and elite in different ways, and this can result in different policies. Left-wing populists turn socio-economic issues into their top priority, focusing on socio-economic inequalities created by elites and favour market-correcting and state-welfare policies as solutions (Roberts 2019). They often stress the people-versus-elite struggle, downplaying insider–outsider differences, which tends to make them more inclusive in their conception of who count as the people (Mudde and Rovira Kaltwasser 2013). Right-wing populists take cultural issues as their top priority, particularly what they see as 'threats' to the national identity of the majority population in their country, such as immigrants and religious minorities. They tend to emphasize differences between the people and outsiders, typically making this kind of populism more exclusive in the way they define the people (Mudde and Rovira Kaltwasser 2013). This is typically reflected in the preference for restrictive immigration policies.

An alternative way of thinking about populism is to look at common traits of populist organizations, especially the role of strong, charismatic leaders with seemingly magnetic personalities. From this point of view, we shouldn't think of populist appeals to the people as anything other than strategic opportunism. It is more important to look at how populist parties play the political game, particularly what they do to win government power and what they do when they have it (Barr 2018). Kurt Weyland, for example, defines populism as 'a strategy through which a personalistic leader seeks or exercises governmental power' (2001: 14, 2017: 59). This strategy is characteristically 'based on direct, unmediated, uninstitutionalized support from large numbers of mostly unorganized followers'. In other words, populism is seen as a strategy where strong leaders build a special relationship with ordinary people, a relationship which side-steps political parties as a tool to bundle ideas about what people want from politics.

Strong leaders undoubtedly mark many populist movements and are probably an important part of their success. In the USA, Donald Trump personified the Republican Party's populist turn from 2016. There are many similarly famous figureheads in Europe: Viktor Orbán in Hungary, the Le Pen family in France, Pablo Iglesias in Spain, Matteo Salvini and Beppe Grillo in Italy among many others. One problem with emphasizing leadership so strongly is that it excludes groups that use populist slogans but thrive on loose or 'grassroots' structures. For example, this fits the transnational Occupy Movement protesting austerity after the 2008 financial crisis with the slogan 'we are the 99%' (Moffitt 2016: 45). It also means excluding parties which mobilize around populist ideas but set up strong party organizations that exist more-or-less independently of individual leaders. This is a problem for studying European populism because there are a good number of established populist party organizations that manage to survive change of leadership.

A closely related approach sees populism as a matter of political style. It can be hard not to notice populists when they communicate through colourfully 'performing' their politics. Populists are often transgressive, ostentatiously sporting the dress and manners of 'ordinary' people and theatrically expressing their contempt for what they see as elite culture (Moffitt 2016; Ostiguy 2017). It meant something when Donald Trump served McDonalds food in the White House, or when the Spanish Podemos parliamentarian Carolina Bescansa breastfed her baby in parliament. There are many ways in which populists can challenge 'the establishment', not just through the words they use.

The Power of Populist Appeals

Appeals to 'popular sovereignty' are incredibly attractive. The promise to 'take back control' can hold the promise of redemption (Canovan 1999, 2002). It seems to pledge sweeping change 'to put things right'. On the back of such claims, populists have found success all over Europe. One way to illustrate this success is to draw on the admittedly uneasy consensus among political scientists about which parties in Europe are populist. I say uneasy consensus because there is considerable debate about whether there is in fact some essential set of ideas, organizational or stylistic features which separate out populist from other parties. As we will see below, some argue that appeals to the people and criticism of elites is so normal in democratic politics that we need to identify populists by referring to the degree to which they make such appeals compared to others.

Despite this important debate, more than 80 leading political scientists have agreed upon the so-called PopuList (Rooduijn et al. 2019). The parties on this list fit Mudde's concept of populism as a 'thin-centred ideology', focusing on antagonism between the 'pure' people and 'corrupt' elite, often combined with other ideologies. It includes parties winning at least one seat or 2% of the vote in a national parliament since 1989 in 31 European countries. In the 31 European countries they surveyed, the PopuList experts counted 61 'far-right' populist parties, 19 'far left' populists, and 24 populist parties that were hard to classify as either far-left or far-right. These hard-to-classify cases are sometimes referred to as 'centrist', 'valence', or even 'pure' populist parties (Zulianello 2020: 322). They are interesting because they tend to pick and choose policies from both the left and right and in addition to anti-establishment themes focus on issues such as corruption, transparency, democratic reform, and moral integrity (ibid.: 329; Roberts 2019: 643). The PopuList shows a dramatic increase in support for populist parties. Since 1992, the share of votes for populist parties of all kinds in Europe rose almost year-on-year from around 4% to nearly one-third of all votes by 2019.

Table 1.1 presents an adapted version of the list, showing populist parties that had seats in national parliaments in 2020, or following elections in that year. There can be large differences in just how successful these parties are. If measured by the percentages of votes that gave them their seats, the top ten in 2020 all got over 20% of the vote. Most of them currently run the government in their country or did so recently. In order of votes, these are the Hungarian Civic Alliance (Fidesz)-led coalition, Poland's Law and Justice, Citizens for European Development of Bulgaria, Italy's Five Star Movement, the Greek Coalition of the Radical Left (SYRIZA), the Czechia's Action of

Table 1.1 Populist parties with representation in European national parliaments 2020 (% vote share)

Country*	Right populist**	Left populist**	(Valance or centrist) populist**
Austria	**Freedom Party (FPÖ) (16.2%)**		
Belgium	Flemish Interest (VB) (12%)		
Bulgaria	**United Patriots (OP) (9.1%)** Will (VOLYA) (4.2%)		**Citizens for European Development of Bulgaria (GERB) (32.7%)**
Croatia	Croatian Democratic Alliance of Slavonia and Baranja (HDSSB) (seat share 0.66%)		Bridge (MOST) (7.4%)
Cyprus		Citizens Alliance (SYM) (6.0%)	
Czechia	Freedom and Direct Democracy—Tomio Okamura (SPD)(10.6%)		**Action of Dissatisfied Citizens (ANO) (29.6%)**
Denmark	Danish People's Party (DF) (8.7%) The New Right (NB) (2.4%)		
Estonia	**Conservative People's Party (EKRE) (17.8%)**		
Finland	**Finns Party (PS) (17.5%)**		
France	National Rally (RN) (13.2%) France Arise (DLF) (1.2%)	Unbowed France (LFI) (11%)	
Germany	Alternative for Germany (AfD) (12.6%)	Left Party (Linke) (9.2%)	
Greece	Greek Solution (EL) (3.7%)	**Coalition of the Radical Left (SYRIZA) (31.5%)** European Realistic Disobedience Front (MeRa25) (3.4%)	
Hungary	**Hungarian Civic Alliance (Fidesz) (49.3%)** Mvt for Better Hungary (Jobbik) (19.1%)		

Country*	Right populist**	Left populist**	(Valance or centrist) populist**
Iceland		People's Party (F) (6.9%)	Centre Party (M) (10.9%)
Ireland		Sinn Féin (SF) (24.5%)	
Italy	League (Lega) (17.4%) Brothers of Italy (FdI) (4.4%) Forza Italia (FI) (14%)		Five Star Movement (5SM) (32.7%)
Latvia	Who Owns the State (KPV-LV) (14.3%)		
Lithuania			Labour Party (DP) (9.5%)
Luxembourg	Alternative Democratic Reform (ADR) (8.3%)		
Netherlands	Forum for Democracy (FvD) (1.8%) Party for Freedom (PVV) (13.1%)	Socialist Party (SP) (9.1%)	
Norway	**Progress Party (FrP) (15.2%)**		
Poland	**Law and Justice (PiS) (43.6%)** Kukiz-15 (seat share 1.3%)		
Portugal	Enough! (CH) (1.3%)		
Slovakia	SME Rodina (SR) (8.2%)	**Direction – Social Democracy (Smer) (18.3%)**	**Ordinary People & Indep. Personalities (OL'aNO) (25%)**
Slovenia	**Slovenian Democratic Party (SDS) (24.9%)** Slovenian National Party (SNS) (4.2%)	List Marjan Šarec (LMŠ) (12.7%) The Left (Levica) (9.3%)	
Spain	Vox (15.1%)	**Podemos (P) (12.8%)**	
Sweden	Sweden Democrats (SD) (17.5%)		
Switzerland	**Swiss People's Party (SVP) (25.6%)** Ticino League (LdT) (0.8%) Federal Democratic Union of Switzerland (EDU-UDF) (1%)		
UK		Sinn Féin (SF) (0.6%)	

Continued

Table 1.1 *Continued*

Country*	Right populist**	Left populist**	(Valance or centrist) populist**
Other major European populist parties (not in national parliaments in 2020)			
UK	United Kingdom Indep. Party (UKIP)/Brexit Party/Reform UK (31.6% EP 2019)		

Sources: PopuList (popu-list.org). Parties and Elections in Europe (parties-and-elections.eu) and ParlGov Project (parlgov.org).
Notes: * Countries in **bold text** have at some point in the last two decades had populist parties dominating the government, holding the position of prime minister, leading a minority government or being the largest party (or equal largest party) in a coalition government.
** Parties in **bold text** have governing experience, participating in a formal coalition government according to the ParlGov.org database. All listed parties had seats in national parliaments in 2020 and are included in PopuList 2.0. The PopuLists' classification of far-right and far-left have been broadened to right and left. This required reclassification of some cases recorded as populist but not far-left or far-right on the PopuList. Reclassification was undertaken with reference to Chapel Hill Expert Surveys from 2010–2019 (LRECON) and relevant secondary literature. The vote share for Fidesz includes votes for its closely associated, but formally separate electoral and governing coalition partner the Christian Democratic People's Party (KDNP). United Patriots is composed of three parties or coalitions of parties: Bulgarian National Movement (IMRO), Attack, and the National Front for the Salvation of Bulgaria (NFSB). The Croatian Democratic Alliance of Slavonia and Baranja participated in the 2020 elections in an election coalition with the Croatian Democratic Union (HDZ). Data on its share of votes is unavailable, so its share of seats is used as an indication of its level of support. Kukiz 15 (Poland) participated in an electoral alliance (Polish Coalition). Data on its share of votes is unavailable, so its share of seats is used as an indication of its level of support.

Dissatisfied Citizens, Swiss People's Party, Sinn Féin in Ireland, the Slovakian Ordinary People & Independent Personalities, and the Slovenian Democratic Party. Other important populist parties sitting in European parliaments in 2020 with over 15% of the vote, including some involved in coalition governments, were the Hungarian Movement for a Better Hungary, the Slovakian Direction – Social Democracy, the Freedom Party in Austria, Conservative People's Party in Estonia, Finns Party, League in Italy, Sweden Democrats, and Spain's Vox.

More generally, of the parties listed in Table 1.1, some 44% (or the 24 parties in bold type) have formally participated in governments at some point in recent years. Fidesz in Hungary and Law and Justice in Poland have dominated coalition governments with a corresponding majority in parliament. Leaders of other populist parties have been important enough to hold the job of prime minister (PM), headed minority governments, or been the largest parties in a coalition government. This includes PM Silvio Berlusconi's Forza Italia and later the Five Star Movement in Italy; the Swiss People's Party; PM Boyko Borissov's Citizens for the European Development of Bulgaria;

PM Alexis Tsipras' Coalition of the Radical Left – Progressive Alliance in Greece; PM Andrej Babiš Action of Dissatisfied Citizens in Czechia; in Slovakia, PM Robert Fico's and PM Peter Pellegrini's SMER-SD and PM Igor Matovič's and PM Eduard Heger's Ordinary People and Independent Personalities; Lithuania's Labour Party; Latvia's Who Owns the State? And PM Janez Janša's Slovenian Democratic Party. That is, nine of the 27 member states in the EU have been dominated by populist parties at some point in recent years. This is not the end of the story of populist party influence. If influence includes populist parties exchanging votes in parliament for policy concessions with parties in government, the number of important populist parties is higher still. The Danish People's Party, the Dutch Party for Freedom and more recently the Sweden Democrats are prominent examples of this kind of influence (Zulianello 2019, 2020).

Table 1.1 is meant to give a picture of how things stood in 2020. If we took in other years, and European Parliament elections, and included more European states, it would look a little different (see Zulianello 2020 for example). Another issue is that leading scholars have become increasingly wary of definitions searching for the 'essence' of populism (Jagers and Walgrave 2007; Rooduijn and Pauwels 2011; van Kessel 2014; Aslanidis 2016; Brubaker 2017; Hawkins and Rovira Kaltwasser 2017; Weyland 2017; Rooduijn 2019). Essentialist approaches aim to identify the traits that *all* and *only* populists have, but non-populists don't have. This was always a difficult task, not least because as Brubaker has pointed out, 'speaking in the name of the people … is a chronic and ubiquitous practice in modern democratic settings' (2017: 357–385; see also: Canovan 1999, 2002; van Kessel 2014). It is probably more accurate to say that populists prioritize appeals to the people against the elite more often than other parties. Populist claims may be 'harder' or 'softer' depending on the speaker, and some populist appeals may not be pitched in moralistic tones. Some might see their competitors uncompromisingly as 'enemies', while others seem more willing to compromise, and treat opponents as mere 'adversaries'. In short, it is probably more useful to speak of populism as a matter of degree.

Measuring the degree of populism is easier said than done. We may recognize the colour and forms painted in populist images of a true, genuine, and good people regardless of the context, but appreciating the shades and finer details can be more challenging. Scholars have used different techniques to rank parties in terms of their populist appeals. Some have analysed political speeches, broadcasts, party manifestos, or Twitter and Facebook posts, some counting and comparing the number of appeals to the people or elites, others interpreting or 'grading' party texts to see how well they fit definitions of populism (Jagers and Walgrave 2007; Hawkins 2010; Rooduijn and Pauwels 2011; Engesser et al. 2017). Another approach is to use expert surveys where political scientists evaluate the degree of populism based on knowledge of parties in their own countries (Meijers and Zaslove 2020 and 2021). These approaches provide evidence that populists are not the only ones to glorify the people and vilify elites, but that many of those who are typically seen as populists tend to do so much more intensely than other parties. A problem though, is that capturing the subtleties in populist appeals across countries is time-consuming, while the quicker computer-aided methods tend to overlook the subtleties. Large 'n' studies comparing the content of political speech of all European populist parties are rare.

The Populism and Political Parties (POPPA) expert survey, undertaken in 2018, has the advantage of providing data on 250 parties in 28 European countries on a range of core dimensions of populist ideology. Country experts were asked to evaluate, on a 0–10 scale, the extent to which each party adopted a Manichean worldview, seeing politics as a moral struggle between good and bad; saw the people as indivisible, or considered 'the people' to be homogeneous; spoke of the 'general will', where ordinary people's interests were considered to be singular; were people-centric, believing that sovereignty should lie exclusively with the ordinary people rather than the elites; and adopted more general anti-elitist attitudes (Meijers and Zaslove (2020 and 2021). These were aggregated into a single populism score for each party, and as Figure 1.1 below shows, populism scores show considerable variation in the degree of populism among European parties.

Figure 1.1 shows some very large differences among the parties typically considered populists. Some populist parties, such as the Dutch Party for Freedom, the Italian Five Star Movement, and Alternative for Germany are seen by experts to take populist positions very often. Parties often seen to embody the populist wave, such as the Hungarian Fidesz and Polish Law and Justice party, also have relatively high populism scores. At the lower end, parties like the Slovakian Smer-SD, Citizens for European Development of Bulgarian, and Forward Italy, all of which have extensive experience of governing, have POPPA scores similar to many mainstream parties (see http://poppa-data.eu). On the whole, scores for populist parties listed on both the PopuList (and shown in Table 1.1) and included in the POPPA dataset is 7.52, compared to the average of 4.38 for all parties with populism scores in the POPPA dataset.

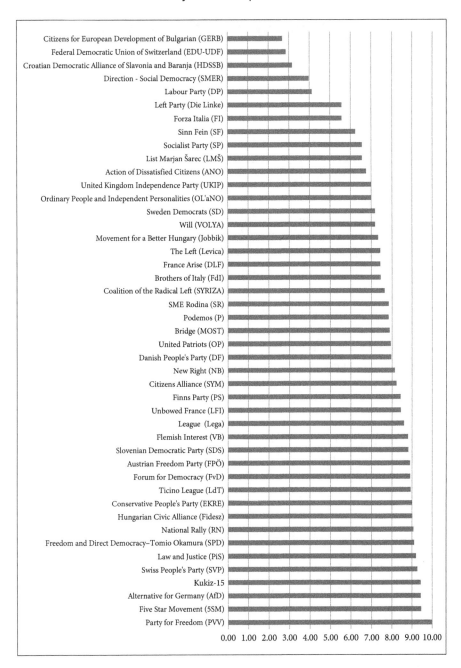

Figure 1.1 'Degrees of populism' for major European populist parties in 2018 (POPPA dataset)

Note: Data is from the Populism and Political Parties Expert Survey (http://poppa-data.eu, Meijers and Zaslove 2020 and 2021). United Patriots (OP) score is average of three coalition members: VMRO, Ataka, and NFSB. Parties listed are from Table 1.1 except for those not included in the POPPA database, namely Greek Solution (EL), Who Owns the State (KPV-LV), Alternative Democratic Reform (ADR), Progress Party (FrP), Enough! (CH), Slovenan National Party (SNS), Vox, European Realistic Disobedience Front (MeRa25), Peoples Party (F), and Centre Party (M).

Populism and Democracy: Threat or Corrective?

Deep uncertainty about whether populists are 'good' or 'bad' for democracy may also bewilder those opposing populist parties. Part of the problem is that there are incentives for any party to avoid openly pursuing alternatives to liberal democracy. Political norms in Europe favour democratic government and open pursuit of non-democratic alternatives can result in jail time or party bans. This is only part of the problem though. Different types of populist parties seem to engage with questions of democracy in different ways. Populists call for real democracy and taking back control from unresponsive elites. Yet populist theories of democracy seem to destabilize many of the usual yardsticks for evaluating democratic standards. In power, populists often speak the language of democracy but may nevertheless challenge and weaken the institutions we usually think of as essential for modern liberal democracy.

Curiously, this uncertainty about populism's effect on democracy contrasts with the early postwar and the Cold War periods. At this time, it was relatively easy to work out which parties opposed liberal democratic systems. The main challengers were neo-fascists and orthodox communists whose revolutionary ideological standpoints pointed to the strong possibility that they would probably dismantle liberal democratic institutions if given a chance. A general tendency to see populism as a threat to democracy lingered into the 1980s and 1990s, even as leading scholars insisted that the rising right-wing populists in Europe were quite different from fascists (Betz 1994; Kitschelt and McGann 1997: 31; Mudde 2004). At this time, Jean-Marie Le Pen's French National Front and Jörg Haider's Freedom Party of Austria were the prototypes. These parties often denigrated religious and ethnic minorities, and their policy ideas impaired minority rights. Among other provocations, these leaders sometimes made taboo-breaking statements openly admiring Nazi policies or minimizing Nazi crimes. However, the emergence of left-wing populists like SYRIZA in Greece and Podemos in Spain following the financial crisis of the 2000s turned the populism versus democracy debate on its head. Following the lead of Chantal Mouffe (2018), the principal theorist of left-wing populism, these parties pitched populism as a revival of the democratic tradition against the excesses of economic liberalism.

Some of the differences between these different populist traditions are captured by what Mudde and Rovira Kaltwasser (2013) described as 'inclusive' and 'exclusive' populisms. Inclusive populism, which they associated with left-wing populists in Latin America, not only favoured a material redistribution of state resources like jobs and welfare provisions to a wider group of people, it also sought to advance the quality of participation and public contestation in democracy by dignifying groups often ignored in politics and finding new ways to encourage their involvement and representation. In contrast, exclusive populism, which Mudde and Rovira associated with right-wing populists in Europe, only sought to improve the quality of democratic representation and address the unacknowledged interests of 'the natives'. Exclusive populists sought to protect the welfare state by excluding outsider groups, especially immigrants, from access to state resources. Those excluded from the definition of the true, authentic, and good people were degraded as political subjects. Mudde and Rovira Kaltwasser's point was not that inclusionary (or left-wing) populism was inevitably more democratic than exclusionary (or right-wing) populism (ibid.: 168–169); they argued that both types could be either a threat or a corrective to democracy. The point was that the relationship of populism to democracy was complicated. It could go both ways, enhancing the quality of democracy in some ways and undermining it in others.

Another controversy is whether populism is always anti-pluralist. Pluralism is often seen as a foundational element of liberal democratic politics, requiring an acceptance that societies are made up of people with sometimes profoundly differing identities, interests, and aspirations. This seems to clash with populist theories of the 'people' and the 'elites' as somehow unified and undifferentiated homogeneous groups. Many scholars have argued that pluralism is the opposite of populism, although Müller (2016b) takes a particularly strong stance in this regard (see also Mudde 2004: 544; Hawkins 2010: 29; Norris and Inglehart 2019). Müller argues that in addition to being anti-elitist, populists are always anti-pluralist (2016b: 3). To be a populist, someone 'must claim that a *part* of the people *is* the people—and that only the populist authentically identifies and represents the real or true people' (ibid.: 22–23). This 'implies that whoever does not support populist parties might not be a proper part of the people' and that populists want to deny those who disagree with them a place in the democratic game (ibid.: 3–4). One issue with this argument is that in practice, populist parties routinely operate in political systems where they have to compete with a plurality of parties and engage with clashing political ideas (Pappas 2019: 30). Many populist parties seem to be willing to live with this, which means that the anti-pluralist label erroneously paints all populists as anti-democrats.

Recent populist successes have also forced us to think more carefully about how liberalism and democracy fit together. Liberal democracy is a form of political rule that delegates popular sovereignty to elected representatives, coupled with rules to keep leaders from abusing power. *Democracy* is based on the idea of a 'sovereign people', or the idea that the people as a whole—not economic interests, technocrats, foreign powers, or some other select group—should ultimately decide how to govern. This is an attractive idea. It is what most people think democracy is about. In practice, finding a formula that will enable the people to govern themselves and yet get on with their daily lives is challenging. Modern *societies* are complex and diverse. Modern *democracies* have therefore come to rely on some process through which people can select some of their number to make political decisions on everyone's behalf. Elections and majority rule are the basic tools of this modern form of representative democracy. The leader or party winning a majority of votes in an election has a very strong claim to legitimately run the government. *Liberalism* justifies limits on government power. Individual rights promise certain freedoms from government interference and equal citizenship. Independent courts guarantee the rule of law. Political opposition and free media provide critical scrutiny of government actions.

Populists characteristically exalt 'popular sovereignty', or rule by the people, and the principle of majority rule. Their rallying cry is typically a call for 'real democracy'. When it comes to the liberal half of the liberal democratic formula, populists are typically less committed. This is why populism has been called 'democratic extremism' (Mudde 2004: 561), or much more commonly 'illiberal democracy' (Mudde and Rovira Kaltwasser 2013; Galston 2018; Pappas 2019). When those who run liberal institutions like the courts or the media are demonized as a 'corrupt elite' controlled by the enemies of the 'people', liberalism as a whole may be discredited. When populists present the 'people' and the 'elites' as somehow united and undifferentiated homogeneous groups, they not only create a political fiction, it seems to dismiss the whole idea that the people should be criticized or opposed. Populists in power experience the tension between democracy and liberalism directly when they face the possibility that liberal checks by independent courts try to block government actions, despite election wins. Sometimes populists in power have responded by changing the rules for recruiting judges and populate courts with party supporters (Scheppele 2013, 2018; Sadurski 2019b). Tensions between the democratic imperative and liberal checks and balances can also be felt when parliamentary manoeuvers by the opposition, or a critical media, challenge the ability of democratically elected governments to implement what the people seem to have shown they wanted when they cast their vote for a populist party. For some populists, this may make it easier to justify measures such as limiting media freedoms and changing electoral rules to make it harder for the opposition to win power.

In 2012, Mudde and Rovira Kaltwasser published a book whose title underlined ambiguity about the relationship between populism and democracy. The book was called *Populism in Europe and the Americas: Threat or Corrective for Democracy?* and has been widely cited. In the book, the authors insisted that populism could be a 'corrective *and* a threat' to the quality of democracy. Populism could have positive effects on democracy, improving political participation by bringing marginalized groups or viewpoints to the forefront of the political game. The idea of populism as a potential corrective chimes with many arguments that link populist success with a profound sense of dissatisfaction with the way existing liberal democracies work (Mair 2002: 82–88; Mény and Surel 2002b: 15; Eatwell and Goodwin 2018: 225). This includes a failure of mainstream parties to confront raising economic inequalities and challenges of multiculturalism in contexts of European integration and globalization. On the other hand, the authors argued, populism could be a threat to democracy where it weakened the ability of the public to contest government power. This usually happened when populists in power were able to increase governmental control and weaken the ability of others to block government decisions. This is an outcome that captures events in several Latin American countries where populists have gained power. But how widespread is it in Europe? The concept of 'democratic backsliding', which I turn to discuss now, helps us to answer this question.

Populism, 'Democratic Backsliding', and Competitive Authoritarianism

Democratic backsliding is typically defined as a state-led weakening or elimination of any of the political institutions that sustain an existing democracy (Greskovits 2015: 28; Bermeo 2016: 5). It is similar to what others have called 'autocratization' (Lührmann and Lindberg 2019) and 'de-democratization' (Enyedi 2016). All these concepts communicate, in slightly different ways, movement away from a situation where at least some democratic institutions work, to one where they no longer work, or work less well. Interestingly, scholars working on this topic have observed that democratic backsliding now takes comparatively 'milder' forms than in the past. Blatant attacks on democratic regimes, such as classic military-led *coups d'état*, executive-led coups, or election-day fraud, are now much less common (see Bermeo 2016; Scheppele 2018; Lührmann and Lindberg 2019). It is more common to see what Nancy Bermeo calls 'executive aggrandizement', where elections are still held but the people running the government gradually weaken the authority of those constitutionally permitted to limit government power (2016: 10; see also Lührmann and Lindberg 2019: 1104–1105). Typically, they do so by packing the courts. They get their friends to take over independent media or hobble them with administrative rules. They make life difficult for opposition parties and critical civil society groups, perhaps cutting funding or tightening registration rules. They tilt political competition to make it easier for themselves to win the next elections. This includes using government resources for election campaigns, keeping opposition candidates off the ballot, hampering voter registrations, packing electoral commissions, and changing electoral rules.

Levitsky and Way's concept of 'competitive authoritarianism' captures how this mixing of liberal democracy and authoritarianism tends to work in practice:

> Competitive authoritarian regimes are civilian regimes in which formal democratic institutions exist and are widely viewed as the primary means of gaining power, but in which incumbents' abuse of the state places them at a significant advantage vis-à-vis their opponents. Such regimes are competitive in that opposition parties use democratic institutions to contest seriously for power, but they are not democratic because the playing field is heavily skewed in favour of incumbents. Competition is thus real but unfair.
>
> (Levitsky and Way 2010: 5)

Put differently, in fully authoritarian regimes, elections aren't used to choose political leaders. In competitive authoritarian ones, political leaders can't be sure they can hold onto power after an election (ibid.: 12). In a liberal democracy, there is also uncertainty about election outcomes, but parties compete under more-or less the same conditions. In competitive authoritarian regimes, powerholders use their control of the state to help them win elections.

So far in Europe, democratic backsliding has at worst created forms of competitive authoritarianism. One way to illustrate this outcome is to look at results of the Varieties of Democracy (V-Dem) project, which like the PopuList is an expert survey involving an international team of political scientists (V-Dem Institute 2021). The V-Dem project classifies regime types from around the world. Countries are first sorted into groups of democracies and autocracies based on whether they meet standards guaranteeing meaningful elections (Lührmann, Tannenberg, and Lindberg 2018: 60). Meaningful elections are guaranteed by institutions ensuring officials are elected, elections are free and fair, there is sufficient freedom of expression, alternative sources of information, associational autonomy, and inclusive citizenship. The next step is to identify stronger and weaker forms of democracy and autocracy. Democracies can be weaker *electoral democracies*, which only satisfactorily meet the 'democratic' standards required for meaningful elections. Stronger *liberal democracies* meet these democratic standards and additional 'liberal' guarantees, such as checks on government power, protection of individual liberties, independent and impartial courts. The strongest type of autocracy is *closed autocracies*, which don't even hold multiparty elections for the head of government or members of parliament. In weaker *electoral autocracies,* multiparty elections are held, but fall short of 'democratic' standards, because of problems like electoral irregularities and limits on party competition (ibid.: 61). Electoral democracies and electoral autocracies fall within the scope of competitive authoritarian regimes discussed above.

Table 1.2 shows how EU states fit into the different types. There are no closed autocracies and the vast majority are liberal democracies. The plus or minus signs show the 'grey zone' between categories. A minus sign shows there is a problem on one or more key standards. A plus sign shows that it would not take much for a state to move into a higher category (ibid.: 60).

Table 1.2 Liberal democracies, electoral democracies, and electoral autocracies in the EU (2020)

Liberal democracy	Electoral democracies	Electoral autocracies
Austria	Lithuania +	Hungary +
Belgium	Malta +	
Estonia	Portugal +	
Finland	Slovakia +	
France	Slovenia	
Germany	Croatia	
Ireland	Czechia	
Luxembourg	Poland	
Netherlands	Romania	
Spain	Bulgaria	
Sweden		
Cyprus −		
Denmark −		
Greece −		
Iceland −		
Italy −		
Latvia −		

Source: V-Dem Project, *Autocratization Turns Viral, Democracy Report 2020,* March 2021, University of Gothenburg, p. 31. https://www.v-dem.net/media/filer_public/74/8c/748c68ad-f224-4cd7-87f9-8794add5c60f/dr_2021_updated.pdf

When this point is understood, we can see that there are nine electoral democracies, including four close to being liberal democracies, and one electoral autocracy, which is itself close to being an electoral democracy. This doesn't tell us anything about how things have changed over time, but can help identify states where there are problems. A more fine-grained picture of variation among states is presented in Figure 1.2, which shows rankings for democracy and liberalism standards, two key indicators used to work out whether states are stronger or weaker democracies, or autocracies.

One obvious question to ask in light of these figures is whether there is a link between populism and competitive authoritarianism. Some specialists in Latin American populism have been quite categorical in their conclusion that 'successful populism almost always triggers a slide into competitive authoritarianism' (Levitsky and Loxton 2013 and 2019: 334). Successful populists, they argue, 'push fragile democracies towards authoritarianism' because populists tend to be 'political outsiders with little experience with (or stake in) liberal democratic institutions', 'earn an electoral mandate to bury the existing elite and its institutions', and 'almost always confront institutions of horizontal accountability controlled by established political parties'

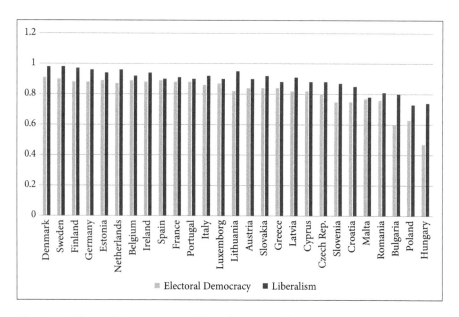

Figure 1.2 Electoral democracy and liberalism scores for EU states (V-Dem)

Source: V-Dem Project, *Autocratization Turns Viral, Democracy Report 2020*, March 2021, University of Gothenburg, p. 34. Shows Electoral Democracy Index and Liberal Component Index Scores. https://www.v-dem.net/media/filer_public/74/8c/748c68ad-f224-4cd7-87f9-8794add5c60f/dr_2021_updated.pdf

(ibid.: 2019: 334). There are reasons to be cautious about such arguments, especially in Europe. At first glance, Levitsky and Loxton's argument relies on a conception of populism that seems to fit the Latin-American experience of populism better than the European one. For instance, many of Europe's most successful populists are career politicians leading well-organized political parties, rather than inexperienced political outsiders. They rarely win power outright. Directly elected presidents able to dominate the government in the Latin-American style are rare in Europe. As Table 1.1 above has shown, most populists must be willing to cooperate with other parties in coalition governments to have any influence.

To be sure, many of the countries at the lower end of the scale of democratic quality—notably Hungary, Poland, Czechia, Bulgaria, Slovakia, and Slovenia—have had long periods of rule by governments dominated by populists. However, if we go into more detail with the V-Dem data, the link between populism and democratic quality seems much more tentative (see Figure 1.3, for more details see Appendix I).

Figure 1.3 shows difference scores for Europe's populist-dominated governments between 2000 and 2020 for the V-Dem Electoral Democracy Index (EDI) and Liberal Democracy Index (LDI). The difference scores are calculated by subtracting country scores in the last year of a populist-dominated government from the country scores in the year before that government

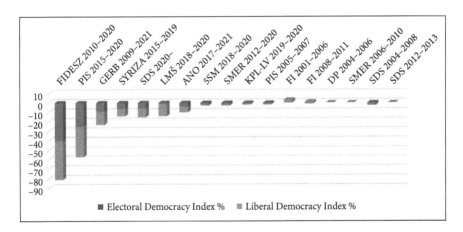

Figure 1.3 Quality of democracy for governments led by populist parties in Europe (2000–2020)

Abbreviations: GERB: Citizens for European Development of Bulgaria; ANO: Action of Dissatisfied Citizens (Czechia); SYRIZA: Coalition of the Radical Left (Greece); FIDESZ: Hungarian Civic Alliance; FI: Forza Italia; 5SM: Five Star Movement (Italy); KPV-LV: Who Owns the State (Latvia); DP: Labour Party (Lithuania); PiS: Law and Justice (Poland); Smer: Direction – Social Democracy (Slovakia); SDS: Slovenian Democratic Party; LMŠ: List Marjan Šarec (Slovenia).)

began. The data confirms the clear and serious deterioration in liberal democratic standards in Hungary (decline of 40% for EDI and 41% for LDI since 2010) and Poland (decline of 25% for EDI and 32% of LDI since 2015) under populist governments. It shows moderate declines in democratic quality following over a decade of populist rule in Bulgaria (decline of 9% for EDI and 14% for LDI since 2009). In Slovenia, where the rather rapid changeover from one populist party (List Marjan Šarec) to another (Slovenian Democratic Party) makes it difficult to assign responsibility, there has also been moderate but negative change of direction (decline of 10% EDI and LDI of 13% since 2017). V-Dem difference scores show low, but notable negative changes in democratic quality in Greece (decline of 6% EDI and 8% LDI since 2015) and over a shorter period in Czechia (decline of 4% EDI and 6% LDI, since 2017). On the other hand, populist-dominated coalitions in Italy, Slovakia, Latvia, and Lithuania have had negligible or almost imperceptible impacts on V-Dem scores. A study using a similar methodology, but different data applied to a larger sample including Western European cases where populist parties were also junior coalition partners or parliamentary support parties, shows a similarly mixed result (Vittori and Morlino 2021).

These mixed results reflect findings of larger studies over longer time-periods, covering more parties and comparing European and Latin American populist governments (Huber and Schimpf 2017; Ruth-Lovell, Lührmann, and Grahn 2019). For example, Lovell et al.'s 2019 study using V-Dem scores for 47 European and Latin American countries between 1995 and 2018 showed that EDI scores did not change more than up or down 5% for most (20 out of 30) populist tenures. It changed substantially in ten populist tenures though, including Hungarian, Polish, and Bulgarian cases (ibid.: 2019: 9). Comparing changes in V-Dem scores for both populist-led and non-populist led governments, the authors observed that populist-led government was associated with an average decline of about 1.8% per year of EDI scores and 1.6% per year for LDI scores (ibid.: 19).

Understanding the hybrid nature of regimes run by populist parties has several important consequences for studying opposition to them. The first is that the legitimation of populist party governments through electoral success means opponents must face the 'uncomfortable truth' that many of those responsible for democratic backsliding 'marshal broad popular support' (Bermeo 2016: 16). As such, it 'means that those seeking to reverse backsliding must cope not only with the state actors who engineer backsliding but with their mobilized supporters', and as Bermeo points out, 'changing their preferences is devilishly difficult and a long-term project at best' (ibid.). Another consequence is that political leaders in backsliding states often take great pains to present themselves as law-abiding democrats. Constitutional lawyers have called this 'autocratic legalism' (Scheppele 2018), or in Sajó's (2021) memorable phrase 'ruling by cheating' (see also: Levitsky and Way 2010: 5; Bermeo 2016: 11; Lührmann and Lindberg 2019: 1096). Scheppele, for instance, has shown how what she calls 'new autocrats' pointedly avoid the Hitler and Stalin 'scenarios', which is how most people imagine the end of democracy (Bermeo 2016: 16; Scheppele 2018: 571–581; Sajó 2021). The so-called new autocrats follow a script which allows them to 'hide' autocratic designs. New autocrats first win elections. This gives them the democratic mandate needed to legitimize their rule. They 'repurpose' existing liberal democratic institutions for their own ends, rather than abolish them. They generally follow the letter of the law. They steer clear of emergency measure and mass violations of human rights: Opposition activists are rarely jailed, nor are parties or NGOs banned. This façade of openness and legality disarms critics and makes authoritarian moves harder to detect.

On the other hand, competitive authoritarianism stops short of outright dictatorship which means rulers must still put up with opposition. To be sure, it is difficult to fight a fight against those who don't fight fair: The opposition may not be outlawed in competitive authoritanism, but government critics are typically 'subject to surveillance, harassment and occasional violence; their access to media and finance is limited; electoral and judicial institutions are politicized and deployed against them; and elections are often marred by fraud, intimidation and other abuse' (Levitsky and Way 2010: 12; Lührmann and Lindberg 2019: 1098). The key point, though, is that in competitive authoritarian regimes a party's hold on power is still relatively precarious. Limits on opposition do not preclude serious contestation, nor occasional opposition victories (Levitsky and Way 2010: 10, 12; Bermeo 2016: 17; Lührmann and Lindberg 2019: 1108). Partial, incomplete, and ambiguous reforms leave some openings for opposition within state institutions. Arenas of contestation are periodically opened, not least by multiparty elections. Ultimately, as Levitsky and Way argue: In competitive authoritarianism, 'Government officials fear a possible opposition victory (and must work hard to thwart it), and opposition leaders believe they have at least some chance of victory … incumbents are forced to sweat' (Levitsky and Way 2010: 12).

In Europe, there are many examples of populists leading governments who later joined the ranks of the opposition (see Appendix I). Victor Orbán's Fidesz government may have been able to form governments after four consecutive election wins and the Polish Law and Justice have so far been able to do so twice. Yet governments led by Silvio Berlusconi's Forza Italia, Alexis Tsipras' SYRIZA, Slovenia's Janez Janša's SDS, Bulgaria's Boyko Borisov's

GERB, and Robert Fico's Smer were all forced out of government, mostly following election defeats. As we will see later in the book election losses happened not just because populists became less popular. They were sometimes the outcome of concerted acts of opposition, such as the withdrawal of support by coalition partners, a successful no-confidence vote, or resignation of the government after nation-wide protests.

In this chapter 1 have sketched the basic contours of the political landscape in which opposition to populist parties takes place. I use the metaphor 'muddy waters' to express the idea that this is difficult terrain. It is not just that the object of opposition is rather slippery, rather, it is hard to separate out appeals to genuine grievances from democratic double talk, or to find the right lessons from history. Populist orientations to liberal democracy are not always clear and there can be important differences between populist parties. Democratic backsliding has not occurred everywhere populists are in power, but where it has occurred, challenging populist parties can be an uphill battle. In the next chapter, I turn to examine how those who disagree with populists navigate this complex field.

2
Mapping Initiatives Opposing Populist Parties in Europe

There are many, many ways to oppose populist parties in Europe. The most familiar forms of opposition take place during elections, where other parties typically do what they can to get voters to switch allegiance. Other parties may try to steal their most attractive policy ideas, sometimes repackaging them in more moderate language. Opponents may try to match populist style, perhaps choosing to dress like them, using folksy language, or adopting habits of the 'ordinary people'. Populists often find themselves the target of demonizing speech. Populist parties may be demonized by opponents who call them Nazis, fascists, communists, racists, extremists, or anti-democrats, or be condemned as one or other kind of nasty disease of the body politic. There may be media campaigns against them, and opponents may spread discrediting information online. If a populist party does well, winning many votes and seats in an election, other parties can decide to exclude it on principled grounds or include it in a coalition government. Coalition partners may think they can teach populist parties new ways by socializing them into governing routines or alternatively, calculating that populists in government will hang themselves on their own radical ideas or inexperience. Every now and again populists end up in court for hate or racist speech, party-funding irregularities, political corruption, or other criminal or civil law violations. Options for repressive measures are widely available but rarely used, including banning a party, state surveillance, or denying registration, party funding, or rights to participate in specific elections. Populist parties may be prevented from joining, or be kicked out of international party federations, and denied prestigious or influential positions within bodies like the European Parliament. Like all governments, populist-led executives will have to deal with manoeuvres by opposition parties in and out of parliament, or from the vantage point of alternative powerbases in local and regional governments. They will probably see protest and civil society opposition to controversial policies or face constraints from Constitutional Courts and other regulatory agencies. Governing populists will, like all governing parties, find themselves subject to monitoring by international organizations and transnational

Responding to Populist Parties in Europe. Angela K. Bourne, Oxford University Press. © Angela K. Bourne (2023). DOI: 10.1093/oso/9780198892588.003.0003

NGOs. They may find themselves subject to diplomatic, political, or economic sanctions, and their policies will probably be subject to review in courts like the Court of Justice of the EU and the European Court of Human Rights.

This is not an exhaustive list, but it is extensive. As a starting point for a theory of effective opposition to populist parties it is daunting. Separately, these forms of opposition mobilize quite different kinds of political power, ranging from coercion to manipulation of incentive structures and persuasion, and involve political actors with vastly differing resources and legitimacy. Taken together, the list also points in many directions when it comes to evaluating appropriate ways of mobilizing against populist parties in a democratic society. In this chapter I develop a typology that sorts through this jumble of initiatives. I identify six types (and various subtypes) of initiatives opposing populist parties (IoPPs) that help map the terrain of opposition to populist parties. This is the first step in clarifying how different types of initiatives opposing populist parties can work.

There are several approaches classifying responses to anti-system actors in general, or the use of specific initiatives, such as party bans (Kirchheimer 1961; Fox and Nolte 2000; Niesen 2002; Pedahzur 2004; Capoccia 2005; Rummens and Abts 2010; Bourne 2012; Downs 2012; Niesen 2012; Malkopoulou and Norman 2018; Sajó 2021). None of these are a good enough fit for studying responses to populism. Efforts to classify opposition to anti-system actors have been strongly influenced by the concept of 'militant democracy'. As mentioned in the Introduction, militant democracy is often defined as legally authorized, but exceptional, restrictions of certain basic political rights—particularly those of association and expression—to pre-emptively marginalize those who are otherwise acting within the law from undermining liberal democracy (Müller 2012: 1253; Tyulkina 2015: 14; Invernizzi Accetti and Zuckerman 2017: 183; Malkopoulou 2019: 12). One obvious problem is that these repressive, state-controlled initiatives are only a small portion of IoPPs deployed in practice. They cannot be justified where parties accept liberal democracy and cannot easily be used against populist parties in government. A larger problem is that the boundaries between initiatives that might be called militant and non-militant is unclear. Some insist militant measures are directed against non-violent actors, others see the logic of militant democracy at work in counterterrorism policy (Tyulkina 2015; Müller 2016a: 250). It is not clear whether militant democracy addresses anti-democratic ideas and/or behaviour (Bourne 2012; Invernizzi Accetti and Zuckerman 2017). Nor is the boundary between exceptional rights limitations covered by the paradigm of militant democracy and ordinary law in practice as clear-cut as it might seem in theory (Kirshner 2014; Malkopoulou and Norman 2018; Tyulkina 2019).

Another set of classificatory schemes typically incorporate a much broader range of responses than rights-restricting measures by public authorities. Capoccia's widely cited typology, for example, distinguishes between initiatives pursuing shorter- and longer-term goals on the one hand, and 'exclusive-repressive' and 'inclusive-educational' initiatives on the other (Capoccia 2005). Down's typology distinguishes between a strategy of disengagement and engagement with anti-system parties on the one hand, and more-or-less tolerant responses on the other (Downs 2012). Others build on theoretical distinctions between 'procedural' and 'substantive' models of democracy (Fox and Nolte 2000; Rummens and Abts 2010). Procedural models conceive democracy as an institutional arrangement for choosing leaders, with majority rule as the basis for legitimacy. Tolerance is a transcendent norm and there are no guarantees that democracy will always prevail. In the substantive model, democracy is conceived as a means for creating a society where citizens enjoy core rights and liberties and asserts that rights should not be used to abolish other rights. In this model, which is often seen to underpin militant democracy, tolerating the intolerant is inappropriate when core values are at stake. Rummens and Abts's 'concentric containment' model of democratic distinguishes between initiatives associated with substantive/militant and procedural conceptions of democracy on the one hand, and whether an anti-system party is politically significant enough to enter formal political institutions on the other (Rummens and Abts 2010). Malkopoulou and Norman introduce a third, 'social democratic' model of democratic defence, which they argue is superior on normative grounds to 'militant democracy' and a 'liberal-procedural' model (Malkopoulou and Norman 2018). Another related set of classificatory approaches by Meguid (2005) and Albertazzi and Vampa (2021) focus on strategies of party-political competitors. The core response categories are *dismissive strategies*, where a party signals that a competing party or its policies are insignificant by ignoring it; *adversarial strategies*, where a party competitor declares its opposition to a party's policy stance or the party itself; and an *accommodative strategy*, where party competitors move closer to the policy positions of another in order to draw votes away from it or accept it as a partner.

These typologies differ in terms of the range of initiatives they encompass and the types of initiating political actors addressed. For example, Downs' (2012), Meguid's (2005), and Albertazzi and Vampa's (2021) typologies narrowly focus on the actions of political parties. Others, such as Capoccia (2005) and Pedahzur (2004) classify a broader range of initiatives ranging from party bans, criminal law, lustration, collaboration with anti-system parties in government, and long-term strategies of civic education. Most typologies prioritize state-based initiatives and the strategies of political parties, although both Pedahzur (2004) and Rummens and Abts (2010) pay attention to civil society responses to anti-system parties.

Despite their many insights, these classificatory frameworks have shortcomings limiting their usefulness for studying contemporary responses to populism. Most assume the initiatives they study oppose 'extremists' posing a readily identifiable threat to liberal democracy. As we have seen in Chapter 1, this is a problematic assumption when dealing with populist parties in Europe. Initiatives of interest in this work are those targeting opposition parties, while populist successes make responses to populists in government increasingly important. It is hard to see where international IoPPs might fit into any of these classificatory schemes (for a partial exception see Kaltwasser and Taggart 2016). In some cases, core types seem outdated, such as Capoccia's (2005) 'purge' category linked to democratic transitions. The problem posed by contemporary populists in contemporary Europe is de-democratization or democratic backsliding rather than the challenges of transition from authoritarian rule. Classifications developed by political theorists are often difficult to operationalize, particularly differences between procedural and substantive democracies.

In light of these problems, new thinking is required to classify responses to contemporary populist parties. Inspired by traditional approaches, but departing from them in important ways, my approach classifies IoPPs with reference to two classificatory criteria. One dimension classifies IoPPs according to the *type of political actor* that initiates a response against populists (public authorities, political parties, and civil society actors). A second classificatory dimension is whether the *modes of engagement* employed by these different types of actors are 'tolerant' or 'intolerant'. This constitutes a typology with six property spaces (see Figure 2.1).

This typology was developed to help researchers systematically record evidence of opposition to populist parties in a project financed by the Carlsberg Foundation's 'Challenges for Europe' programme. It has been tested, adjusted, and improved in collaboration with researchers studying opposition to populism in Poland, Hungary, Germany, Denmark, Sweden, Spain, and Italy.[1]

---

[1] Data on IoPPs was collected by Francesco Campo, Mathias Holst Nicolaisen, Aleksandra Moroska-Bonkiewicz, Bénédicte Laumond, Franciszek Tyszka, Katarzyna Domagala, and others.

		IOPP INITIATOR		
		Guardians (Public Authorities)	Gatekeepers (Political Parties)	Advocates (Civil Society)
MODE OF ENGAGEMENT	Intolerant (exceptionality, illegitimacy/threat)	Rights-restrictions	Ostracism	Coercive confrontation
	Tolerant ('normal' politics, despite disagreement)	'Ordinary' legal controls and pedagogy	Forbearance	Adversarialism

Figure 2.1 Typology of initiatives opposing populist parties (IoPPs)

Populist Opponents: Public Authorities, Parties, and Civil Society

The first way to classify IoPPs is to distinguish between initiatives undertaken by public authorities, political parties, or civil society actors. Each category potentially incorporates political actors engaged in local, regional, state, and international territorial arenas.

Public authorities encompass individuals or organizations empowered by constitutional or ordinary law, or by international agreements, to act in the public interest. Within states this includes the judicial, legislative, and executive branches of government, the bureaucratic apparatus, state agencies, and territorial governance structures. International organizations such as the EU and the Council of Europe can be considered public authorities with delegated authority to make authoritative policy and judicial decisions on behalf of the member states and European citizens. Also included in this category are international agencies carrying out the mandate of their founding governments, and initiatives of foreign governments against populist parties (either in opposition or government).

Political parties are typically organizations which, in Alan Ware's (1996: 1–6) formulation, 'seek influence in a state', often, but not always, fielding candidates in elections to occupy positions in legislative and executive bodies at various territorial levels. They may formulate a programme of government, sets of preferred policies, future-oriented programmes for political change, or simply serve as a vehicle for the political ambitions of individuals.

Civil society actors are private groups or institutions organized by individuals for their own ends. Civil society actors differ from political parties insofar as parties are typically set up to pursue government office or influence public policy by contesting elections. Civil society actors include a very wide range of non-governmental actors, including lobby and advocacy groups, social movements, businesses, churches, trade unions, neighbourhood groups, cultural associations, mainstream and social media. Some civil society actors operate transnationally, such as some churches, or human rights organizations like Amnesty International or Human Rights Watch, or social movements like Occupy, Black Lives Matter, or #MeToo.

Public authorities, political parties, and civil society actors deploy different sources of authority and resources and play different roles when opposing populist parties. To the extent they have not been 'captured' by the supporters of populist parties, *public authorities* can be conceived as *guardians* of the liberal democratic status quo. At the state level, public authorities have the power to adopt legal regulations, as well as deploy the administrative, financial, and coercive apparatus of the state. To supplement these activities, states can additionally choose to delegate or share their powers and resources with international organizations. Outside of public office, *political parties* are *gatekeepers* guarding entry to the formal seat of political power. Sometimes they can do this by deciding who takes office (e.g., deciding who to form a coalition with, or in investiture or confidence votes). Sometimes they can do this by influencing the kinds of policies pursued (e.g., by offering parliamentary votes to support legislation). They also have a decisive role in shaping the political agenda, through their strategic engagement with voters and their role in aggregating and filtering political ideas. *Civil society actors* lack the legal authority and formal gatekeeping abilities but may serve as *advocates* of liberal democratic (or other) political projects. Civil society opponents may engage with populist parties in a wider variety of often more diffuse registers, including threatening or intimidating populist parties or their supporters; creating practical difficulties for party organization, communication, and mobilization; challenging the moral authority and legitimacy of populist parties; and pressuring others to act on their behalf against populists.

One difficulty with the approach is that it draws boundaries between spheres of political life that are often overlapping. The problem is fundamental for public authorities and political parties, especially in Europe where party government dominates. That is, governments in Europe are usually formed by parties able to sustain a majority of parliamentary seats after an election. We can acknowledge this complexity by conceiving relations between public authorities, political parties, and civil society actors as interconnected spheres (see Figure 2.2). Where they overlap, we can identify recognizable mixed categories, namely party-controlled public authorities, movement parties, and party-linked organizations. Thus, the broader category of *public authorities* would typically include courts, the bureaucracy, government agencies, the ombudsman, and international organizations,

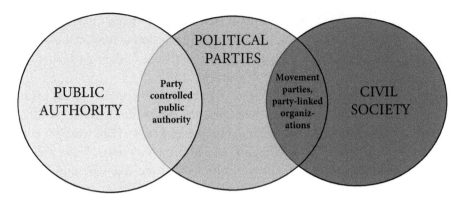

Figure 2. 2 Actors opposing populist parties: overlapping fields

which exercise constitutionally and legally defined public functions theoretically independently of political parties. On the other hand, the offices of president, prime minister, minister, the cabinet, and those running local and regional governments are typically controlled by political parties.

Tolerant and Intolerant Modes of Engagement with Populists

The second way to classify IoPPs is to distinguish between 'tolerant' or 'intolerant' modes of engagement. This dimension acknowledges the line drawn in some form or other in all classifications of responses to political extremism. This is the distinction between initiatives considered 'intolerant' (or 'coercive', 'repressive', 'exclusive') on the one hand, and 'tolerant' (or 'persuasive', 'accommodative', 'inclusionary') on the other. In my approach, the difference between intolerant and tolerant modes of engagement can be observed explicitly with reference to criteria of 'exceptionality' and 'normality' (see Figure 2.3).

Intolerant modes of engagement subject populist parties to 'exceptional' treatment. Within liberal democracies, 'exceptionality' occurs when populist parties are denied the rights, privileges, and respect which political parties would usually enjoy, either by law or in practice, because of their representative function in a democratic society and/or a governing party in the international sphere. Rights-restricting initiatives of militant democracy clearly meet this criterion because they curtail basic rights that parties otherwise enjoy as a fundamental right in liberal democracies. Intolerant modes of engagement include a wide variety of legal and political initiatives, including restrictions on the right of association (such as party bans); of expression (such as displaying Nazi paraphernalia); and collusion among mainstream parties to reduce anti-system party success at elections or their participation in government (cordon sanitaire, or ostracism).

In the international sphere, exceptional treatment for populist parties principally entails the denial of rights, privileges, and respect due to those running state institutions by virtue of agreements between states (like treaties) and international norms (like sovereignty and non-intervention). However, in highly developed international organizations like the EU, where populist parties may have important representative functions (like participating in the European Parliament), exceptionality also entails a denial of the rights, privileges, and respect which political parties would usually enjoy. Examples of such initiatives include the expulsion or suspension of a state led by populists from an international organization, and the imposition of political and economic sanctions on such a state, party, or its representatives for actions within the state deemed to threaten liberal democratic institutions, principles, and values.

Exceptionality is observed empirically when, first, it can be shown that a norm or rule with general application is suspended in the case of a populist party. Such rules can be a formal rule, such as the legal provisions of a constitution establishing a general right to association and free speech, legislation regulating state funding for political parties, or regulations permitting the proportional distribution of positions of power (e.g., in a parliament). Rules may also be informal, including political practices permitting (at least theoretical) collaboration, for example in elections or government, between political parties with differing ideological positions, and norms of non-violence and civility regulating political engagement in the public sphere. Exceptionality is often observed when the suspension of a general rule, practice, or norm is accompanied by a justification which explicitly or implicitly claims that the ideas and behaviours of populist parties are illegitimate and/or constitute a threat to liberal democracy.

Tolerant modes of engagement subject populist parties to the *same* norms, rules, and practices in democratic politics and international relations as those applied to other parties and states not led by populists. Tolerant modes of engagement are the negation of *intolerant* modes of engagement, in that they subject populist parties to 'normal', rather than 'exceptional' treatment. This distinction between 'exceptional' and 'normal'/ 'ordinary' responses to anti-system parties is a common theme in studies of responses to anti-system parties. Many scholars draw a line between militant democracy restrictions on fundamental rights on the one hand, and 'ordinary law', which can itself sometimes be mobilized against anti-system parties (for example when they commit criminal code violations) (Müller 2012; Tyulkina 2015: 46–48; Malkopoulou and Norman 2018: 449). A similar distinction has been draw in relation to EU law provisions for sanctions (like Article 7 TEU voting suspension procedures) and procedures used to deal with rule of law violations in 'normal times' (like infringement proceedings) (Blauberger and Kelemen 2017: 332). Regarding party responses, the strategy of ostracism has been described as 'a drastic one, which must be justified by portraying the other as some kind of evil party that should not be dealt with in any way' (van Spanje 2018: 38). In contrast, the decision to invite a party into a governing coalition has been described as treating them as 'normal' parties, or as 'ordinary political opponents' (Van Spanje and Van Der Brug 2007; Rummens and Abts 2010: 649).

In other words, initiatives classified as tolerant engage with populist parties through the modalities of 'normal politics': 'ordinary law', criminal and civil codes, and the courts; application of parliamentary and administrative procedures; information campaigns and civic education; competition among political parties to win 'office', 'policy', and 'votes'; and protest, contestation, persuasion, and accommodation in the public sphere. Importantly, tolerance does not require a passive attitude towards populist parties, nor accepting their ideas and behaviour uncritically. Tolerance entails, as McKinnon defines it, 'putting up with what you oppose', even if another person's life choices or actions shock, enrage, frighten, or disgust (McKinnon 2006: 4). A robust opposition to populist parties is thus compatible with treating populist parties as 'normal' political opponents.

As the negation of exceptionality, 'normal' treatment can be observed empirically when opposition to populist parties nevertheless follows norms, rules, and practices with general applicability, even in cases where opponents regard the ideas or behaviour of a populist party as highly objectionable. Tolerant modes of engagement may be justified by appeal to a criterion of 'normality', including a reference to the rights of citizens voting for populists to have their voices heard or positions represented in the political system like other citizens. Alternatively, they may be accompanied by discourses demonizing populist parties and claims that populists pose a threat to liberal democratic institutions. In short, whatever the justification, tolerant modes of opposing populist parties will not lead to suspension of norms, rules, or practices of general application of interest here.

In less abstract terms, application of the framework to classify IoPPs with colleagues from the Carlsberg Foundation's 'Challenges for Europe' project led to the observation of three sets of norms, rules, and practices of general

OPPONENTS' MODE OF ENGAGEMENT

INTOLERANT	TOLERANT
Exceptional Treatment	**Normal politics**
Opposition *suspending* a general norm, rule or practice of general application which grants rights, privileges and respect to parties by virtue of a) their representative function in democratic politics or b) their role as governing parties in the international sphere.	Opposition *observing* a general norm, rule or practice of general application which grants rights, privileges and respect to parties by virtue of a) their representative function in democratic politics or b) their role as governing parties in the international sphere.

Norms, rules and practices of general application granting rights, privileges and respect to populist parties by virtue of their a) representative function and/or b) leading role in government

Public authorities: free exchange of political ideas within states (rights to expression and association) and non-interference in domestic political affairs of states in the international sphere.

Political parties: parties keep their options open regarding their political platform and/or alliances strategies

Civil society actors: non-coercive forms of expressing disagreement with political opponents

Figure 2.3 Tolerant and intolerant modes of engagement with populist parties

application which were suspended or observed, depending on the type of populist opponent. That is, IoPPs undertaken by *public authorities,* which were in accordance with constitutional norms and rules providing for the *free exchange of political ideas within states* and the *principle of non-interference in the domestic political affairs of states in the international sphere*, met the criteria of 'normality' for tolerant IoPPs. IoPPs suspending or contravening those principles meet the criteria of 'exceptionality'. IoPPs undertaken by *political parties* meeting the criteria of 'normality' were consistent with the general practices of democratic competition whereby *parties keep their options open regarding their political platform and/or alliance strategies*. IoPPs meeting the criteria of exceptionality did not keep their options open. IoPPs undertaken by *civil society actors* met the criteria of 'normality' when they were in accordance with norms, practices, and rules favouring *non-coercive forms of expressing disagreement with political opponents*.

Intolerant Initiatives Opposing Populist Parties

Intolerant IoPPs subject populist parties to 'exceptional' treatment at odds with norms, rules, or practices granting rights, privileges, and respect to parties by virtue of (a) their representative function in a democratic society and (b) their governing roles in the international sphere.

Rights restrictions by public authorities

When intolerant IoPPs are undertaken by public authorities they seek to delimit the participation of populist parties in the public sphere and/or the impact of their ideas and actions on public policy by (a) *restricting certain kinds of political rights*, including rights of association and expression exercised by populist parties and their representatives, as well as (b) *rights to obtain access to public goods* (such as funds) which they would otherwise have a right to obtain.

IoPPs that restrict such rights are often typical of militant democracy. Tyulkina helpfully distinguishes between rights restrictions justified with the preventive rationale of militant democracy on the one hand, and 'ordinary' types of rights-restrictions on the other (Tyulkina 2015). This distinction helps clarify the nature of the exceptionality criteria for *rights-restricting* IoPPs. Distinguishing between 'militant' and 'ordinary' forms of rights-restriction is also important because civil and political liberties are never absolute and are often subject to limitations quite apart from those justified as preventing harm to the liberal democratic system. Militant democracy, according to Tyulinka, has a narrow area of application, targeting a limited range of rights related to 'participation in political and public discourse', rights whose abuse has 'the potential to affect the operation of the state as a constitutional democracy' (Tyulkina 2015: 46–47). Thus, limitations on rights like family and private life, and social and economic rights, are difficult to justify with militant democracy rationales because their application is unlikely to affect the operation of the state as a constitutional democracy (Tyulkina 2015: 46). Rights limitations under militant democracy 'usually only have a direct effect on a limited number of citizens compared to ordinary rights limitations' and 'are applied mainly in a case-by-case manner and cannot be invoked in relation to the whole political community' (Tyulkina 2015: 46). In other words, the *criterion of exceptionality* is met because those subject to restrictions of their political rights are *denied the right to freely exchange their political ideas* under the same conditions as others. Another way to think about this is to note that *rights-restricting* IoPPs suspend tolerance for political speech in relation to two core features of democracy, or what one of the foremost theorists of democracy Robert Dahl (2000) describes as 'effective participation' and 'enlightened understanding'. To satisfy these, members of a polity ought to have, respectively, 'equal and effective opportunities for making their views known to other members' and a chance for 'learning about the relevant alternative policies and their likely consequences' before new policies are adopted (ibid.: 37).

Germany, long the prototypical case of a militant democracy, provides many examples of rights-restricting IoPPs (Braunthal 1990; Kommers 1997; Backes 2006; Michael and Minkenberg 2007: 1115; Tyulkina 2015; Bourne 2018). Parties may be banned or denied public funding in Germany if they, 'by reason of their aims or the behaviour of their adherents, seek to undermine or abolish the free democratic basic order or to endanger the existence of the Federal Republic of Germany' (Article 21(2–3), Basic Law). Parties that may better fit the definition of an association may also be banned for such reasons (Article 9, Basic Law). In addition, rights to freedom of expression, the press, of teaching, assembly, association, privacy of correspondence, posts and telecommunications, rights of property, and of asylum may be denied if used to 'combat the free democratic basic order' (Article 18, Basic Law). Other rights limitations include surveillance and reporting of political activity by the Federal Office for the Protection of the Constitution (Verfassungsschutz) for parties considered a threat to the free democratic basic order, and bans on use of symbols of anti-constitutional organizations.

Rights-restricting IoPPs include both of what Müller has described as 'hard' and 'soft' measures of militant democracy (Müller 2016a: 259). Hard measures are responses like 'party bans or restricting rights to certain kinds of speech … [or] the complete loss of political rights'. In contrast, soft measures 'would leave a party in existence but officially limits its possibilities for political participation, or de facto make its life difficult'. Soft measures include not allowing a party to register for elections, but letting it exist nonetheless (as in Israel); banning certain kinds of speech (on religious or ethnicity themes) only during election campaigns (as in India); or denying parties financing or access to broadcast media for election campaigns. The effectiveness of such rights-restricting IoPPs are discussed in Chapter 4 on 'Enforcement through the Constitution, Courts, and Coercion'.

In the international sphere, 'exceptional' treatment by public authorities entails a denial of 'rights' to states led by populist parties. Although the concept of 'rights' has a different hue in national compared to international law, we can conceive of rights in the international sphere as entitlements granted by virtue of a state being party to an international agreement such as a treaty, or in case of the EU, its laws and regulations. Exceptional treatment in this arena can include denying rights to participate in international institutions (including expulsion, suspension of voting rights), or the application of sanctions preventing access to public goods (like funds) which a state would otherwise have a right to receive.

Application of Article 7 of the Treaty on the European Union is a prime example of *rights-restricting* IoPPs in the international sphere. The article permits the Council to suspend voting rights of a member state deemed to be in breach of the common values of the EU. An example of provisions restricting a member state's right to public goods to which it would otherwise be entitled on the grounds of a threat to liberal democratic values are new rules permitting the EU to withhold funds where rule of law conditionality is not met. Effectiveness of international *rights-restricting* IoPPs are discussed in the section of Chapter 5 on leverage and international sanctions.

Ostracism by other political parties

When intolerant IoPPs are undertaken by other political parties, they aim to delimit participation of populist parties in the public sphere and/or the impact of their ideas and actions on public policy *by refusing to cooperate with populist parties*, thereby denying them access to positions of political power and signalling their illegitimacy in democratic politics (Downs 2001; Art 2007; Van Spanje and Van Der Brug 2007; Downs 2012; Akkerman and Rooduijn 2015; van Spanje 2018). Ostracism is the act of intentionally excluding someone from a social group or activity. For political parties, ostracism is a strategy most commonly available when populist parties are not large enough to establish single-party governments. In the literature on democratic defence, there is no consensus on usage of the term, with many using it synonymously with 'cordon sanitaire' to signify the principled exclusion of 'pariah parties' from coalition governments (Van Spanje and Van Der Brug 2007; Downs 2012; Akkerman and Rooduijn 2015). Nor is there agreement regarding its scope, with most focusing on its consequences for government formation, and some acknowledging a broader set of exclusionary practices (Art 2007: 338–339; Pauwels 2011: 61; Ripoll Servent 2019). Adopting this broader meaning of *ostracism*, I use it to describe IoPPs undertaken *by political parties to exclude a populist party from a collaborative political activity on principled grounds, or more specifically, because they consider populists illegitimate and/or a threat to liberal democracy.*

Ostracism meets a *criterion of exceptionality* because it suspends the general practice in democratic politics whereby political parties keep their options open regarding their policy positions and/or alliance strategies.

This practice does not seem to be linked to specific norms or rules of democratic politics but contributes to the goal of representation at the heart of modern liberal democracies insofar as it permits parties to respond to changing citizen preferences (Dahl 2000: 85; Rummens and Abts 2010: 654). That parties keep their options open does not require they weigh all other parties as equally attractive partners. The literature on coalition formation makes it clear that cooperation choices are influenced by goals of 'office', 'policy', and 'vote' (among other things) (Laver and Schofield 1998; Müller and Strøm 1999; Martin and Stevenson 2001).

Four subtypes of ostracism can be identified. *Electoral ostracism* takes place where parties compete to win votes, but decide to exclude, on principled grounds, a populist party from electoral alliances, or from being favoured in other ways, such as being named as a preferred option in two-vote electoral systems (Van Spanje and Van Der Brug 2007: 1028; Bardi and Mair 2008: 158). In the parliamentary arena, where legislation, political accountability, and the building and maintaining of government coalitions take place, political exclusion on principled grounds can take different forms. The most widely researched of these is *governmental ostracism* (or cordon sanitaire), or exclusion of parties from governing coalitions (see Table 3.1 for examples). A third form is *parliamentary ostracism*, including a principled refusal to support all parliamentary initiatives of a populist party, no matter how minor (Art 2007: 338–339); a refusal to allocate parliamentary positions (e.g., committee chairs) to populist parties (e.g., in the European Parliament see Startin 2010; Ripoll Servant 2019); or suspension, expulsion, or exclusion of parties from parliamentary groups (Haugton 2014; Kelemen 2020). A final form is *public ostracism* (ignoring), or the intentional exclusion, by competing parties, of populist parties, from activities or events in the public sphere, including a refusal on principled grounds to invite populist parties to public debates, or a refusal to attend debates where a populist party has been invited. Effectiveness of ostracism is discussed further in Chapter 3 on 'Manipulation of Voter and Party Choice'.

Coercive confrontation by civil society actors

When intolerant IoPPs are undertaken by civil society actors they seek to delimit the participation of populist parties in the public sphere and/or the impact of their ideas and actions on public policy *by using coercion*, which in contemporary Europe is usually undertaken to *exclude, intimidate, or express contempt,* rather than to eliminate opponents as a rival. As used here, coercion is a form of advocacy involving what Tilly defines as 'collective violence', or a form of contentious claim making which 'inflicts physical damage on persons and/or objects' (Tarrow, McAdam, and Tilly 2001: 105–107; Tilly 2003: 3).

Coercive IoPPs meets a *criterion of exceptionality* because they suspend the general norm, rules, and practice in liberal democracies whereby non-state actors make political claims without coercion. As John Keane observes, a unique characteristic of those living in contemporary democracies is a self-understanding of their system of political rule as, ideally, a 'bundle of non-violent power-sharing techniques' and a 'learned quality of non-violent openness' (ibid.: 3, 9). While it never eliminates violence, the ambition to control it is institutionalized in procedures where 'the violated get a fair public hearing, and fair compensation ... that those in charge of the means of violence are publicly known, publicly accountable to others—and peacefully removable from office' (ibid.: 9; see also: Tarrow 2011: 110). The very concept of 'civil society', as Keane observes, has a close affinity with a norm of non-coercion, conceived as 'a site of complexity, choice and dynamism' and the 'elimination of violence from human affairs' (2004: 44, 52). It is associated with the notion of 'civility', or a 'more or less ... peaceful outlook', a 'strong distaste for cruelty, a genuine interest in others' way of life, or a simple commitment to ordinary courtesy and respect' (ibid.: 3). Those willing to deploy coercion tend to regard their opponents as illegitimate actors undeserving of 'civility', and/or believe coercion is justified to protect liberal democratic institutions or values. In many cases, they may approximate Mouffe's (2000) conception of 'antagonistic' opponents, engaged in a struggle to eliminate an enemy, in a battle over mutually incompatible political projects and identities.

In one form or another, coercion is one of the main tactical repertoires available to civil society actors engaged in contentious politics (Tarrow, McAdam, and Tilly 2001: 5; Tilly 2003; Taylor and Van dyke 2007; della Porta 2008). *Coercive confrontation* can take various forms. There are four main subtypes, including *damage to property* (eg. smashing windows, defacing public statues, or hacking websites), *diffuse threats of violence* (eg. physically blocking movement in a public place, throwing food at populist politicians, or use of smoke bombs) and *political violence* (eg. forcible occupation of building, fights with opposing protestors, rioting, shooting into a crowd, assassination, and harm to self through hunger strikes and self-immolation). A fourth subtype - *organized armed conflict*, which includes civil and international war, insurrection, and terrorism – is absent in Europe. This suggest that in Europe, coercion against populist parties is mostly used to exclude, intimidate, or express contempt rather than to eliminate an enemy.

Effectiveness of coercive confrontation is discussed in Chapter 5's section on disruption and when in the form of symbolic action, as part of Chapter 6's section on framing and stigmatization.

Tolerant Initiatives Opposing Populist Parties

Tolerant IoPPs observe the norms, rules, and practices typically granting rights, privileges, and respect to political parties by virtue of their representative function in a liberal democratic society, and in the international sphere, by virtue of their governing roles. As their name signals, tolerant IoPPs may require opponents to put up with what they dislike or abhor and may therefore be accompanied by harsh critique and claims of grave disagreement with populist parties.

'Ordinary' legal controls and pedagogy by public authorities

When tolerant IoPPs are undertaken by public authorities, they seek to delimit the participation of populist parties in the public sphere and/or the impact of their ideas and actions on public policy by (a) *deploying ordinary legal controls,* such as constitutional checks and balances, civil and criminal litigation, as well as (b) *practices of public pedagogy,* such as civic education and condemnatory declarations. These measures meet a *criterion of normality* because they observe the general practice of liberal democratic and international politics whereby political parties, or governments run by them, may freely express their political ideas, or obtain access to public goods under the same conditions as others. That is, IoPPs in this category use rules and procedures designed to affect all parties and states, address illegal behaviour in general, and/or seek to change political ideas through education, dialogue, or discourse. There are three main subtypes discussed in this book.

The first deploys *checks and balances* of liberal democratic politics, institutionalized in varying (usually constitutionally entrenched) rules for separate but interdependent judicial, executive, and parliamentary bodies. Additionally, it includes use of procedures vetting executive and judicial appointments; dismissal of governments or ministers in no-confidence votes; impeachment; establishing investigatory committees; the rulings of constitutional courts; and acts of secondary supervisory bodies like ombudsmen or independent media regulators. In the international sphere, rulings of human rights courts, such as the European Court of Human Rights, provide additional checks against rights violations (Alter 2012: 23). This vast and potentially very powerful set of tools for responding to populist parties is chronically under-theorized in the relevant literature, despite its obvious importance for dealing with populist parties approaching, or occupying, positions of political power.

A second subtype is *judicial controls*. This IoPP subtype includes invocations of ordinary law against populist parties for infractions mostly spelt out in civil and criminal codes (or equivalent). It includes investigations, proceedings, and convictions for corruption and abuse of office, violation of party funding rules, as well as hate speech and hate crimes. While hate speech rules clearly limit freedom of expression, they typically aim to protect the dignity of victims and public peace rather than the subversion of democratic institutions per se (Bleich 2011; Niesen 2012: 548). Holocaust denial sits closer to the boundary between this subtype and *rights-restricting* IoPPs, given that it has a been 'closely linked … to efforts on the right to restore the "positive" image of Nazism and prewar fascism' (Wistrich 2012: 13; see Behrens, Terry, and Jensen 2019 on other political effects). Nevertheless, it can also be interpreted as being a 'particularly malevolent form of racist incitement', which justifies its inclusion within this category (Bleich 2011; Wistrich 2012: 25). In the EU, IoPPs prosecuting illegal acts include tactical use of infringement proceedings against illiberal or anti-democratic practices of member states (Blauberger and Kelemen 2017: 322; Scheppele et al. 2020). The effectiveness of checks and balances and judicial controls are discussed in Chapter 4 on 'Enforcement through the Constitution, Courts, and Coercion'.

A final category of tolerant IoPPs by public authorities is *public persuasion*, which includes speech and symbolic action aiming to dissuade populist parties from undertaking actions, such as those that may undermine liberal democratic institutions, or to persuade others not to support populist parties or their ideas. It can include speech by representatives of public authorities (presidents, prime ministers, the EU's Commission president) condemning or demonizing populist parties. Demonization is defined as a moral judgement 'portraying a person as the personification of evil' (van Heerden and van der Brug 2017: 37). While what constitutes evil will vary over time and according to context, portraying someone as a Nazi or a fascist in contemporary Europe (and elsewhere) is widely recognizable as demonization, with the fascist branded as a morally defective person who should be shunned (van Heerden and van der Brug 2017: 37). Public persuasion can also include dialogical processes, whereby populist parties or their supporters are persuaded, through rational argumentation, social learning, moral discourses, emotional appeals, or new issue frames, to adopt new opinions, identities, and/or interests (Risse et al. 1999; Risse and Ropp 2013). This can take place locally, when for example participation of populist parties in governmental or parliamentary institutions may restore populist party members' 'faith in politics' (Rosenblum 2008), as well as international fora, such as the European Commission's 'Rule of Law' framework, or the EU Council's Rule of Law dialogue (Sedelmeier 2017). Public persuasion can also take the form of information which may 'name and shame' its targets, which is produced by public authorities such as government departments and agencies, or international bodies such as the Council for Security and Cooperation in Europe and the European Commission against Racism and Intolerance.

Forbearance by political parties

When tolerant IoPPs are undertaken by other political parties, they aim to delimit the participation of populist parties in the public sphere and/or the impact of their ideas and actions on public policy by (a) *using ordinary tactics of party-political opposition* and (b) *cooperating with, or copying, populist parties* (Bale 2003; Capoccia 2005: 63–66; Akkerman and de Lange 2012; Downs 2012; Zaslove 2012; Akkerman, de Lange, and Roodouijn 2016; van Spanje 2018). Forbearance involves self-restraint, preventing oneself from saying or doing something otherwise preferred, or sufferance, unwillingly granting someone else permission to do something. As Downs has put it in the case of tolerant responses to extremists, there is a 'tendency to exercise restraint in the face of objectionable pariah parties, even when such tolerance is at odds with other democratic values (protection of minorities, for example)' (2012: 31). Like ostracism, forbearance is a strategy available to political parties when populist are not large enough to run the government, and becomes attractive when populist parties become large enough to obtain 'blackmail' or 'coalition' potential (Sartori 1976). For parties opposing populist governments, forbearance may be more of a necessity than a choice.

Forbearance in the form of parties' decisions to cooperate with or copy populist parties they oppose meet a *criterion of normality* because they observe the general practice in democratic politics whereby political parties keep their options open regarding their policy positions and/or alliance strategies. As noted above, this contributes to the goal of representation at the heart of modern liberal democracies insofar as it permits parties to respond to changing citizen preferences (Downs 1957; Dahl 2000: 85; Rummens and

Abts 2010: 654). As such, a party which exercises forbearance in relation to a populist opponent engages with a populist party principally to achieve strategic goals of 'office', 'policy', and 'votes' (Akkerman and de Lange 2012; Akkerman, de Lange, and Roodouijn 2016; van Spanje 2018).

Cooperation with populist parties is widely regarded as a 'tolerant' or 'accommodatory' response to anti-system parties (Capoccia 2005: 63–66; Downs 2012: 2; Albertazzi and Vampa 2021: 59–62). Inspired by van Spanje's distinctions (2018: 40), I distinguish four main types of cooperation, mirroring the four types of ostracism mentioned above. *Electoral cooperation* occurs where a populists' opponents are willing to form electoral alliances with them. In the parliamentary arena, *governmental cooperation,* or inclusion of populist parties in governing coalitions is now very common (see Table 3.3). A third form is *parliamentary cooperation,* or routinized cooperation with a populist party to pass legislation and manage parliamentary business. Examples of populist parties remaining outside formal coalition governments, but systematically providing support to minority governments could be found in Denmark (Danish People's Party), where then leader Pia Kjærsgaard was elected speaker of parliament in 2015, and in the Netherlands (Party for Freedom). It can also include less formalized forms of engagement in parliamentary business such as involvement in budget negotiations. A final form is *public cooperation,* or the routine inclusion of populist parties in activities or events in the public sphere, such as television debates or hustings, and informal dialogue between populist and non-populist parties.

Policy cooptation involves 'parroting' or 'copying, at least partially [a] party's core issue positions' (van Spanje 2018: 24), with the paradigmatic example being 'contagion to the right' on immigration policy (Bale 2003; Akkerman and Rooduijn 2015). Downs classifies policy cooption as militant (intolerant), being a strategy where 'the political establishment … engages the pariah directly with the issue or issues fuelling its electoral success and tries to aggressively combat the threatening party by recapturing the policy space (even when doing so results in some compromise of pre-existing moderate principles')' (Downs 2012: 31). Similarly, van Spanje argues that the best strategy to combat anti-system parties is to combine ostracism and 'parroting the pariah' (van Spanje 2018). Nevertheless, I follow Meguid (2005) and Albertazzi and Vampa (2021) in conceiving policy cooption as a routine kind of strategic interaction in democratic competition, something which parties in general do to win over competitor's supporters, and thus a tolerant mode of engagement with populist parties. The effectiveness of cooperation with populist parties and policy cooptation is discussed in Chapter 3 on 'Manipulation of Voter and Party Choice'.

An additional subtype of forbearance is *oppositional politics*, where populists' partisan opponents aim to defeat populists using ordinary tactics of electoral campaigning or parliamentary procedure. It includes initiatives of opposition parties to defeat or amend the legislation of a governing populist party, to interpellate government representatives, establish investigatory committees, and challenge government acts in the courts. Some oppositional politics IoPPs, such as a motion of no-confidence in the government or a minister, or impeachment, may overlap procedurally with *checks and balances,* a subcategory of tolerant IoPPs by public authorities. Nevertheless, these can be considered largely acts of political parties until such initiatives achieve their goal. That is, a no-confidence motion against a populist government remains an act of opposition politics until it succeeds, after which it becomes a check on the executive branch. The effectiveness of *oppositional politics* is discussed in Chapter 4 on 'Enforcement through the Constitution, Courts, and Coercion'.

And finally, *political persuasion* is analogous to *public persuasion*, involving acts or speech by political parties, their leaders, or members aiming to persuade others not to support populist parties or their ideas. It can take the form of condemnation, demonization, 'naming or shaming', or dialogue, among other things. It can also include symbolic actions, such as when ignoring a party aims to signal to voters that a party's policy proposals lack merit (Meguid 2005: 349; Downs 2012: 32–33; Albertazzi and Vampa 2021: 54–56). The effectiveness of oppositional politics is discussed in Chapter 6 on 'Persuasion, Talk, and New Ideas'.

Adversarialism by civil society actors

When tolerant IoPPs are undertaken by civil society actors they seek to delimit the participation of populist parties in the public sphere and/or the impact of their ideas and actions on public policy by *using non-coercive means of public protest demonstrating a claim in public* (Tarrow 2011: 98). Adversarial IoPPs meet a *criterion of normality* by observing norms of civility, at a minimum committing to non-violent engagement with political opponents, but often involving some level of acceptance of political pluralism and the open-ended nature of political struggle (Mouffe 2000; Keane 2004; Rummens 2020). It is named after Mouffe's (2000) conception of the 'adversary' in her model of democratic politics as 'agnostic pluralism'. As Mouffe argues, the adversary is 'someone whose ideas we combat but who's right to defend these ideas we do not put into question' (ibid.: 192). This is 'liberal-democratic' tolerance, she argues, in the sense that it 'does not entail condoning ideas that we oppose or being indifferent to the standpoints that we disagree with, but treating those who defend them as being legitimate opponents' (ibid.: 192). Adversarial IoPPs thus tend to treat populists as one opponent among others in political life and use forms of opposition typically deployed against other types of parties as well.

Adversarial IoPPs are forms of contentious politics, which 'demonstrate a claim, either to objects of the claim, to power holders, or to significant third parties', but can take a very wide variety of forms (Tarrow and Tilly 2006; Tarrow 2011: 98). They include demonstrations, marches, strikes, litigation, lobbying, boycotts, civil disobedience, hunger strikes, art and satire, public debate, and (dis)information campaigns using both traditional and social media. Such actions may involve exclusively local actors or transnational networks. It often involves formation of alliances between civil society actors and more powerful actors such as political parties or pressuring public authorities to use their resources to constrain populist parties. Protest may employ a tactical repertoire pursuing *instrumental* goals, such as publicizing a grievance, challenging legislation, or stigmatizing an opponent; or take *expressive* form, for example, by modelling through performance some desired alternative forms of social relations, decision-making, or political culture (Taylor and Van Dyke 2007: 266–267). Protestors may use non-confrontational *insider tactics*, such as letter-writing, leafletting, lobbying, press conferences, and lawsuits or more confrontational *outsider tactics*, such as sit-ins, demonstrations, blockades, and strikes (Taylor and Van Dyke 2007: 267). Protest may be *conventional* 'ritualized public performances', using tried and tested action forms accepted as legitimate by elites and easily understood by bystanders (Tarrow 2011: 99). Or they may be more innovative, perhaps illegal, *disruptive* action forms which 'break with routine, startle bystanders and leave elites disoriented, at least for a time' (Tarrow 2011: 99).

Adversarial IoPPs may follow a more traditional logic of *collective action*, or digitally enabled, networked forms of what Bennett and Segerberg (2013) call *connective action*. As these authors explain, collective action is generally *organizationally brokered*, involving coalitions of formal, leadership-based, professionally run, resource-intensive organizations, with members integrated through collective identities, perhaps emotional commitments to a cause, and common ways of defining issues and acting in concert (ibid.: 10, 13). Newer, digitally networked forms of *connective action* are built around looser gatherings of individuals, formal organizations and technologies, which use more inclusive, easily personalized action frames acknowledging growing preferences for more flexible and individualized engagement with political causes (ibid.: 2–6).

Adversarialism can be divided into five main subtypes: *Classic modes of protest*, including public demonstrations, civil disobedience, petitions, strikes, boycotts or establishing new opposition group or network; *Legal initiatives,* involving court cases, including the initiation of court cases or administrative proceedings which fail, and parliamentary acts such as proposing legislative initiatives; *Challenging speech and communication*, including incitement to violence or hatred, demonizing discourse, condemnation, symbolic protest, political art, investigation such as media reports or NGO studies, and acts of exclusion; *Appeals for change and intervention and factual statements*, including appeals, dialogue, declarations, or reform proposals; and *other initiatives*, including online initiatives and interventions in election campaigns.

Effectiveness of adversarial IoPPs is mainly discussed in Chapter 6 on 'Persuasion, Talk, and New Ideas'.

Initiatives and National Patterns of Opposition to Populist Parties

In this chapter, I have sought to map the terrain of contemporary opposition to populist parties. Despite an ambition to address a broad range of responses to populist parties, it should be noted that the typology presented here deliberately leaves out a IoPP subtype which can be observed empirically. That is, the category of tolerant IoPPs by public authorities may also include a more diffuse set of *policy and legislative responses.* IoPPs that could be included in such a subtype include (a) new legislation, reforms, or public programmes which aim to address problematic behaviour of populist parties (e.g., online hate speech) or (b) longer-term programmes of civic education (e.g., in the school curriculum, or training of public officials) (Pedahzur 2004; Capoccia 2005). Programmes run by international organizations for democratic education could also be included in this category (Capoccia 2005: 54). The subtype could also include (c) changes in electoral rules, such as requirements for internal party democracy, or rules affecting populist party vote-to-seat ratios (Pedahzur 2004; Downs 2012), and forms of what Capoccia calls (d) 'anti-extremist legislation', which typically empowers public authorities (especially the executive) with special powers to deal with an immediate extremist threat (among other things) in a state of emergency or siege, or in cases of sedition or treason (Capoccia 2005: 56; Tyulkina 2015). This policy and legislative IoPP subtype could also include (e) policy reforms of the kind linked to the grievance model of responses to populism (see Introduction) which aim to address issues underpinning populist party support. Among other things, these can include reforms of taxation and welfare provision to address social and economic inequality (Galston 2018: 16–17; Mounk 2018); or anti-corruption legislation, electoral and institutional reforms to address problems of democratic governance (Mény and Surel 2002a; Eatwell and Goodwin 2018; Zielonka 2018). Overall, IoPPs in this subtype are relatively rare, but are excluded from further analysis because their impact is much more difficult to detect over the short to medium term. A further difficulty is the methodological challenge of specifying whether these kinds of legislative and policy responses are actually an *IoPP*, given many policy responses will pursue multiple, general political goals which may have little to do with populists. The empirical burden of classifying *policy and legislative IoPPs* is thus often substantially higher that others discussed in this chapter, requiring detailed knowledge of the policy fields in question which is beyond the scope of this book.

Despite this shortcoming, there are several advantages to the new approach I present here. The typology integrates initiatives we know a lot about, such as repressive, state-based initiatives and responses by political parties, with initiatives rarely discussed in the literature, such as judicial review, opposition politics, the actions of other states and international organizations, and protest by civil society actors. Additionally, the typology retains distinctions between tolerant and intolerant modes of engagement with populists, reflecting broad lines of long-standing debates about how to address the dilemma of 'tolerating the tolerant' in liberal democracies (Rawls 1971; Waldron 1981; Scanlon 2003; Rummens and Abts 2010; Kirshner 2014; Müller 2016a; Rijpkema 2018; Malkopoulou 2019). As such, typology facilitates dialogue between empirical and normative analysis, opening a new terrain for normative theories on lesser-known types of IoPPs (such as ordinary legal controls and pedagogy, coercive confrontation, adversarialism and international IoPPs more generally).

The typology is built on operationalizable definitions and recognizable empirical illustrations of IoPP types and subtypes, which is an advantage over many earlier classification schemes based on often difficult-to-operationalize ideal or constructed types. Cross-national comparison of broader patterns in use of IoPP-types allows us to draw a more accurate picture of how opposition to populist parties varies in different countries, or in relation to the different types of left, right, and centrist governing and opposition populist parties. For example, many scholars have observed that distinctions between 'intolerant' and 'tolerant' modes of engagement are broadly in line with variation in responses to anti-system actors, often linked to varying constitutional traditions and political cultures (Kirchheimer 1961; Gordon 1987; Fox and Nolte 2000; Pedahzur 2004; Backes 2006; Klamt 2007; Bligh 2013; Bourne 2018). This typology classifies *initiatives* opposing populist parties, not *country-traditions*, or responses to *anti-system parties* in general. However, data classified according to the typology and compared across countries allows us to evaluate whether contemporary IoPPs 'fit' longer-standing distinctions between tolerant and intolerant response traditions observed in the literature. Where the fit is poor, more nuanced models of IoPPs can be developed.

Early results of data collection for the Carlsberg Foundation's 'Populism and Democratic Defence in Europe' project suggest a need for more nuanced models to capture patterns of IoPPs in different countries (Bourne 2023). In Germany, the prototypical 'militant democracy', a broad range of both intolerant and tolerant IoPPs are deployed against the right-wing populist party of permanent opposition, Alternative for Germany. This includes deployment of traditional, rights-restricting actions by the state, such as covert party surveillance, ostracism by political parties at state and regional levels and violent, confrontational acts of opposition by some civil society groups. This is matched by a full range of tolerant types of IoPP, including ordinary legal proceedings on illicit party funding, policy cooptation and limited cooperation at the local level, and non-coercive, adversarial forms of opposition by civil society actors. By contrast, in the Italian case, with a relatively tolerant tradition towards anti-system parties, opposition to right wing League and the ambiguous, post-ideological Five Star Movement (5SM) has predominantly been tolerant, involving ordinary legal proceedings, collaborative deal-making, policy cooptation among political parties, and political protest in civil society. There is, however, a striking contrast between civil society responses to the 5SM, which is generally non-coercive or adversarial and to the League, which also includes notable instances of coercive confrontation. In Poland, the governing Law and Justice Party, has been predominantly met by tolerant responses from domestic opposition actors, and many reactions from international actors. These include various court cases using tolerant ordinary treaty infringement procedures and the initiation of what could (at least theoretically) end with the intolerant and exceptional Article 7 TEU sanctions procedure. Opposition to the right-wing populist party, Danish People's Party, which has intermittently supported minority 'bourgeois' block governments, is predominantly characterized by tolerant responses within the realm of normal party politics and with only a few attempts at ostracism. While further work is needed to refine country-specific models and their generalizability, these findings show the advantages of identifying IoPP types drawing on distinctions between both tolerant and intolerant modes of engagement *and* different types of political actors opposing populist parties.

For the purposes of this book, sorting through the jumble of known forms of opposition to populist parties was a necessary first step for working out a theory of effective opposition to populist parties. A better understanding of the range of initiatives used by populist parties' opponents and the kinds of actors who deploy them directs analytical attention to relevant scholarly literatures discussing the effectiveness of different types of legal and political interventions. As the following chapters show, scholars specializing in the study of political parties, social movements, national and international law, the European Union, and International Relations, have theories to explain the impact of political initiatives in their field. From this research I identify the four main tools or 'mechanisms' linking the IoPPs identified here to the goals pursued by opponents of populist parties. As Figure 0.1 in the introduction showed, I argue that responses to populist parties are effective if they achieve at least one of four goals: Reducing support for a populist party, diminishing their resources, inducing ideological moderation, or curbing their ability to implement illiberal or anti-democratic policies. These should be achieved without producing unwanted or perverse effects of increasing support for populist parties, boosting their resources, or inducing radicalization. The goals are typically achieved using one or some combination of the following four mechanisms: The manipulation of strategic incentives for voters and parties in the context of democratic competition (Chapter 3); enforcement of national and international law (Chapter 4); exploitation of interdependence to leverage change (Chapter 5); and persuasion (Chapter 6). In the next four chapters, I knit these together to provide a new theory, illustrated with empirical examples, of how initiatives opposing populist parties can effectively achieve their goals.

3
Manipulation of Voter and Party Choice

In this chapter I examine how initiatives opposing populist parties (IoPPs) work by manipulating the strategic choices of populist parties and their supporters. In a liberal democracy, electoral contests and the struggle among political parties to win governing power and influence policy is one of the most important settings for opposition to populist parties. In the context of democratic competition, the actions of other parties—particularly decisions to *ostracize, cooperate* with, or *coopt the policies* of populist parties—affects the ability of supporters and populist parties to achieve opposition goals.

As it will be recalled, I argue that IoPPs are effective if they contribute to the achievement of one or more goals typically pursued by those opposing populist parties without producing perverse effects. The main goals of opponents are reducing support for populist parties among voters or sympathizers, diminishing their resources, or inducing their moderation, as well as curbing illiberal and anti-democratic policies of governing populist parties. Perverse effects are increasing support for populist parties, enhancing their resources, and radicalization.

In the first section of the chapter, I elaborate on the proposition that IoPPs affect the strategic choices of populist parties and their supporters, an approach that draws on rational choice theories of voting and party competition (e.g., Meguid 2005; Downs 2012; van Spanje 2018, Albertazzi and Vampa 2021). In this tradition, modern democratic politics is conceived, following Schumpeter (1947), as competition among potential leaders and political parties for votes and a chance to run the government. Voters are conceived as self-interested individuals who vote for the parties offering policies closest to their own preferences (Downs 1957). Politicians join forces in political parties to maximize votes, control government, or exert pressure on those in power. This party competition literature provides theories and concepts for understanding how *ostracism, policy cooptation,* and *cooperation* between populist and mainstream parties can affect *support for populist parties* or *induce moderation and radicalization.* Complementing this is research from the resource mobilization tradition of social movement studies (e.g., Klandermans 1984; McCarthy and Zald 2002; Edwards, McCarthy, and Mataic 2018). In this tradition, mobilization and successful realization of movement goals is seen to depend not only on the existence of social grievances, but also the resources of social constituencies supporting a movement. The resource mobilization literature provides theories and concepts for understanding how party-based IoPPs may affect parties' *moral, material, and organizational resources*. The rest of the chapter explores the plausibility of the theory in light of existing research, statistical data measuring populist parties' voting records and ideological change, and the rich secondary literature on populist parties.

How IoPPs Work by Manipulating Strategic Incentives

Winning and losing votes

A starting point for much subsequent work on party-based IoPPs is Meguid's (2005) work on the effects of mainstream parties on the vote share of what she calls 'niche' parties. Meguid develops a modified version of Downsian (1957) spatial theories of voting and party behaviour, modelling party strategies on the perceived salience of the policy issues 'owned' by radical right, anti-immigration, and green parties. Where mainstream parties *dismiss* or ignore niche parties, Meguid argues, they signal that the core issue on which a niche party mobilizes lacks merit, *reducing support for that party* (2005: 349). If other parties *accommodate* the niche party *by coopting* its signature policy, this will also *reduce support for that party* because they 'draw voters away from a threatening competitor' (ibid.: 348–349). In contrast, if other parties adopt an *adversarial* strategy, openly opposing the niche party's signature policy, they will *increase support* for it by 'encouraging voter flight to the competing party' (ibid.: 349). More recently, Albertazzi and Vampa (2021) extend Meguid's arguments to model interactions beyond 'niche' and established, mainstream parties to encompass all parties in a political system. Among other things, the authors add new subcategories not unlike some of the IoPP types identified in this book, including 'clashing' (similar to *political persuasion* in my typology) and 'marginalization' (or *ostracism*, and some kinds of *rights-restrictions* in my typology) (see Chapter 2).

Van Spanje (2018) also builds on Meguid's work, adding theories of strategic coalition voting to model effects of *ostracism* on support for what he calls 'pariah parties'. The author argues that 'where voters are rational actors who aim to have an influence on real-life policy outcomes, they are expected to not vote for a party that will not be able to come to power' (ibid.: 40). In short, *ostracisim reduces support* for a party because for instrumentally oriented citizens voting for an ostracized party is a wasted vote. However, the most important theoretical insight of van Spanje's work is that a strategy combining *ostracism* and *policy cooptation* will most consistently *reduce support* for the targeted party (ibid.; van Spanje and van der Brug 2007; van Spanje and Weber 2019). The argument is that when a party is 'parroted and treated as a pariah at the same time, a challenger party loses its attractiveness to policy-oriented voters. This is because the challenger is not the *only* option any more for voters who are swayed by its policy proposals (because it is parroted by others) and because the challenger is not the *best* option anymore for these voters either (because it is treated as a pariah by others)' (van Spanje 2018: 69). While voting for a pariah party can be an attractive option if it signals the intensity of voter feeling on an issue, this 'signalling function' is no longer effective when other parties parrot it by offering similar policies (ibid.: 74; van Spanje and Weber 2019: 748).

Down's work provides theoretical grounding for understanding why *ostracism* may increase support for populist parties, arguing that it 'gives disenchanted voters further reasons to embrace ... anti-establishment messages' (2012: 103–104). More specifically, *ostracism* may 'strengthen the credibility of populists in claiming that the established parties are forming a "cartel"'(Hellström and Nilsson 2010: 60, 64; Müller 2016b: 83–84). In other words, *ostracism* may *increase support for populist parties* if that opposition is framed as the machinations of a corrupt and self-interested elite aiming to marginalize those defending the interests of ordinary people. In relation to *policy cooptation*, Betz's work suggests that the decision of other parties to copy another party's signature policies may *increase support for populist parties* by providing incentives to vote for that party 'precisely because previous support for them proved so effective at achieving desired policies' (2002: 209).

It follows from van Spanje's (2018) argument about *ostracism*, that if other parties are willing to *cooperate* with populist parties, they may see an *increase in support* because it gives policy-oriented voters hope that their preferences might become government policy. If *cooperation in government* is successful, it may increase support by providing evidence of their competence and respectability (Eatwell 2000: 423). There are, though, other reasons to expect that *cooperation* may *reduce support for populist parties*. One commonly recognized challenge is the obvious disjuncture between the anti-elitist core of populist messages and participation in government (Heinisch 2003: 91–92; Zaslove 2012: 424; Akkerman et al. 2016: 16, 46; Heinisch and Mazzoleni 2017: 116; Norris and Inglehart 2019: 416). Similarly, there is a risk that the policy compromises required of governing will alienate core supporters

(Dézé 2003; Akkerman and Rooduijn 2015; Akkerman, et al. 2016). As Norris and Inglehart describe the dilemma, 'populists typically attract disproportionate support among disillusioned citizens distrusting parliament, parties and politicians' and therefore 'may have a problem campaigning as radical outsiders fighting mainstream elites once they join the parliamentary backbenches, enter governing coalitions or even hold executive office' (2019: 416). Rather than providing an opportunity to demonstrate competence and respectability, populist parties may be punished electorally for their lack of governing experience given that many voters make decisions after 'evaluat[ing] the performance of government officials' (Berman 2008: 6; Akkerman and de Lange 2012: 580; Norris and Inglehart 2019, 417). Heinisch argues that populist parties may be more prone to encounter difficulties 'translat[ing] a novel (and at times even radical) agenda into public policy', which could affect the party's 'the ability to work effectively with a coalition partner' (2003: 113).

Moderation and radicalization

Müller and Strøm's (1999) theoretical work on party strategies, and the trade-offs between party vote, office, and policy goals, has guided various studies on the effects of party-based IoPPs on moderation and radicalization of populist party electoral appeals. According to the authors, parties with *office-seeking goals* aim to maximize control over the 'private goods bestowed on recipients of politically discretionary governmental or sub governmental appointments' which are obtained by 'controlling the executive branch or as much of that branch as possible' (ibid.: 5–6). A party's *policy-seeking* goals 'seek to maximize its impact on public policy', while *vote-seeking* goals pursue vote maximization, or at least getting sufficient votes to achieve other goals (ibid.: 7, 9). The pursuit of some goals is necessary for, or facilitates, achieving others: 'Pure vote seekers, office seekers or policy seekers are unlikely to exist' (ibid.: 12). Thus, winning votes is clearly necessary for obtaining office, while winning office facilitates achievement of policy goals. On the other hand, 'party leaders rarely have the opportunity to realize all these goals simultaneously' because 'the same behaviour that maximizes one of their objectives may not lead to the best possible outcome with respect to the others' (ibid.: 9). For example, coalition partners can rarely obtain all their policy preferences, incumbency often leads governing parties to lose votes in subsequent elections, and some party policy preferences may be an electoral liability (ibid.: 9–10).

Dézé's (2003) reflections on the 'adaptation dilemma' facing European 'extreme right-wing parties' illustrate many of the 'tradeoffs' and 'hard choices' that leaders of populist parties routinely make between office, policy, and vote-seeking goals. This adaptation dilemma involves a choice to 'either adapt themselves to the system, hence running the risk of losing a part of their original identities and of the support of their most orthodox members, or distinguish themselves from the system, thereby running the risk of being excluded from it, or being marginalized' (ibid.: 20). Party-based IoPPs often force parties subject to *ostracism*, *policy cooptation*, and *cooperation* to make 'hard choices' about whether to prioritize vote, policy, and office goals. As I show below, in some circumstances it provides incentives to voluntarily moderate political appeals, while in others it provides incentives for maintaining the status quo or radicalization.

A party 'moderates' in ideological terms if it aligns its policy bids towards some kind of 'mean' policy position (Akkerman and Rooduijn 2015: 1141; Akkerman et al. 2016). The most common way of working out the 'mean' policy position is by reference to 'a centrist position on the classic left–right scale … that attributes importance to socioeconomic issues' (Akkerman et al. 2016: 7). The mobilization of populist parties on issues like immigration, European integration, multiculturalism, the family, and sexuality (Kriesi et al. 2005; Pytlas 2016; Norris and Inglehart 2019), suggests moderation should also be conceived with reference to socio-cultural dimensions of political competition. Moderation has also been 'defined on the basis of [a party's] loyalty to the political system', in contrast to 'parties that seek to reform or overthrow the existing system and the norms and values on which it is based' (Akkerman et al. 2016: 7; Zulianello 2019).

A second way to define moderation refers to behaviour or informal rules of politics, which may include style of speech or dress, modes of argumentation, or practices of representation. A focus on moderation as 'political style' fits well with the study of populism, which is sometimes defined in these terms. Part of the populist style may be performance of what Moffitt (2016) calls 'bad manners', or what Ostiguy (2017) calls the 'flaunting of the low'. 'Bad manners' perform a contrast between the virtues of 'the establishment', which includes 'seriousness, earnestness, gravitas, intelligence and sensitivity to the positions of others' on the one hand, with the virtues of the 'outsider', including 'directness, playfulness, a certain disregard for hierarchy and tradition, ready resort to anecdote as "evidence"' on the other (Moffitt 2016: 44). 'Good manners' for Moffitt and 'the high' for Ostiguy correspond to forms of political moderation identified by Akkerman et al., including 'cultivating more respectable profiles', or adopting behaviour showing 'commitment to the principles of liberal democracy and to the formal and informal rules of the political game' (2016: 7; see also Akkerman and Rooduijn 2015: 1141). In more concrete terms, Akkerman et al. argue that moderation of political style can also involve disregarding extremist language, avoiding anti-democratic references and symbols, or loosening ties to extremist movements (ibid.).

Radicalization can be conceived as the opposite of moderation as just defined. That is, radicalization refers to a shift of parties' ideological position 'away from the mean towards the extremes of the political spectrum' (Akkerman and Rooduijn 2015: 1141). This movement away from the mean can occur on the socio-economic or socio-cultural dimensions of political competition, decreasing support for the liberal democratic status quo, adoption of increasingly extremist language, increasing use of anti-democratic references and symbols, or tighter ties with extremist movements.

By placing office goals beyond reach, *ostracism* may provide incentives for populist parties to *radicalize or at least retain radical policy positions*. Many have observed that *ostracism* provides a breeding ground for ideological rigidity and radical policies, a strategy which helps keep radical supporters happy (Betz 2002: 212; Dézé 2003: 20–21; Mudde 2007: 89; van Spanje and van der Brug 2007; Downs 2012: 101; Akkerman and Rooduijn 2015: 1141; Luardie et al. 2021: 216). Where other parties successfully *coopt* a populist parties' signature policies, populists have incentives to differentiate their policy programmes from the copycats, either by *radicalizing* (Akkerman et al. 2016: 16) or more rarely, *moderating their policy positions* (Krekó 2017; Kim 2021: 137). It has often been observed that where there is a chance to reach office through *governmental cooperation*, parties have incentives for moderation (van Spanje and van der Brug 2007: 1023; Akkerman and Rooduijn 2015: 1143; Akkerman et al. 2016: 15). That is, populist parties 'interested in office ... have incentives to demonstrate to their potential partners that they are reliable and credible allies—for example by toning down their anti-establishment rhetoric, obeying the parliamentary rules and "sanitizing" their party' (Akkerman et al. 2016: 15). Once in government, populist parties may also be under pressure to moderate because of the need to 'make policy compromises and shed some of their populist rhetoric when they enter government coalitions' (Akkerman and de Lange 2012: 581). On the other hand, populist parties may be able to use a strategy of 'one foot in and one foot out of government' to resist such pressures and retain radical positions (Akkerman and de Lange 2012: 595; Zaslove 2012: 431; Albertazzi and McDonnell 2015). This strategy allows a party to pursue some radical policies while it compromises on other policies with governing partners.

Boosting and diminishing party resources

Resource mobilization theory from social movement studies helps conceptualize the effects of IoPPs because acts of opposition can create costs and benefits for populist parties and those who consider supporting one (Klandermans 1984; McCarthy and Zald 2002; Edwards et al. 2018). Distinctions are helpfully drawn between different types of resources: *Human resources* include the time, skills, experience, and knowledge of talented individuals and the political weight a large membership brings (Edwards et al. 2018: 80). *Material resources* include money, as well as infrastructure such as property, office space, and equipment (ibid.). *Organizational resources* include formal institutional structures which help maintain solidarity, recruit members, cultivate new leaders, and run effective campaigns, as well as a social organization's network with affinity groups. *Moral resources* can include a social organization's legitimacy or authenticity, the sympathy of its supporters, or celebrity endorsement (ibid.: 83).

Social organizations, such as movements and political parties, often generate their own resources through individual activists' contributions of time, money, labour, and expertise. Their resources may also come from the outside, including from institutional actors such as churches, media outlets, philanthropic bodies, and governmental programmes (McCarthy and Zald 2002: 536). Social organizations typically seek to 'cultivate, maintain and preserve numerous exchange relationships' in order to 'gain access to the specific mix of resources supporting their endeavours' (Edwards et al. 2018: 89). These exchange relationships 'bring a reciprocal set of expectations and obligations between the parties, with each relationship having widely varying potential for either social control or facilitation' (ibid.).

Party-based IoPPs may affect party resources in complex and sometimes contradictory ways. *Ostracism* may *diminish the key organizational resource* of party unity, if the party 'is divided on the issue of how to respond to the other parties' strategies' (van Spanje 2018: 40; see also van Donselaar 2003). This may also *decrease support for populist parties* because, as Van Spanje argues, 'rational voters will, all things being equal, prefer to vote for a party that is united to a divided, conflict ridden-party, as the former can be expected to be more effective in policy-making than the latter' (ibid. 2018: 40, see also van der Brug et al. 2005; Zulianello 2019: 74). In other cases, *ostracism* may *boost organizational resources* by helping to 'keep the *Fundis* and *Realos* together, as exclusion by the established parties takes away the incentive to moderate' (Mudde 2007: 89). *Ostracism* may also boost organizational resources by strengthening the dynamics of positive and negative partisanship, which studies show make European right-wing and left-wing populist party supporters more likely to develop both strong psychological attachments to populist parties and strong antipathy toward other parties and their supporters (Meléndez and Rovira Kaltwasser 2021; Harteveld et al. 2022). Regarding *policy cooptation*, it has been argued that this IoPP subtype may *boost a party's moral resources* by increasing the salience and respectability of issues that win votes for populist parties, with immigration policy a prime example (Eatwell 2000; 423; Bale 2003: 69; Meguid 2005: 28). *Cooperation in government* may also *boost moral resources* by formally recognizing the party and its policies as legitimate (Eatwell 2000: 423; Bale 2003: 74–76; Downs 2012). Governing roles come with ministerial posts and the spoils of office, which may *boost a party's material resources*. They also bring greater public visibility and access to the media, which may also *boost a party's organizational resources*. On the other hand, entering government may generate internal conflicts which *diminish the organizational resource* of party unity. As various scholars have argued, the transition from vote-seeking to office-seeking strategies tends to create internal tensions for all types of radical challenger parties (Akkerman and de Lange 2012: 581; van Spanje 2018: 40). More specifically, participation in government may exacerbate tensions between 'realos' (pragmatists) and 'fundis' (fundamentalists) because 'they have to make policy compromises and shed some of their populist rhetoric when they enter government coalitions' (Akkerman and de Lange 2012: 581). Like *ostracism*, internal party disunity accompanying cooperation in government can *reduce support for a party*.

It is beyond the scope of this book to systematically test these theoretical propositions. This would require a complex research design permitting control of alternative explanations for voter choices and detailed knowledge of institutional contexts and decision processes within populist parties. However, it is possible to demonstrate the plausibility of these theoretical insights by looking at the findings of existing studies, data on vote share change, moderation and radicalization, and case studies exploring the internal dynamics and evolution of European populist parties.

The Mixed Blessings of Ostracism

Ostracism is defined in this book as an intolerant initiative undertaken by some political parties against another political party. It involves a refusal by those parties to cooperate with another in either election campaigns, in routine parliamentary decision-making, or in the formation of government coalitions. It can also involve a refusal to appear in public with the targeted party, such as in televised debates. Ostracism is an exception to the general practice where parties keep their options open regarding their alliance strategies and is often justified with a claim that the targeted party is illegitimate and/or a threat to liberal democracy. Sometimes ostracism is comprehensive. Alternative for Germany, for instance, faces competitors who refuse electoral, governmental, and parliamentary cooperation, and it is frequently subject to public ostracism (Pautz 2021). In other cases, ostracism can become progressively more or less encompassing over time. From its founding in 1995 up to 2001, for instance, the Danish Peoples Party was subject to both governmental and parliamentary ostracism (Juul Christiansen 2016). This weakened to governmental ostracism and the Danish People's Party became a support party for various Liberal (V)-led 'bourgeois bloc' governments (see Table 3.3 below). By 2014 the Liberals were open to forming a government with the Danish People's Party, and by 2017 the Social Democrats were too. The case of the Dutch Party of Freedom (PVV) shows further variation. The party was not ostracized by its right-wing competitors when it was formed in 2006 and was a support party for a centre-right government between 2010 and 2012 (Akkerman 2021: 136) (see Table 3.3 below). From 2017 though, the party was excluded as a potential coalition partner by mainstream parties (Akkerman 2021: 136).

In a review of party strategies towards populist parties in ten Western European states between 2007–2018, Vampa and Albertazzi (2021) observe that strategies of marginalization (which captures initiatives including ostracism) is relatively rare these days. The small number of parties listed on Table 3.1 confirms this observation. It shows populist parties with representation in European national parliaments in 2020 (as shown earlier on Table 1.1) currently subject to electoral, parliamentary, and governmental ostracism.

Ostracism is the only party-based IoPP that directly *curbs the ability of populist parties to implement illiberal and anti-democratic policies*. Ostracism is often referred to as a policy of 'cordon sanitaire', which as Downs points out, invokes the idea of preventing 'contamination from some perceived menace or danger' by 'keeping the threat at some safe, sanitary distance' (Downs 2012: 82; see also van Spanje 2018). Ostracism is also often seen as a way of preventing the 'Weimar-scenario', or as Levitsky and Ziblatt put it, a way to avoid the 'fateful mistake: willingly handing over the keys of power to an autocrat-in-the-making' (2018: 13).

Over and above excluding a party from government there are theoretical reasons to expect *ostracism* will be a mixed blessing for populist parties. As discussed above, *ostracism* may *reduce voter support* for a populist party,

Table 3.1 Populist parties represented in national parliaments in 2020 subject to electoral, parliamentary, and governmental ostracism

Country	Populist party
Belgium	Flemish Interest (VB)
France	National Rally (RN)
	Unbowed France (LFI)
Germany	Alternative for Germany (AfD)
Greece	Greek Solution (EL)
Ireland	Sinn Féin (SF)
Luxembourg	Alternative Democratic Reform (ADR)
Sweden	Sweden Democrats (SD)*

Source: Author's own elaboration, combining populist parties listed on Table 1.1, and other sources including van Spanje 2018; Zulianello, 2020; Albertazzi et al. 2021.
* *Note*: SD was subject to long-term ostracism until October 2022, when it was accepted as a support party in a centre-right government.

essentially because a vote for an ostracized party may be a wasted vote. That is, ostracized parties 'become increasingly less attractive over time' and 'instrumental ideologically driven voters' in particular are likely to 'opt for other parties instead or stay at home' (van Spanje and van der Brug 2009; Pauwels 2011; van Spanje 2018). On the other hand, if populist parties can plausibly frame ostracism as a confirmation of anti-elitist appeals, it may *increase support for the party*. By taking office goals off the table, ostracism provides incentives for populist parties to retain radical policy positions rather than adopt more moderate appeals. In some cases, ostracism may *boost the organizational resource* of party unity because moderates and fundamentalists can put aside potential conflicts over the advantages or appropriateness of moderation. In other cases, it may do the opposite, provoking disagreement within the party about how to respond, a situation which may *reduce support among voters*.

Van Spanje's research has shown that ostracism had a negative effect on the vote share of postwar communist parties (2018: 87–88). Similarly, some ostracized radical right parties such as the Republicans or National Democratic Party in Germany, never managed to break through electorally. Nevertheless, ostracism can be an 'asset', which has sometimes been the case for European anti-immigrant parties (van Spanje 2018: 99). Figure 3.1 shows that important contemporary right-wing populist parties have managed to survive—and indeed strive—despite being subject to ostracism, in some cases over very long periods of time. This includes Flemish Interest in Belgium,

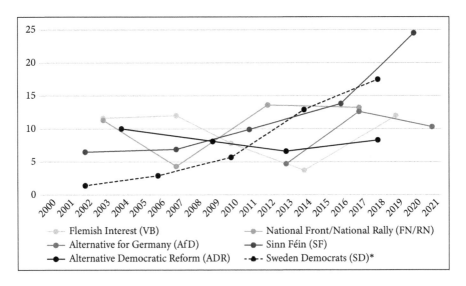

Figure 3.1 Vote share for established populist parties subject to long-term policies of ostracism (represented in national parliaments in 2020)

Note: SD was subject to long-term ostracism until October 2022, when it was accepted as a support party in a centre-right government.

the French National Front/National Rally in France, Sweden Democrats (until October 2022, when accepted as a support party for a centre-right government), and Alternative for Germany (see also Art 2018: 78).

In the case of the right-wing populist Flemish Interest (VB) (previously called Flemish Block), Downs has argued that ostracism 'helped fuel and sustain popular support for the party as a vehicle of protest' (2012: 103–104). VB has been excluded from participating in government at all territorial levels since 1989 and according to various authors ostracism was seen as a form of 'life insurance' used by the party to 'mobilize voters on the "undemocratic" exclusion of the VB by the establishment' (ibid.: 74; see also: Akkerman et al. 2016: 80; Lucardie et al. 2021: 216). Indeed, for a long time the electoral success of VB made it the paradigmatic case for arguing ostracism didn't always work (Mudde 2007: 289; van Spanje and van der Brug 2009: 376; Pauwels 2011; Downs 2012: 95). Sijsterman also suggests ostracism *may boost the organizational resource* of party unity, at least in the sense that 'members' feeling of exclusion from mainstream Belgian politics' bolsters 'community feeling' in the VB (2021: 278). For example, one West Flemish provincial councillor was quoted in the research as explicitly linking personal experience of exclusion to this identity construction, explaining that exclusion 'ensures that we have the bond of "us" versus the rest … All the attacks that we receive ensure that we have a very high "Robin Hood" feeling' (ibid.). It also meant that '[f]riendships are more meaningful' because 'you are in the same boat; you don't have anyone else' (ibid.).

Studies examining the impact of ostracism on moderation and radicalization show mixed results. Van Spanje and van der Brug's research (2007) showed that ostracized parties tended to remain radical because they lacked 'any incentive to tone down their rhetoric' and because they could be 'dominated by their most radical factions' (ibid.: 1036). This study measured policy change on the left–right dimension as perceived by respondents in the European Election Studies between 1989–2004. A later study by Akkerman and Rooduijn, however, rejected the argument that ostracism had this kind of 'freezing effect' on party positions. The authors drew their conclusion after observing policy positions of ostracized parties along a different, nationalism–cosmopolitan dimension of political competition (2015: 1149).

More current data from the Chapel Hill Expert Survey, which includes data on both socio-economic and socio-cultural dimensions of political competition, suggests that populist parties subject to long-term policies of ostracism tend to stick to what were often already rather radical policy positions (see Table 3.2). The Chapel Hill Expert Survey estimates the relative policy position of major European parties at regular intervals on socio-economic (left–right) and socio-cultural (libertarian/postmaterialist-traditionalist/authoritarian) dimensions of political competition as well as major issues, such as European integration. This data can be used to estimate the extent to which populist parties subject to ostracism moderate, radicalize, or basically retain their ideological positioning on these topics (indicated by the dash in the Table 3.2) (see Appendix II for details on data and methodology).

The data summarized in Table 3.2 paints a picture of quite limited ideological change over the medium to longer term on most dimensions. More often than not, the populist parties subject to long-term policies of ostracism tend not to vary their ideological position (66.6%). The main exception is a trend towards moderation on socio-economic issues, reflecting the already well-known journey of many radical right populist parties from neoliberal or anti-tax parties towards welfare chauvinism. Changes on the socio-cultural or EU dimension were limited but have tended towards moderation. Overall, the data tends to support van Spanje and van der Brug's (2007) 'freezing' hypothesis, while also acknowledging that policy change can differ depending on issue-dimension, as Akkerman and Rooduijn's (2015) study suggests.

Table 3.2 Moderation and radicalization of ostracized parties' ideological positions (1999–2019)

Party (CHES data availability)	Overall ideology	Socio-economic	Socio-cultural	European integration	Anti-elitism
Flemish Interest (1999–2019)	–	high moderation	moderation	–	–
National Front/National Rally (1999–2019)	radicalization	high moderation	moderation	–	–
Alternative for Germany (2014–2019)	–	moderation	–	–	radicalization
Sinn Fein (1999–2019)	–	–	–	moderation	–
Alternative Democratic Reform (2014–2019)	–	–	–	moderation	high moderation
Sweden Democrats (2010–2019)*	–	–	–	–	–

Type of change	Frequency	Percentage
High moderation	3	10%
Moderation	5	16.6%
No change	20	66.6%
Radicalization	2	6.6%
High radicalization	0	0

Source: Seth Jolly, Ryan Bakker, Liesbet Hooghe, Gary Marks, Jonathan Polk, Jan Rovny, Marco Steenbergen, and Milada Anna Vachudova. 'Chapel Hill Expert Survey Trend File, 1999–2019'. *Electoral Studies*. https://doi.org/10.1016/j.electstud.2021.102420
* *Note*: SD was ostracized between 1999–2019, but accepted as a support party for a centre-right government in October 2022.

Policy Cooptation and the 'Original' versus the 'Copy'

Policy cooptation occurs when one party, in van Spanje's words, 'parrots' or 'copy[ies], at least partially [another] party's core issue positions' (2018: 24). It is a tolerant initiative, observing the general practice of democratic politics where parties alter their policy offerings to win over voters inclined to vote for another party (see Chapter 2). In their review of practices in ten Western European states between 2007–2018, Vampa and Albertazzi observe that this is the most widely used strategy employed by populist parties' right-wing (non-populist) competitors and the second most used strategy by left-wing (non-populist) competitors (2021: 273, 276). The highest profile, and most studied, form of policy cooptation is the appropriation of right-wing populist parties' policy ideas for restricting immigration by centre-right and centre-left party competitors (Downs 2001; Bale 2003; Meguid 2005; Bale et al. 2008; Downs 2012; van Spanje 2018, Abou-Chadi and Krause 2020). Studies have also focused on cooptation of the environmental policies of green parties (Meguid 2005), cooptation of communist parties' policy proposals on market regulation (van Spanje 2018: 26–28), cooptation of populist parties' nationalist and Eurosceptical positions (Pytlas 2016; Pirro and Taggart 2018) and pro-welfare state policies (Krause and Giebler 2020).

As discussed above, *support for populist parties may be reduced* when mainstream parties *coopt* populist parties' signature policies, especially when combined with *ostracism*. Or, on the contrary, *policy cooptation* may *increase support for a populist party* if voters realize that votes for populist parties may force other parties to take on and implement their preferred policies. Where other parties successfully *coopt* a populist parties' signature policies, populists have incentives to differentiate their policy programmes from the copycats, sometimes by *radicalizing their positions*, at other times *moderating them*. Policy cooptation can also be expected to *boost a party's moral resources* by increasing the salience and respectability of issues that win votes for populist parties, with immigration policy a prime example.

Van Spanje's research show that policy cooptation works most consistently to *reduce a party's support* in combination with *ostracism*, or what van Spanje and his co-authors call 'parroting the pariah' (van Spanje and van der Brug 2009; van Spanje 2018; van Spanje and Weber 2019). This is because the 'challenger is not the *only* option anymore for voters who are swayed by its policy proposals (because it is parroted by others) and because the challenger is not the *best* option anymore for these voters either (because it is treated as a pariah by others)' (van Spanje 2018: 69). Examining this theory in a study of 28 anti-immigrant and communist parties in 15 west European countries between 1944 and 2011, van Spanje found that the strategy of 'parroting the pariah' is both 'quite a common strategy' and a 'strikingly effective' way in which 'established parties can damage the [targeted] party electorally' (2018: 1, 99). More specifically, the research identifies '39 occasions in post-war Europe in which a country's established parties have reacted in this way to a particular other party' and in '21 out of 39 cases, that party lost a quarter of its vote share or more' (ibid.: 2).

Pauwel's (2011) study of the precipitous decline of the electoral fortunes of Flemish Interest (VB) in the 2010s illustrates the combined effect of ostracism and policy cooptation. As discussed above, the VB had capitalized on its pariah status over many years. However, by the late 2000s, Pauwels argued, repeated, deliberate exclusion from office, even in its own stronghold of Antwerp, diminished 'the hope that the VB would ever be part of a coalition' (ibid.: 75). While ostracism 'cast a shadow on the party's electoral fortunes', the VB also had to compete with two new rivals mobilizing on its signature policies. These were the New Flemish Alliance (N-VA), campaigning on Flemish nationalism, and List Dedecker (LDD), which adopted a populist platform. According to Pauwels, the combination of *ostracism* and *policy-cooptation* explained the precipitous decline of the VB's electoral fortunes in the 2010 election at the hands of its new rivals. Policy-oriented voters chose to vote for parties offering similar policy platforms to the VB but who had a better chance of influencing policy through involvement in governing coalitions.

While the VB was able to make a comeback by the end of the decade (see Figure 3.1), in other cases *policy cooptation* has *reduced support* to such an extent that the party disappeared. Perhaps the most dramatic case is the collapse of the United Kingdom Independence Party (UKIP) after the Brexit referendum. After the 2016 Brexit referendum, the Conservatives positioned themselves as the party for whom, under Theresa May, 'Brexit meant Brexit', and the party which would, under Boris Johnson, 'get Brexit done' (Vampa 2021). The Labour Party also accepted that the outcome of the Brexit referendum meant the UK would leave the EU. As Vampa observed, once the political establishment committed to leaving the EU, they effectively 'neutralized' any attempt by UKIP, or former leader Nigel Farage's Brexit Party, to maintain 'issue ownership' (Vampa 2021: 222). Similarly, the League of Polish Families, which was in a government coalition between 2006–2007, faded into insignificance after the Law and Justice Party coopted its core national-Catholic positions (Pytlas 2016: 32). The Slovak National Party (SNS), also a governing party (2006–2010), lost many votes to Robert Fico's Direction –

Social Democracy (SMER-SD) after the SMER-SD party began in 2001 to coopt SNS's radical right narrative (Pytlas 2016: 33–34).

Akkerman et al. argue that *policy cooptation* creates incentives for radical right parties to *radicalize* their policy bids to avoid 'losing voters and issue ownership' (Akkerman, de Lange, and Roodouijn 2016: 16). However, there is also evidence that policy cooptation can lead to ideological and behavioural *moderation*. In Hungary, for example, Fidesz successfully coopted many policy ideas from its (then) far right competitor Jobbik (Krekó 2017; Kim 2021: 137). This included many of Jobbik's signature policies, such as its tougher law and order stance, obligatory moral/religious education, extension of citizenship and suffrage to ethnic Hungarians abroad, nationalization of pension funds, constitutional references to Christian values, a tougher immigration policy, and a referendum on the EU's 'quota system' for refugees (implemented by Fidesz in 2016) (Enyedi and Róna 2018; Kim 2021: 137). Rather than being outbid on the extremes, Jobbik differentiated itself through moderation (Krekó 2017; Enyedi and Róna 2018: 264; Kim 2021: 137). Leader Gábor Vona adopted a new 'people's party' strategy, toning down the party's virulent anti-semitism, anti-Roma positions and its hard Euroscepticism, becoming what Ágh described as a 'moderate centre-right and pro-European party' (2021: 26; see also Enyedi and Róna 2018: 264; Kim 2021: 143–153). This also included stylistic moderation, or an 'attempt to move away from the image of uniformed paramilitaries' to a portrayal of the party as a 'competent government-in-waiting' (Kim 2021: 148).

In contrast, another study by Krause et al. (2023), focusing on a narrower, but more current set of radical right parties (many of which are populists) in Western Europe, suggests that *policy cooptation* tends to *increase support for these parties*. Examining consequences of *policy cooptation* using data on both radical right parties' overall electoral successes and voters switching in their favour, the authors conclude that *policy cooptation,* 'is fruitless in the best case and can be detrimental in the worst case'. More specifically they show that 'voters are on average more likely to defect to the radical right when mainstream parties adopt anti-immigrant positions, a pattern that has been particularly pronounced for established [Radical Right parties]' (ibid.). Several case studies support such conclusions.

Policy cooptation has generally been seen as an ineffective tool for reducing support for the French National Front (FN)/National Rally (Schain 2006: 272; Evans and Ivaldi 2021; Shields 2021). Since its electoral breakthrough in the mid-1980s, the National Front's competitors have taken on many of its anti-immigration and Eurosceptical positions and in the notable recent case of Emmanuel Macron, its populist anti-establishment style (Shields 2021).

In 2007, for example, French presidential candidate Nicolas Sarkozy successfully won over a substantial number of FN voters after a 'systematically populist campaign with strong nationalist and authoritarian overtones' and a policy agenda challenging the FN's 'issue ownership' on immigration (ibid.: 97). However, the FN was soon able to recover ownership on the immigration issue (ibid.: 105), lifting its vote share from Jean-Marie Le Pen's 10.44% in the first round of the 2007 presidential elections to Marine Le Pen's 21.3% in the first round and 33.9% in the second round of the 2017 presidential elections (see also Figure 3.1 above). As Jean-Marie Le Pen famously put it, voters preferred the 'original' to the 'copy'.

Evans and Ivaldi argue that the efforts of the political mainstream to coopt the FN's immigration agenda helped *boost the party's moral resources*, or legitimacy (2021: 127). Juul Christiansen (2016) makes a similar argument about the Danish People's Party (DF). While DF was famously declared 'undomesticated' by the Social Democratic Party Prime Minister Poul Nyrup Rasmussen in 1999, Juul Christiansen argued the DF's public legitimacy increased subsequently as a result of the centre-right Liberals (V) increasingly critical stance on the country's liberal immigration policies and later embrace of much of the DF's restrictive immigration agenda (ibid.: 102–103).

Populists in Government as the 'New Normal'

Some twenty years ago, the decision of a European centre-right party to cooperate with a populist party in government was so controversial it provoked international sanctions. The 2000–2002 Austrian People's Party (ÖVP) coalition government with the right-wing populist Freedom Party of Austria (FPÖ) was met with (short-lived) diplomatic sanctions by Austria's EU partners (Merlingen et al. 2001). The political reality is now very different. As Table 3.3 shows, electorally successful populist parties often participate in coalition government, sometimes as the largest party holding the position of prime minister, sometimes as junior coalition partners. Sometimes populist parties participate in governing as extra-parliamentary support parties. On rare occasions, populist parties run single-party majority governments.

As discussed above, there are theoretical reasons to expect that populist parties face significant costs of incumbency. That is, populist parties are *likely to lose support* if members and voters think the party's anti-elitist stance is compromised, or if the party performs badly in office. In addition, populist parties with office ambitions or who participate in government have *incentives to moderate* their ideological positions and political behaviour. On the

Table 3.3 Governing status of populist parties and change in percentage vote share after incumbency 1999–2021

Country	Party	Governing status	Years	Change of % of vote	Change of vote share (% of previous election)
Austria	Freedom Party (FPÖ)	Coalition partner	2000–2002	−16.9	−63
			2002–2005	1	10
Bulgaria	Citizens for European Development of Bulgaria (GERB)	Led single-party minority government	2017–2019	−9.8	−38
		Prime minister and largest party in coalition government	2009–2013	−9.2	−23
			2014–2017	0	0
			2017–2021	−6.8	−21
	Patriotic Front (PF)	Coalition partner	2017–2021	–	–
Croatia	Bridge of Independent Lists (Most)	Coalition partner	2016–2017	−2.5	−25
Czechia	Action of Dissatisfied Citizens (ANO)	Coalition partner	2014–2017	10.9	58
		Led single-party minority government	2017–2018		
		Prime minister and largest party in coalition government	2018–2021	−2.5	−8
Denmark	Danish Peoples Party (DF)	Support party	2001–2005	1.3	11
			2005–2007	0.6	5
			2007–2011	−1.6	−12
			2015–2019	−12.4	−59
Estonia	Conservative People's Party (EKRE)	Coalition partner	2019–2021	–	–
Finland	Finns Party (PS)	Coalition partner	2015–2017	−0.1	−1
Greece	Coalition of the Radical Left (SYRIZA)	Prime minister, largest party	2015–2015	−0.8	−2
			2015–2019	−4	−11
		Led single-party minority government	2019–2019	–	–
Hungary	Hungarian Civic Alliance (Fidesz)	Prime minister, largest party in coalition government	2010–2014	−7.8	−15
			2014–2018	4.4	10
			2018–	–	–

Italy	Forza Italia (FI)	Prime minister, largest party in coalition government	2001–2006	−5.7	−19
		Coalition partner	2008–2011	−15.8	−42
			2021–		
	League (prior to 2018, Legal Nord, LN)	Coalition partner	2001–2006	0.7	18
			2008–2011	−4.2	−51
			2018–2019	–	–
			2021–2022	–	–
	Five Star Movement (5SM)	Largest party in coalition government	2018–2019	–	–
			2019–2021	–	–
Latvia	Who Owns the State (KPV-LV)	Equal largest party in coalition government	2019–2021	–	–
Lithuania	Labour Party (DP)	Largest party in coalition government	2004–2006	−19.4	−68
Netherlands	Party for Freedom (PVV)	Support party	2010–2012	−5.4	−35
Norway	Progress Party (FrP)	Coalition partner	2013–2017	−1.1	−7
			2017–2020	−3.5	−23
		Support party	2020–2021	–	–
Poland	Law and Justice (PiS)	Prime minister, minority government	2005–2006	5.1	19
		Prime minister largest party in coalition government	2015–2019	6	16
			2019–		
Slovakia	Direction – Social Democracy (Smer)	Led single-party majority government	2012–2016	−16–1	−36
		Prime minister, largest party in coalition government	2006–2010	5.7	20
		Prime minister, largest party in coalition government	2016–2020	−10	−35
	Ordinary People and Independent Personalities (OĽaNO)	Prime minister, largest party in coalition government	2020–	–	–
	SME Rodina (SR)	Coalition partner	2020–	–	–

Continued

Table 3.3 Continued

Country	Party	Governing status	Years	Change of % of vote	Change of vote share (% of previous election)
Slovenia	Slovenian Democratic Party (SDS)	Prime minister, largest party in coalition government	2004–2008	0.2	1
			2012–2013	–5.6	–21
			2020–	–	–
	List Marjan Šarec (LMŠ)	Prime minister, largest party	2018–2020	–	–
	The Left (Levica)	Support party	2018–2020	–	–
Spain	Podemos	Coalition partner	2020–	–	–
Switzerland	Swiss People's Party (SVP)	Mostly largest member of power-sharing executive1	1999–2003	4.2	19
			2003–2007	2.2	8
			2008–2011	–2.3	–8
			2011–2015	2.8	11
			2015–2019	–3.8	–13

Governing status	Cooperation type	No. post-incumbency election with vote increases or no change	No. post-incumbency election with vote loss	Average change in % votes before and after incumbency (%)
Junior partners	Support or junior coalition partner	5	11	–17.4
Seniors	Largest party in coalition holding prime minister post, single-party government	6	11	–10
Powersharing		3	2	3,3
Total		14	24	–11.4

Source: Parlgov.org and Parties and Elections in Europe.
Notes: Costs of incumbency were not calculated for Patriotic Front in Bulgaria because the three parties in the coalition participated in the April 2021 election separately. In 1999–2003, the Swiss People's Party was the second largest member of the powersharing executive.

other hand, populist parties may be able to resist such pressures, by pursuing at least some radical policies at the same time as it reaches compromises with other governing parties. *Cooperation in government* may also *boost a populist parties' moral and material resources*, and so long as party unity can be sustained, its *organizational resources*.

There is some scholarly disagreement about whether radical challenger parties, such as populist parties, bear additional 'cost of governing' over and above those which other governing parties bear. Van Spanje's (2011) research, which examined incumbency costs for the broader category of anti-political-establishment parties, showed they tended to lose votes over and above the loses of other types of governing parties. On the other hand, Akkerman and de Lange (2012), studying incumbency effects for seven radical right parties in Western Europe, showed that on average governing populist parties suffered similar vote losses as mainstream parties. It is beyond the scope of this study to examine whether the much larger list of contemporary populist parties experience higher than average costs of governing, or whether there is something distinctive about the reasons why populists might be punished by voters for governing. Nevertheless, it is possible to substantiate the point that populists tend to lose votes after a period of governing.

Table 3.3 shows that, on average, incumbency *reduces support for populist parties*. Populist parties almost always govern in coalition governments. *Junior partners* are support parties, smaller coalition partners, or larger coalition partners that do not hold the post of prime minister. They can be expected to exert less influence on government policy overall. Those with *senior governing status* are the largest party in a coalition and hold the post of prime minister. They may also be the parties running single-party minority or majority governments. The last two columns of Table 3.3 show the magnitude of gains or losses in populist parties' party vote share obtained in the election after governing compared to the election before they participated in government. Effects of incumbency in the Swiss case, where successful parties jointly govern in a power-sharing executive (Bernhard et al. 2021), reflect a different logic to the other cases examined here and are thus calculated separately.

The data shows that, on average, populist parties lose votes after a period of governing, regardless of their junior or senior governing status. Between 1999 and 2021, populist parties governing as junior partners lost on average 17.4% of their vote share in the next election, with losses experienced in 11 out of 16 cases. Some parties experienced very big losses following a period of governing including the Austrian Freedom Party (−63% in 2002 and −38% in 2019), the Labour Party in Lithuania (−68% in 2008), the Danish Peoples Party (−58% in 2019), Northern League (−51% in 2013), and the Dutch Party for Freedom (−35% in 2012). Others lost a moderate share of their votes after a period of incumbency, such as the Bridge of Independent Lists in Croatia (−25% in 2020), and the Norwegian Progress Party (−23% in 2021). In a few cases, junior governing populist parties gained votes, notably the Action of Dissatisfied Citizens in the Czech Republic (+58% in 2017), and the Northern League (+18% in 2006).

Where a populist party held the post of prime minister and was the largest party in a coalition government or ran the government alone, there were, on average, still incumbency costs, but these were generally lower than for those with junior governing status. On average, populist parties with senior governing roles lost 10% of their vote share in the election after governing, with losses experienced in 11 out of 17 cases. The biggest losses were for Forza Italia (−42% in 2011 and 19% in 2006), Direction – Social Democracy (SMER-SD) (−36% in 2016 and −35% in 2018), Citizens for European Development of Bulgaria (−23% in 2013 and −21% in 2021) and for Slovenian Democratic Party (−21% in 2013). On the other hand, the Slovakian Direction – Social Democracy (SMER-SD) increased its vote share after governing (+20% in 2010), as did Fidesz and its coalition partner Christian Democratic People's Party (+10% in 2018). Law and Justice increased its vote share on two occasions after governing (+19% in 2007) and (+16% in 2019).

While we lack studies examining how much the change of vote share observed in Table 3.3 can be attributed to participation in government, or why voters might change their mind, single and comparative case studies provide many insights. Akkerman and de Lange (2012), for example, show some radical right populist parties increased their vote share where they were able to influence legislative change on immigration and integration of foreigners. For example, the Danish People's Party's (DF) increased its share of votes after it influenced the tightening of immigration and integration policies of the Liberal-Conservative government led by Anders Fogh Rasmussen (2001–2005) (ibid.; see also Juul Christiansen 2016). Voters rewarded the Freedom Party of Austria (FPÖ) and its offshoot, the Alliance for the Future of Austria (BZÖ), following a move to the right in Austrian immigration policy during the second cabinet government led by the Austrian People's Party chancellor Wolfgang Schüssel (2002–2006) (Akkerman and de Lange, 2012). Yet the study also suggests 'policy achievement cannot fully explain the variation in post-incumbency results' (ibid.: 587). In other cases, governing radical right populist parties increased their vote share, despite moderate or low influence on government policy; respectively, the Swiss People's Party during the 2003–2006 powersharing coalition, and the Northern League during the 2001–2006 coalition under Berlsuconi's leadership (ibid.; see also Albertazzi and McDonnell 2015).

Akkerman and de Lange's study also showed that poor performance in government, measured by the turnover rate of radical right populist ministers 'for reasons of incompetence', could lead to vote losses (ibid.: 595). The poor performance of the Austrian Freedom Party (FPÖ) and the now defunct List Pim Fortuyn in the Netherlands was a 'likely reason why voters punished these parties severely after incumbency' (ibid. 595; see also Zaslove 2012: 442). On the other hand, the authors argue, parties with more institutionalized party structures, allowing them to recruit more competent leaders, did not appear to suffer costs of governing for this reason (Akkerman and de Lange 2012: 595; Zaslove 2012: 440).

While voters initially rewarded the Danish People's Party (DF) for delivering on its hardline immigration policies, there is evidence to suggest that policy compromises while supporting Lars Løkke Rasmussen's right bloc government (2015–2019) led to dramatic vote losses in the 2019 general election. In that election new far-right competitors New Right (NB) and Hard Line (SK) successfully won over many DF voters in the 2019 election (Meret 2021: 181–182). Among other things, the new parties accused DF of 'having moderated its original positions on immigration and asylum as a consequences of its support to mainstream governments' (Kosiara-Pedersen 2020: 1015; Meret 2021: 182).

Similarly, the moderates of the Blue Reform (SIN) in Finland, which split from the radicalizing Finns Party (PS) while the party governed with the Centre and National Coalition parties led by Juha Sipilä (2015–2017), failed to win any seats in the 2019 election. As Jungar observed, the new party was 'much more inclined than the PS to compromise and accept policies that its leadership had previously contested, such as cuts in social welfare, EU bailouts and rising immigration' (2021: 199). The radicals remaining at the helm of the PS nearly equalled their 2015 vote share.

The Five Star Movement's (5SM) rapid decline after it entered government in 2018 has also been linked to compromises of coalition government, many of which discredited its anti-establishment claims. As Cotta has observed, in government the 5SM compromised on many signature policies, including bank bailouts, high-speed trains, and parliamentary immunity, making it 'resemble the elites against which the party had mobilized political support' (2020: 130; see also Moschella and Rhodes 2020: 116). In the 2019 European Parliament elections, which were widely seen as a vote on the League–5SM coalition government (2018–2019), the 5SM halved its vote share and has not since recovered (Chiaramonte et al. 2020).

In a study of ten Western European anti-immigrant parties, including some of those examined in this book, van Spanje and van der Brug (2007) found that those permitted to participate in government moderated their ideological positions, at least along the left–right axis. In contrast, Akkerman and Rooduijn's (2015) study, which examined changes along a cosmopolitan–nationalist ideological dimension, concluded that while ideological moderation sometimes followed cooperation in government, radicalization also occurred. Moreover, while initially less radical than ostracized parties, non-ostracized parties eventually radicalized to the extent that they came to 'draw level with ostracized parties' (ibid.: 1151–1153). Similarly, the study showed that the 'gap in positions between radical right parties and their mainstream right-wing competitors has increased rather than decreased, notwithstanding coalition agreements and cooperation in office' (ibid.: 1154). Data from the Chapel Hill Expert Survey, which permits the comparison of ideological change on both socio-economic and socio-cultural dimensions, among other things, suggests these trends may occur simultaneously for contemporary populist parties (see Tables 3.4 and 3.5 and Appendix II for more details on data and methodology).

Data shown on Tables 3.4 and 3.5 points to considerable ideological stability for governing populist parties, something which both studies cited appear to underestimate. Most of the time, both junior and senior governing populist parties appear to have avoided making changes to their policy appeals. Otherwise, the data suggests that governing is more likely to be associated with radicalization than moderation, in line with Akkerman and Rooduijn's (2015) conclusions. Senior governing parties are more likely to radicalize than junior governing parties, perhaps because their size means they face weaker pressure from moderate partners. Governing populist parties may also be able to mitigate some of the pressures for moderation (and possible costs of incumbency) using a 'one foot in and one foot out of government' strategy (Akkerman and de Lange 2012: 595; Zaslove 2012: 431; Albertazzi and McDonnell 2015). Existing studies suggest this can take a variety of forms: the Swiss People's Party, for example, was able to maintain issue ownership by combining long-standing participation in government with a radical policy agenda by sponsoring referenda and citizens initiatives; the Northern League was able to exploit heterogeneity among coalition partners in Silvio Berlusconi's Forza Italia-led coalition to continue criticizing other smaller governing parties; and for a long time, the Danish People's Party was able to capitalize on the insider/outsider nature of its status as support

Table 3.4 Moderation and radicalization of ideological positions when populist parties become junior governing parties

Party	Overall ideology	Socio-economic	Socio-cultural	European integration	Anti-elite
Danish People's Party					
2001–2011	moderation	moderation	radicalization	–	no data
2015–2019	–	–	–	–	moderation
Aust. Freedom Party					
2000–2005	radicalization	moderation	high radicalization	–	No data
2017–2019	–	radicalization	–	–	–
National Front for the Salvation of Bulgaria					
2017–2021	–	–	–	–	–
Finns Party					
2015–2017	high radicalization	–	–	–	–
League					
2001–2006	radicalization	–	high radicalization	radicalization	no data
2008–2011	–	–	–	moderation	no data
2018–2019	–	–	–	–	–
Party of Freedom					
2010–2012	–	high moderation	–	–	no data

	Type of policy change	Frequencies	Percentages
	High moderation	1	2.33%
	Moderation	5	11.63%
	No change	29	67.44%
TOTALS	Radicalization	5	11.63%
	High radicalization	3	6.98%

Table 3.5 Moderation and radicalization of ideological positions for populist parties with senior governing status

Party	Overall ideology	Socio-economic	Socio-cultural	EU	Anti-elite
SYRIZA					
2015–2019	–	–	–	moderation	high moderation
Forza Italia					
2001–2006	–	–	–	–	No data
2008–2011	–	–	radicalization	–	No data
Five Star Movement					
2018–	–	–	moderation	high moderation	Moderation
Citizens for European Devt of Bulgaria					
2009–2021	–	–	moderation	–	high moderation
Action of Dissatisfied Citizens					
2014–2021	–	–	–	–	moderation
FIDESZ					
2010–	radicalization	–	high radicalization	high radicalization	high radicalization
Law and Justice					
2005–2006	–	high radicalization	radicalization	radicalization	No data
2015	–	–	–	–	radicalization
Direction- Social democracy					
2006–2010	–	radicalization	–	–	No data
2012–2018	–	moderation	high radicalization	–	–
Slovenian democratic party					
2004–2008	radicalization	–	high radicalization	–	No data
2012–2013	radicalization	high radicalization	–	–	No data

Type of policy change	Frequencies	Percentage
High moderation	3	4.62%
Moderation	6	9.23%
No change	35	53.85%
Radicalization	8	12.31%
High radicalization	7	10.77%

TOTALS

party (Zaslove 2012: 431; Juul Christiansen 2016; Ravik Jupskås 2016; Meret 2021: 172). At the same time, and in accordance with van Spanje and van der Brug's study, moderation can be observed, especially on the socio-economic dimension. Data on the salience of anti-elitist appeals is limited, but what is available also suggests that parties participating in government are more likely to temper than to intensify the salience of anti-elitist appeals.

In addition to the *moral resources* obtained from legitimately winning government office, governing parties also obtain many other *material or organizational* rewards of office. These are obviously large for parties with senior governing roles, who control part of the machinery of state, allowing them to pursue their policy goals. There are also rewards for junior governing partners too, especially where the party can strengthen its issue profile in an area through prominent ministerial posts. For example, when the Norwegian Progress Party first entered government in 2013 its leader Siv Jensen became minister for finance, and Robert Eriksson was appointed minister for labour and social affairs (Salo and Rydgren 2021: 104). The party also held minister of justice, minister of immigration, and the minister for health. As Salo and Rydgren observe, all together the party held 'ministerial positions in precisely the policy areas where it had claimed issue ownership prior to the elections' (ibid.: 104). Similarly, when it was first formed, Podemos leaders Pablo Iglesias and Irene Montero held, respectively, positions of second deputy prime minister and minister of social rights, and minister of equality. During the short-lived League and Five Star Movement government in Italy (2018–2019), League leader Matteo Salvini was deputy prime minister and minister of the interior, and the party held ministerial portfolios for agriculture, family, and European affairs, among others. During this government, Five Star Movement leader Luigi Di Maio was deputy prime minister and the party held departments of justice, defence, health, economic development, labour and social policy, infrastructure and transport, parliamentary relations, and direct democracy. As some have observed, even support parties, such as the Danish People's Party, may see their legitimacy enhanced through cooperation with governing parties (Juul Christiansen 2016: 102–103; Meret 2021: 172).

On the other hand, there are cases showing that participation in government has undermined populist parties' organizational unity, causing party splits in some important cases. The Austrian Freedom Party (FPÖ) split in 2005 while governing with the Austrian People's Party (ÖVP). According to Heinisch, policy compromises while in government caused tensions between a moderate, office-oriented leadership and more radical, protest, and policy-oriented party officials and supporters (2003; Heinisch et al. 2021: 82). As a consequence, leader Jörg Haider left the party, taking the moderate leadership and government ministers with him to form the Alliance for the Future of Austria (BZÖ). This party remained in coalition with the ÖVP, but always came second in terms of vote share to the radicalized FPÖ. A similar pattern can be observed in Finland and Switzerland. Tensions between traditionalists and nationalist radicals in the Finns Party (PS) led to a split while in coalition with the Centre Party (KESK) and the National Coalition Party (KOK) under Prime Minister Juha Sipilä. When Jussi Halla-aho, leader of the nationalist faction, replaced the more moderate traditionalist leader Timo Soini in June 2017, the PS's governing partners refused to continue the coalition under Halla-aho's leadership. Soini and a group of PS ministers and parliamentarians formed a new party later known as Blue Reform (SIN), continuing in government until 2019. As mentioned above, this party was a poor competitor to the radicalized Finn's Party. In Switzerland, when in 2008 other parties chose to include a moderate member of the Swiss People's Party (SVP) (Eveline Widner-Schlumpf) rather than radical party leader Christoph Blocher in the Federal Council, moderates were expelled from the SVP (Bernhard et al. 2021: 152). The moderates formed the Conservative Democratic Party (BDP), whose electoral results (ranging between 2.4% (2019) and 5.4% (2011)) made it a poor competitor to the SVP, which has been the largest party in Switzerland since 2003.

To conclude, party-based IoPPs affect populist parties in complex and sometimes contradictory ways. *Ostracism* directly *curbs the ability of populist parties to implement illiberal or anti-democratic policies* by excluding a party from government. It may also *reduce support for populist parties* by making a vote for ostracized parties a wasted vote for policy-oriented voters, especially when combined with *policy cooptation*. On the other hand, where populist parties can plausibly frame *ostracism* as a confirmation of anti-elitist appeals, *ostracism* might *increase support for populist parties* or help them maintain electoral successes. By taking office goals off the table, *ostracism* provides incentives for populist parties to *retain radical policy positions* to keep its core supporters on board, even if this does not exclude the possibility of moderation on some policy dimensions. In some cases, *ostracism* may *boost the organizational resource* of party unity, allowing moderates and radicals within the party to put aside potential conflicts, while in other cases it may spark potentially vote-losing disputes about how best to respond to *ostracism*.

As mentioned, where mainstream parties *coopt* a populist parties' signature policy, *populist parties may lose support*, especially when combined with *ostracism*. Or, on the contrary, *policy cooptation* may *increase support for a populist party* if voters realize that votes for populist parties may force other parties to take on and implement their preferred policies. Populist parties have incentives to respond to *policy cooptation* by trying to differentiate their appeals from the copycats, sometimes through *moderating*, other times *radicalizing their positions. Policy cooptation* may also *boost a party's moral resources* by increasing the salience and respectability of issues it campaigns upon.

Populist parties that *cooperate in government* are likely to see a *decrease in support* for their party, especially when members and voters may think the party's anti-elitist stance is compromised or because the party performs badly in office. In addition, populist parties that want to, or do, *cooperate in government* have incentives to *moderate their ideological positions and political behaviour* to establish or maintain good relations with governing partners. At the same time, populist parties have incentives to *retain radical policies* at least in some areas while participating in government, especially if this helps them avoid losing support from core voters. *Cooperation in government* may also *boost a populist parties' moral and material resources*, and if it can avoid damaging disunity, *cooperating in government* can *boost organizational resources*.

More research is needed to understand why the same IoPP—*ostracism*, or *policy cooptation*, or *cooperation*—often affects different parties in different ways. Existing studies provide some clues for why this might be. Various authors suggest populist party characteristics may at least partly account for differential effects. Heinisch has argued that organizational traits associated with populist parties such as the Austrian Freedom Party (FPÖ)—that is, charismatic leadership, spectacular forms of self-presentation, and a tendency to operate as relatively de-institutionalized movement parties—may 'impair the long-term prospects for populist parties in government' (2003: 91; see also Heinisch et al. 2021: 82). Among other things, such organizational features make it difficult for populist parties 'to resolve conflicts between competing leading personalities' (Heinisch 2003: 113). Others have observed that better organized parties more effectively deal with internal dissent (Pauwels 2011: 61; Akkerman and de Lange 2012; Zaslove 2012: 441–442). For example while serious internal conflicts within the FPÖ during its period in government in the 2000s were punished by voters, parties like the Danish People's Party (at least initially), and Swiss People's Party, with better functioning party organizations, were better able to handle such challenges and were not punished by voters (Heinisch 2003; Pauwels 2011: 61; Akkerman and de Lange 2012; Zaslove 2012: 441–442; Juul Christiansen 2016: 94). Akkerman and de Lange have argued that effective organization allowing populist parties to recruit more competent leaders may help reduce incumbency costs linked to poor governance (2012: 595). Mudde has argued that an established, well-organized and well-led party will be better placed to deal with challenges posed by *ostracism* (2007: 269–270). In addition to the characteristics of party organization, institutional context may also help explain variation. For example, van Spanje and van der Brug (2007) argue that institutional structures can explain varying effects of *ostracism*. In some contexts, they point out, opposition parties can be influential even if they never get into government, such as political systems with powerful parliamentary committees or where minority government is common.

This chapter has shown that an important way to understand how *ostracism*, *policy cooptation*, and *cooperation* work is through the manipulation of the strategic choices of populist parties and their supporters. In the next chapter I examine how other kinds of IoPP work through enforcement of the law.

4
Enforcement through the Constitution, Courts, and Coercion

This chapter examines how initiatives opposing populist parties (IoPPs) work through enforcement of the law. Various types of opposition initiative—particularly *rights-restrictions, judicial controls*, and *checks and balances* by public authorities—rely heavily on the courts, procedural rules, and constitutional guarantees to have an effect. Where political parties and civil society organizations have standing to institute proceedings against a populist party, enforcement is necessary for understanding how IoPPs in the form of *oppositional politics* and *adversarialism* work. Where they rely on convincing others to act on their behalf, these initiatives may indirectly rely on enforcement.

As it will be recalled, I argue that IoPPs are effective if they contribute to the achievement of one or more of the goals typically pursued by opponents of populist parties without producing perverse effects. I argue the main goals of those opposing populist parties are reducing support for populist parties among voters or sympathizers, diminishing their resources or inducing their moderation, as well as curbing illiberal and anti-democratic policies of governing populist parties. Perverse effects are increasing support for populist parties, boosting their resources, and radicalization.

In the first part of the chapter, I draw on concepts and theories from political science, sociology, international relations, and international law to examine how IoPPs contribute to the achievement of opposition goals or produce perverse effects. At heart, enforcement relies on the use—or threat—of the coercive power of the state and, as new institutionalist approaches from political science point out, on enabling and constraining effects of the institutional environment (e.g., Steinmo et al. 1992; Hall and Taylor 1996; March and Olsen 1996; Pierson 2000; Schmidt 2008). Through coercion and institutional constraint, IoPPs may *curb the ability of populist parties in government to implement illiberal or anti-democratic policies*. This is perhaps clearest in relation to *rights-restrictions*, such as party bans, *checks and balances*, and *oppositional politics* where public authorities and political parties use constitutional powers and legislative procedures to block such policies. In addition, research on effectiveness of international and supranational law, especially international human rights and EU law, help us to understand how *international checks and balances* and *international judicial controls* can *curb the ability of populist parties in government to implement illiberal or anti-democratic policies* (e.g., Keohane 1997; Helfer and Slaughter 1997; Guzman 2008; Simmons 2009; Moravcsik 2012; Alter 2012; Kosař et al. 2020). The political process tradition of social movement studies can also be bought into focus to show how some forms of *adversarialism* by civil society actors work *to curb illiberal and anti-democratic policies of governing populists* through alliances with the courts and political parties empowered to block such policies (e.g., Burstein et al. 1995; Kriesi et al. 1995; Giugni 2004; Tarrow 2011). In addition, a focus on coercion and institutional constraint, supplemented by concepts and theories from party politics and resource mobilization literatures introduced in the previous chapter, help us to understand how *rights-restrictions* and *judicial controls* may *diminish or boost a populist party's resources*, which may, in turn, *increase or reduce support for a populist party* or *induce moderation or radicalization*.

The rest of the chapter explores the plausibility of theoretical propositions drawn from the theory in light of existing research, particularly the rich secondary literature on populist parties both in and out of government, and studies on the Court of Justice of the EU and European Court of Human Rights cases concerning Hungary and Poland.

How IoPPs Work through Coercion and Institutional Constraint

Political opportunity structures and constrained democracy

Enforcement sometimes relies directly on the coercive power of the state. Other times, it lurks in the background. Where IoPPs rely on the use, or threat, of this coercive authority, they can be conceived as acts of state repression. That is, they are initiatives taking the form of 'obstacles by the state (or its agents) to individual and collective actions by challengers' (Davenport 2004; McCarthy and McPhail 2006: 3; Earl 2011), or 'efforts of authorities to inhibit or suppress activity by dissidents' (Tilly 2004: 218). As Ferree (2005) observes, repression can be 'hard' or 'soft'. 'Hard' repression can be understood as initiatives undertaken by the state and denotes 'mobilization of force to control or crush oppositional action through the use or threat of violence' (ibid.: 138–142). As Davenport adds, hard repression 'may be legitimate or illegitimate, but is always essential to the very definition of the state ... [in fact] one of the most basic functions of the institution' (2005: 35). Hard repression approximates many of the IoPPs discussed in this chapter. Enforcement of many *rights-restricting* IoPPs and *judicial controls*—such as party bans, surveillance, fines, and prison sentences—may require intervention from various state (and sometimes international) authorities to ensure implementation, including the judiciary, police, and security and prison services. In extreme situations, *checks and balances* may also rely on the coercive power of the state to preserve the institutional status quo. In contrast, 'soft' repression involves 'mobilization of non-violent means to silence or eradicate oppositional ideas' (ibid.). IoPPs such as *ostracism* and demonizing discourses, discussed elsewhere in this book, can be considered forms of 'soft repression'.

Enforcement also takes place through adaptation to, or conformity with, opportunities and constraints of the institutional environment, as new institutionalist theories propose (Steinmo et al. 1992; Hall and Taylor 1996; March and Olsen 1996; Pierson 2000; Schmidt 2008). In this approach, institutions are defined, in Goodin's (1996) definition, as 'stable, recurring patterns of behaviour'. They can be specific organizations such as courts, parliaments, governments, bureaucracies, states, firms, NGOs, or political parties. They may also be 'formal or informal procedures, routines, norms, and conventions embedded in the organized structure of the polity or economy' (Hall and Taylor 1996). Social institutions are more generalized patterns of activity and include practices as diverse as religious rituals, marriage, handshakes, and international principles like 'sovereignty' (Keohane 1989: 162–163). Institutions are seen to affect political behaviour in various ways. On the one hand, they provide 'enforcement mechanisms for agreements' and 'penalties for defection' (Hall and Taylor 1996; March and Olsen 1996). However, they also provide moral or cognitive templates for interpretation and action (ibid.). New institutionalist approaches also draw attention to the ways in which institutions may embed worldviews and principled ideas, which then create a tendency, through 'path dependence', for future choices to gravitate towards actions in accordance with those ideas (Hall and Taylor 1996; March and Olsen 1996; Schmidt 2008).

The institutional environment can be conceived as an element of the 'political opportunity structure' in which populist parties operate. Political opportunity structures are made up of the institutional, political, cultural, or social environment in which social groups operate and can affect their activities, influence, and organization (Gamson and Meyer 1996; Kriesi 2004;

Tarrow 2011). As research on the radical right shows, the concept of 'political opportunity structures' is easily transferred to the study of populist parties (Mudde 2007, ch 10; see also Kitschelt and McGann 1997; Minkenberg 2003; van der Brug et al. 2005; Arzheimer and Carter 2006; Norris and Inglehart 2019). For instance, this literature shows how the *cultural context* might enable or constrain populist parties, depending on the resonance of their appeals with the prevailing intellectual climate, a political 'subculture', historical legacies, or prevailing societal norms. Or, the *political context* may constrain or enable populist parties, depending, for instance, on the extent to which there is issue consensus among moderate right (and/or left) parties, or the inclinations of other parties to deploy the kind of party-based IoPPs discussed in Chapter 3. The *institutional* context might constrain or enable populist parties, depending for instance on electoral rules, territorial structure of the state (federalism versus unitary), parliamentary rules, prevalence of corporatist state–society relations, or prevailing practices of adversarial, consociational, or consensus politics. They also include the legal framework for setting out *checks and balances* by public authorities, and procedures enabling *oppositional politics* by political parties.

The concept of political opportunity structures also provides important clues about why IoPPs may work differently in different countries and in relation to different parties. That is, in addition to providing a conceptual framework for understanding the interaction of individual populist parties with their external environment, political opportunity structures affect their opponents too. In other words, an examination of the political, cultural, and institutional environment in which opponents operate provides important clues for why IoPPs may work differently in different countries.

More specifically, enforcement through the use, or threat, of coercion and institutional constraint helps us to understand how *checks and balances* and *oppositional politics* can *curb illiberal and anti-democratic policies by populists in government*. As Jan-Werner Müller has observed, 'the whole direction of political development in post-war Europe' has been towards a form of 'constrained democracy', based on a 'profound distrust of unrestrained popular sovereignty and even unconstrained *parliamentary* sovereignty' (2014a: 156–157). The historical experience of 'legislative representative assemblies handing all power to Hitler and to Marshal Pétain, the leader of Vichy France, in 1933 and 1940 respectively' shaped a 'basic structure' of European democracies, such that:

> parliaments in post-war Europe were systematically weakened, checks and balances were strengthened and non-elected institutions (constitutional courts are

the prime example) were tasked not just with defending individual rights, but with defending democracy as a whole.

(ibid.: 157)

International bodies, such as the Council of Europe, with the European Court of Human Rights at its heart, complements the institutions of constrained democracy within European states.

This edifice of procedures, routines, rationales, penalties, moral and cognitive templates provide the institutional framework for IoPPs deploying *checks and balances* by public authorities and for the manoeuvres of *oppositional politics* by political parties. In autocratizing or 'democratic backsliding' states, at least some law-enforcement bodies or institutions with authority to check executive power may retain autonomy, and challenges may be launched in international courts. Insofar as the institutions of constrained democracy limit populist parties and enable their opponents, *checks and balances* and *oppositional politics* may permit opponents to *curb illiberal and anti-democratic policies of populists in power.*

The institutional environment also shapes opportunities for populist opponents which do not have a formal role in checking governmental power, such as civil society actors. As the political process approach of social movement theories suggest, civil society actors deploying *adversarial* initiatives opposing populist parties may sometimes achieve their goals indirectly through enforcement by influential allies (Kriesi et al. 1995; Tarrow 2011: 163, 166). Among other things, the approach focuses attention on how the allies of civil society actors may be 'acceptable negotiators on their behalf', 'friends in court', or 'guarantors against repression' (Giugni 2004: 120; Tarrow 2011: 166, 169). Alliances with political parties may be important for achieving civil society goals because 'it is only by entering parties' agendas' that the demands of civil society actors 'gain wider attention, and are more likely to produce broader, possibly long-term societal and political consequences' (Burstein et al. 1995: 289; Giugni 2004: 122–126, 170; Piccio 2016: 279). More specifically, political parties may use their formal authority, where the legal framework allows it, to deploy *oppositional politics* to support civil society campaigns (or vice versa), and this may help them to *curb illiberal and anti-democratic policies of populists in government.*

In addition, as Kolb's work highlights, civil society actors can sometimes use a 'judicial mechanism' to achieve political goals 'using the power of the courts on their behalf' (2007: 86). Constitutional Courts, for example, can 'overturn whole pieces of legislation on behalf of social movements, while lower courts can play important roles in the proper implementation of passed legislation' (ibid.). Governments and other political actors may make concessions to avoid 'risks of losing a court case' (ibid.: 86). Not all groups will be able to jump the hurdles for accessing courts though, which often require financial resources and legal knowhow, and significant change, if it occurs, may be slow because courts necessarily proceed on a 'case-by-case basis' (Simmons 2009: 133–134).

In a process analogous to the potentially perverse effects of *ostracism* giving 'disenchanted voters further reasons to embrace ... anti-establishment messages' (Downs 2012: 103–104), populist parties may be able to turn initiatives deploying *checks and balances* and *oppositional politics* into an opportunity for *increasing their support*. These initiatives are particularly vulnerable to populist counter-discourses because they are steered by public authorities and political parties, which through the populist prism look like the work of a prototypical corrupt and self-serving elite. Particularly for initiatives involving the courts, as Rovira Kaltwasser put it, 'Populists can claim that actors who are neither elected nor controlled by "the people" have decided to censor the party which gives voice to the "silent majority"'(2019: 89). In this way, populists can discredit opponents through frames presenting IoPPs as 'evidence' supporting core anti-establishment themes and invoking a corresponding need to renew popular sovereignty.

Repression and its effect on resources, votes, and moderation

The most repressive form of *rights-restricting* IoPP, the party ban, directly *curbs the ability of a populist party to implement illiberal or anti-democratic policies*. They do so by preventing a party from participating in the main mechanism available in liberal democracies to access governmental power, namely contesting elections (Bourne 2018). Given that party bans are rare, it is more useful to look to concepts and theory from the resource mobilization tradition of social movement studies to explain how IoPPs relying on state repression—that is *rights-restricting* IoPPs more generally and *judicial controls*—might *diminish or boost a populist party's resources* which may, in turn, *increase or reduce support for a populist party* or *induce moderation or radicalization*.

As discussed in Chapter 3, resource mobilization theory sheds light on how IoPPs may affect a party's material, human, organizational, and moral resources. The effects of repressive IoPPs on resources is perhaps clearest where they may deplete a party's *material resources* by, for example, cutting access to state funding or scaring off 'outside sources of funding and support' (Boykoff 2007: 295; Davenport 2005: xvi). Banned parties are typically dissolved and their goods are confiscated (Bourne 2018), while parties deemed a threat to the liberal democratic order may be denied access to state funding, as in Germany. Entanglement in financially burdensome legal proceedings may deplete resources that could otherwise be used for other objectives (ibid.). Where depleted material resources affect the ability to run effective party organizations or electoral campaigns, they may *reduce support for the populist party*.

Repressive IoPPs targeting party leaders may reduce a party's *human resources*. Charismatic, personalistic leadership is widely regarded as a primary resource of populist (and other) parties, so much so that some definitions of populism put charismatic leadership centrestage (e.g., Moffitt 2016; Ostiguy 2017; Weyland 2017). Heavy reliance on the leadership qualities of particular individuals make a party vulnerable to the fortunes of that individual. Some criminal offences may lead to the leader's imprisonment or disqualification from electoral contests. Repressive IoPPs may undermine confidence in the leader internally. As van Donselaar has observed:

> The leader who adapts too much to repressive conditions runs the risk of being regarded as 'lax' and 'weak', and hence runs the risk of endangering his own position. A leader who adapts too little and holds on to too radical a profile can be just as controversial, just as endangered; for with him his fellow group members are criminalized. Leaders are also vulnerable who have an insufficient moderating effect on party members who have been discredited because of extreme ideas or behaviour.
>
> **(2007: 734)**

Theories on the electoral success and failure of radical right populist parties emphasizing the importance of internal party characteristics, or 'supply side' explanations (e.g., Kitschelt and McGann 1997; Mudde 2007; Akkerman et al. 2016, 17–20; Mudde and Rovira Kaltwasser 2017: 97–118), suggest that IoPPs weakening the leader may *reduce support for the party* among voters and sympathizers.

Repressive IoPPs may also generate negative social and material consequences for rank-and-file party members who may end up in the courts for acts in support of the party. As various scholars have observed, dissidents involved in legal proceedings may face 'large legal fees, lost wages, and other pecuniary losses', 'reputations can be tarnished or destroyed in the public arena', and those who find themselves imprisoned may be 'so traumatized as to drop their dissident stances or temporarily put them on hold' (Boykoff 2007: 289; Lichbach 1987: 270). Such actions may have a broader deterrent effect where 'current supporters and potential supporters in bystander publics are discouraged from putting forth dissident views' (Boykoff 2007: 289; on deterrence see also Lichbach 1987: 270; Koopmans 2005; Earl 2011). Where costs generated by repressive IoPPs are high, members and sympathizers have incentives to withdraw, *reducing support for the populist party*.

Repressive IoPPs may additionally *diminish a group's organizational resources,* including their ability to maintain solidarity, recruit members, cultivate leaders, and run effective campaigns (Boykoff 2007: 294; Edwards et al. 2018: 84). Repression 'imposes a new logic' on a social organization, forcing participants to 'look internally and consider what state actions their political beliefs might instigate' (Boykoff 2007: 299–300). It may 'contribute in significant ways to foster inter- and intra-group strife and strain' (Boykoff 2007: 298; Mudde 2007: 273; van Donselaar 2017). As van Donselaar has argued, parties subject to state repression need to 'stringently undertake and control impression management' and this can make the organization unstable (2017: 734). Impression management often requires presenting the party to the outside world, or 'front-stage behaviour', in a way that differs from 'goings on behind the scene', or 'back-stage behaviour'. This can cause problems internally if, for example, party leaders fail to publicly acknowledge ideas of radical members 'for fear of confrontation with the judiciary or other authorities' (ibid.: 724). And yet, '[r]adical supporters may be alienated or repelled by silence or denial of ideological principles and membership in extreme right groups may suffer as a result' (ibid.: 723). As discussed in Chapter 3, a lack of internal cohesion can *reduce support for a populist party* because, as van Spanje argues 'rational voters will, all things being equal, prefer to vote for a party that is united to a divided, conflict ridden-party, as the former can be expected to be more effective in policy-making than the latter' (2018: 40, see also van der Brug et al. 2005; Zulianello 2019: 74).

Some kinds of *rights-restricting* IoPPs and *judicial controls* may damage the reputation or legitimacy of a populist party, thereby *undermining its moral resources* and potentially *reducing support for the party*. In a society where democratic principles are valued, *judicial controls* confirming violations of such principles *may reduce support for the party*. This is also likely to be the case where a party or its leader are involved in corruption cases, which tarnish the plausibility of populist claims targeting others as 'corrupt elites'. Cases involving racism or hate speech may also discredit defendants insofar as these charges clash with norms rendering blatant discrimination socially undesirable (Jacobs and van Spanje 2020: 914).

In some circumstances though, existing scholarship shows that repressive IoPPs may *boost party resources*. All IoPPs that generate controversy may potentially boost populist parties' *organizational resources* by providing 'free publicity', which may increase the salience of populist ideas on the political agenda or enhance the appeal of a populist party for certain audiences (van Spanje and de Vreese 2015: 117–118; van Heerden and van der Brug 2017: 38; Jacobs and van Spanje 2020). This may be especially so with high-profile court cases, such as party bans, racism and hate speech trials. High-profile initiatives of this kind may profitably enhance a party's 'issue ownership' or the stature of a populist leader if he or she is considered effective in the face of such IoPPs (ibid.).

Similarly, repressive IoPPs resulting in harsh financial penalties or detention of leaders and members may inadvertently bolster *organizational resources* by creating a sense that the party is a 'community under seige' (Zúquete 2007: 36–47). As Levite and Tarrow put it, such strategies may produce 'sectarian closure', where 'members of an organization become a cult of true believers' and 'substitut[e] intense subcultural solidarity for the support they lack among the mass public' (1983: 298). Like *ostracism* and demonizing discourses discussed elsewhere, repressive IoPPs may strengthen internal cohesion by sharpening a sense of injury and victimhood, as well as distance from, and distrust of, the political mainstream among supporters (van Spanje and van der Brug 2007: 1023; Fallend and Heinisch 2016: 330; Rovira Kaltwasser 2019: 89; Meléndez and Rovira Kaltwasser 2021; Harteveld et al. 2022).

Where repressive IoPPs create high costs for leaders or rank-and-file party members, and where material or organizational resources are threatened, populist parties, like other social organizations, will have incentives to alter their behaviour to mitigate or avoid future repression. This may take the form of demobilization but may also *induce moderation* (Lichbach 1987; Moore 1998; Tilly 2004; Rummens and Abts 2010; Earl 2011). On the other hand, repressive IoPPs *may induce radicalization* if parties 'retreat and go underground', opening the possibility that 'the apathetic become politicized, the reformers become radicalized, and the revolutionaries redouble their efforts' (Lichbach 1987: 269; Koopmans 2005: 159; van Donselaar 2017: 733; Tilly 2004; Davenport 2004).

Like other IoPPs relying on enforcement through coercion or institutional constraint, *rights-restrictions* and *judicial controls* are vulnerable to populist counter-discourses because they are typically steered by public authorities and political parties. As mentioned above, public authorities and political parties are the prototypical corrupt and self-serving elite of populist discourse, which gives those targeted by repressive IoPPs an opportunity to maintain or *increase support* by framing them as 'evidence' supporting core anti-establishment themes (Downs 2012: 103–104; Rovira Kaltwasser 2019: 89).

Compliance with international and supranational law

Enforcement of *international checks and balances* and *international judicial controls* principally rely on the extent to which state governments can be compelled to comply with international and supranational (or EU) law. A clear limitation to the enforceability of international law and even the EU's highly developed legal system is the lack of centralized mechanisms analogous to those within states authorizing coercion to enforce laws. There is no international equivalent to the extensive state-based apparatus for administering justice, typically including police and public prosecutorial services, specialized tribunals, and prisons for the most serious wrongdoers.

International relations theory provides many insights into why states often comply with international law, despite the lack of international centralized enforcement mechanisms. The realist tradition of international relations tends to hold that compliance with international law is generally quite good but is sceptical about the *independent* effect of international law on state behaviour (Steinberg 2012: 163). That is, compliance with international law should not be read as something that necessarily makes states change their behaviour. In this tradition international law is seen as subordinate to state interests and the relative power of states (Goldsmith and Posner 2005; Steinberg 2012). States sign up to international agreements they are willing to comply with in the first place, so that compliance 'requires [states] to do little more than they would in the absence of a treaty' (Goldsmith and Posner 2005: 163; Thompson 2012). International law cannot 'pull states towards compliance contrary to their interests' (Goldsmith and Posner 2005: 13). These basic assumptions are refined by realist emphasis on the role of power in generating compliance. As such 'social norms', like the promotion of democracy and human rights, 'may become part of international law when advanced by powerful states' (Steinberg 2012: 158). Powerful states though are unlikely to comply with international law when it is not in their interests and weaker states may be pressured to comply under the 'shadow of coercive action' of powerful ones (Steinberg 2012: 163; Goldsmith and Posner 2005).

A second approach developed from liberal theories of international relations focuses on 'self-enforcement'. From this perspective, states entering into international agreements have incentives to keep their commitments because benefits of cooperation over the long term outweigh short-term advantages of breaking them (Keohane 1989; Guzman 2008; Simmons 2009: 116–118). Compliance with self-enforcing agreements is regulated by *reciprocity*. That is, states have incentives to comply with international law because a failure to do so will end cooperation as other states calculate their interests will no longer be served by the agreement (Guzman 2008: 33). On the other hand, reciprocity will not be effective for broken promises relating to democracy and human rights, especially where these are not linked to other forms of cooperation (Keohane 2002: 6; Guzman 2008: 45; Simmons 2009: 124). This is because a violating state is unlikely to care much about another state's refusal to respect human rights as a response to its own violation. States may also want to comply with international law to uphold a good *reputation*. When a state keeps its agreements—or when it violates them—it sends a signal about its general willingness to honour international obligations (Guzman 2008: 33). As Guzman points out, maintaining a reputation for compliance can be 'valuable because it makes promises more credible and therefore, makes future cooperation both easier and less costly' (ibid.). On the other hand, the effectiveness of reputational constraints may be limited if a state can conceal violations, or if it can offset reputational deficiencies in one domain (e.g., human rights and the rule of law) with excellence in another (e.g., compliance with trade rules) (Keohane 1997; Simmons 2009: 118, 124; Schimmelfenig and Sedelmeier 2020). A third approach for understanding why states often obey international law draws on the constructivist tradition in international relations, focusing on the pull of international norms and state identities. I take this perspective up in Chapter 6 on persuasion, shaming, and negotiation.

International courts can help states enforce international law, despite wide variation in institutional design and effectiveness (Helfer and Slaughter 1997; Keohane et al. 2000; Simmons 2009; Alter 2012). Most international courts are set up to 'flag' non-compliance by reviewing the actions of states, public authorities, and in some cases individuals (Alter 2012: 350). International courts may also undertake *administrative review*, evaluating 'administrative actors in cases raised by private litigants'; *constitutional review*, assessing the legal validity of state actions in relation to international legal obligations; and *dispute settlement,* issuing binding interpretations of international agreements where there is disagreement (Alter 2012: 345).

While performing these tasks, a court's effectiveness can be defined as a 'power to compel parties to appear before it and to comply with its judgments' (Helfer and Slaughter 1997: 283). An effective court will make its authority felt both following judgments and where 'parties in a similar legal position to actual litigants are likely to comply with the court's judgement "in the shadow" of prospective litigation' (ibid.). Nevertheless, as Simmons puts it, 'litigation cannot force [government] compliance' with international treaties and will not 'render a demonic government angelic' (ibid.: 14–15). International courts cannot 'nullify "illegal" national acts' (Alter 2012: 353; Kosař et al. 2020: 22). They must also confront the general reluctance of states to bring cases against each other (Helfer and Slaughter 1997: 285–286; Keohane et al. 2000: 463, 473). They can expect states to try to take the easiest path to compliance. For example, many states 'comply fully with rulings [by international courts on human rights violations] by paying compensation while still maintaining the contested practice' (Alter 2012: 353).

In these challenging conditions, an international court's ability to compel states to pay attention to its rulings may rest on the ability to harness the coercive power of the very states that set up international courts in the first place. Rather than relying on 'horizontal' state-to-state mechanisms of enforcement, such as reciprocity and the reputational constraints discussed above, effective enforcement of international law may rely on 'vertical' enforcement, which is carried out as part of routine legal and political processes within the state (Helfer and Slaughter 1997; Keohane, Moravcsik, and Slaughter 2000; Simmons 2009; Moravcsik 2012). Where vertical enforcement mechanisms have been established, national executives 'no longer need to take positive action to ensure enforcement of international judgements' because 'enforcement occurs directly through domestic courts and executive agents who are responsive to judicial decisions' (Helfer and Slaughter 1997: 288–290; Keohane et al. 2000: 476; Moravcsik 2012: 96).

Importantly, vertical enforcement systems may empower domestic opponents by creating additional sources of political pressure for compliance. In the first place, an 'executive determined to violate international law must override his or her own legal system', which may pitch it not just against the governments of other states but a 'legally legitimate domestic opposition' (Helfer and Slaughter 1997: 289; Keohane et al. 2000: 477). Indeed, 'even in a political system that is otherwise corrupt or oppressive, it is possible a particular government institution—a court or administrative agency or even a legislative body—will choose to forge a relationship with a supranational tribunal as ally in a domestic political battle against corruption or oppression'(Helfer and Slaughter 1997: 334–335; Simmons 2009: 130). For courts to play this role, however, they must possess sufficient autonomy from the executive, be committed to the rule of law and responsive to civil society groups (Helfer and Slaughter 1997: 334; Simmons 2009: 14, 132).

In addition, international courts may also be allies for civil society actors undertaking *adversarial* initiatives deploying an international version of Kolb's 'judicial mechanism' to achieve political goals (2007: 86). Civil society actors can use rights of access to supranational courts to bring 'test cases' and create international pressure for domestic reforms (Helfer and Slaughter 1997: 368; Simmons 2009: 133). An authoritative ruling against a government in an international tribunal may help 'authenticate' complaints against the government, especially where international treaties are 'the clearest statement available about the content of globally sanctioned decent practices' (Simmons 2009: 130, 147). International courts may thus open 'space for the domestic opposition to catch the government in their own rhetoric' and make it 'very hard for the government to deny the validity' of the international norm it signed up to, even if it denies violation or continues to repress those who challenge it (Risse and Sikkink 1999: 15, 27). As Simmons has argued, governments that fail to meet their publicly ratified commitments may face 'inconsitsency costs', which 'risk loss of a degree of domestic legitimacy' or *moral resources*, and which may, under certain conditions, '*erode their domestic support*' (my italics, 2009: 145).

International IoPPs involving courts—as well as other kinds of international initiatives such as *rights-restricting* sanctions (see Chapter 5) and even some forms of *public persuasion* (see Chapter 6)—may provoke a 'populist backlash' of a different kind. Where states and international organizations criticize a state government, they may enter a field of 'normative contestation' with that state (Finnemore and Sikkink 1998: 893). That is, international interventions will often be met by counter-discourses insisting that the international norms on which initiatives are based are incompatible with domestic norms (Risse and Ropp 2013: 21; Risse and Sikkink 2013: 290–291). These often take the form of 'sovereignty' counter-discourses, which easily resonate with populist appeals to popular 'sovereignty'. As Risse and Sikkink put it, sovereignty counter-discourses claim that international initiatives are an 'illegitimate intervention in the internal affairs of the country' and 'opposes the suggestion that its national practices in this area are subject to international jurisdiction' (1999: 223; Bermeo 2016: 15–16). Likewise, appeals to the illegitimacy of international IoPPs can easily be expressed through the populist juxtaposition of 'the pure people' and 'corrupt elite', not least because populist conceptions of the elite often incorporate international actors (Heinisch and Mazzoleni 2017: 108; Schlipphak and Treib 2017: 355). Where sovereignty counter-discourses are deployed to 'rally-round-the-flag', they may *increase support for a populist-led government* (Fallend and Heinisch 2016: 336; Schlipphak and Treib 2017: 354; Closa 2021: 4) or be used to 'de-certify', or 'invalidate' actors making appeals against the government (McAdam, Tilly, and Tarrow 2001: 158).

Checking Populists in the Executive

Checks and balances by public authorities are a type of IoPP authorized by the rules, procedures, and institutions of constrained democracy (Müller 2014a: 156–157). They are designed to block or 'check' the abuse of power by individuals or groups exercising formal positions of authority in the political system. The most potent *checks and balances* include the judicial review of legislative and administrative acts, and procedures permitting dismissal of governments or ministers, such as no-confidence votes or impeachment. Other formal rules permitting those who oppose populist parties to check governmental power include procedures vetting executive and judicial appointments, parliamentary procedures permitting deputies to question government ministers or set up investigatory committees, and acts of secondary supervisory bodies like ombudsmen or independent regulators. Initiatives I call *oppositional politics* include acts of opposition by political parties which include initiating some checks on executive power, such as judicial review, no-confidence votes or impeachment, as well as use of parliamentary procedures to defeat or amend legislation proposed by a governing populist party.

As discussed above, these *checks and balances* and *opposition politics* IoPPs may *curb the ability of populist parties in government to implement illiberal and anti-democratic policies.* The institutional apparatus authorizing such IoPPs may constrain populist parties and enable their opponents, and are ultimately backed up by the use, or threat, of coercion by the state. Where *adversarialism* by civil society actors takes the form of alliances with those able to initiate checks on executive power, such as political parties or the courts, the threat of coercion and institutional constraints may indirectly allow civil society initiatives *to curb illiberal and anti-democratic policies by governing populists.* On the other hand, such initiatives may also provoke a populist backlash, reinforcing anti-establishment themes and *increasing support for populist parties.* There are many examples of such effects, but limitations of space permit mention of only a few notable illustrative examples.

While testing support for governing populist parties through no-confidence motions is common for parliamentary oppositions, there is a case where this procedure ended in the ejection of a governing populist party. In February 2013 in Slovenia Janez Janša's Slovenian Democratic Party (SDS) lost power when coalition partners supported a constructive motion of censure in favour of a new governing coalition (Fink-Hafner and Krasovec 2014: 281). The no-confidence vote followed a wave of anti-austerity and anti-corruption protests engulfing the country through the previous year (Bucik 2013; Kirn 2018). As a response to the 'unprecedented protests' the SDS's coalition partners withdrew support (Fink-Hafner and Krasovec 2014: 281). The party subsequently lost 5.6% of its vote share in the 2014 national elections (from 26.3% to 20.7% of the vote) and Janša and his party were not able to return to government again until March 2020.

In Italy, the formal constitutional powers of the president of the republic, which includes appointment of ministers, a legislative veto, and the dissolution of parliament, have allowed successive presidents to constrain the activities of populist-led governments (Verbeek and Zaslove 2016: 311). For example, President Sergio Mattarella was able to influence the formation of the Five Star Movement (5SM)–League Government (2018–2019) led by Prime Minister Giuseppe Conte by insisting on inclusion of Finance Minister Giovanni Tria and Foreign Minister Enzo Moavero Milanesi (Cotta 2020: 127). In this way, Cotta has argued, Mattarella created a third 'technocratic' pillar in the government: The 'two anti-establishment parties had to accept a sort of "cohabitation" with the state establishment in the leadership of two ministries that are crucial for relations with the EU and with Italy's other international partners' (ibid.: 127). Later, when the League leader Matteo Salvini withdrew from government to force new elections, Mattarella blocked Salvini's chance to build on its victory in the 2019 European Parliament elections and nominated Giuseppe Conte to head a new government with 5SM, the Democratic Party (DP), and Free and Equal (LeU) (ibid.: 136).

In the midst of mass protests in 2017, Polish President Andrzej Duda used legislative veto powers to delay two laws central to Law and Justice's judicial reforms, which weakened the autonomy of the Polish courts (Bojarski 2021: 1373). Protests beginning in front of the Supreme Court in Warsaw 'grew into hundreds of local protests in front of court buildings, grouping thousands of people through Poland for several days' (Bojarski 2021: 1373). An amended version of the disputed laws vetoed by the president, which dealt with the National Council of the Judiciary and Supreme Court, were passed a few months later, but later challenged in the Court of Justice of the EU (Bojarski 2021: 1373).

Czech opposition parties have actively constrained the ability of Action of Dissatisfied Citizens (ANO) leader Andrej Babiš to implement several controversial measures. Guasti has argued that despite the fragmentation of the Czech parliamentary opposition, and more general opposition party 'struggles to hold the executive accountable and investigate its overreach', they have 'united to prevent executive aggrandizement' (2020: 476, see also Pospíšil 2020). For example, in 2017 when ANO was a coalition partner in the Czech Social Democratic-led government, ANO's coalition partner and opposition parties joined forces to enact what has been dubbed 'Lex Babiš' (Stephens 2020; Guasti 2020). This law introduced new rules limiting media ownership for cabinet ministers as well as their ability to own companies receiving state funding. As a consequence, Babiš was forced to put his business holdings in trust, including the MAFRA publishing house and the Agrofert holding company at the centre of EU funding corruption scandals (Stephens 2020). The legislation survived a presidential veto when overturned by opposition parties and following an unsuccessful appeal to the Constitutional Court (Guasti 2020). More generally, Pospíšil (2020) has argued that the Czech Constitutional Court has played an active role guarding the independence of the judiciary, repeatedly annulling legislation that could undermine the separation of powers. There are various other examples of opposition to controversial initiatives by Babiš' government during the COVID pandemic—including proposed rules that would decrease transparency in conflict of interest cases like those facing Babiš over EU funds—which were blocked by opposition parties and the courts, or by the threat of court action (Guasti 2020: 480).

In Poland and Hungary, opposition parties have deployed a variety of parliamentary procedures to challenge governing majorities. According to Ilonszki and Dudzińska (2021: 610), this has included joint initiatives, interpellations, and filibuster, although more often in Poland than in Hungary. Between 16 December 2016 and 12 January 2017, for example, Polish opposition parties occupied the plenary hall of the parliament to protest changes in the 'organisation of the work of journalists in the Sejm and exclusion of an opposition MP from the plenary' (ibid.: 611). Supported by street protests, the initiative led to restoration of '[b]oth the former rules of journalists' work and the MP's participation in the plenary' (ibid.: 611–612).

The Italian Constitutional Court blocked various legislative initiatives promoted by Forza Italia and the Northern League (now League). It blocked a 2008 law providing immunity from criminal prosecutions for the highest office holders in the country, including Forward Italy's (FI) former Prime Minister Silvio Berlusconi, who was subject to various criminal investigations throughout his period in office (Hardt and Eliantonio 2011; Albertazzi and McDonnell 2015: 111). A League-led initiative legalizing vigilante groups (*ronde*) patrolling cities and towns was declared partially unconstitutional in June 2010 (Faraguna 2011; Albertazzi and McDonnell 2015: 109). The Italian

Constitutional Court also ruled in June 2010 that new provisions of the criminal code making irregular immigration status an aggravating circumstance justifying tougher penalties was not constitutional (ibid.).

During the first PiS-led populist coalition between 2006–2007, the Constitutional Court, according to Stanley, 'proved the most damaging to [the coalition's] ambitions', striking down key legislation deemed incompatible with the constitution on several occasions (2016: 271). This included laws threatening the independence of a media oversight body and a lustration law, whose effects would strip newly elected mayors of their mandates and undermine the prerogatives of the judiciary. As the Constitutional Court and many parts of the judiciary were captured by PiS supporters following the 2015 election, judges in independent courts fought back, using among other things petitions to the Court of Justice of the EU (see for example, Pech et al. 2021). The ombudsman, Adam Bodnar, used his powers to campaign against reforms undermining judicial independence, including challenging government actions in the courts.

Even in Hungary, where dismantling checks on executive power is advanced (see for example Scheppele 2018), the actions of the Fidesz government have met with some resistance in the courts. In 2017 the Hungarian Supreme Court (Curia) reached a controversial verdict ruling that police actions against Roma in the town of Gyöngyöspata were unlawful and violated the right to equal treatment (Hungarian Civil Liberties Union 2017). In another controversial case in 2020, the court awarded damages to segregated Roma school children from the same town (Dunai 2020). The ruling confirmed findings reached earlier by the ombudsman.

Repressive IoPPs: Rights Restrictions and Trouble in the Courts

Rights-restricting IoPPs are undertaken by public authorities and seek to delimit the participation of populist parties in the public sphere by restricting certain kinds of political rights, including rights of association and expression, or public goods such as state funding or free broadcast time. *Judicial controls* are initiatives opposing populist parties that typically end in the courts. At the national level, such initiatives usually make use of ordinary law, including civil and criminal codes (or equivalent), to launch legal proceedings against populist parties or their leaders for crimes such as corruption, misuse of public funds, holocaust denial, hate speech or racism. Although *rights-restricting* IoPPs are classified as intolerant modes of engagement with populist parties and *judicial controls* as tolerant ones, in terms of effects, they have much common. That is, both rely directly on the coercive apparatus of the state for enforcement, including the courts, the police, security services, and sometimes prison services.

There are very few current examples of *rights-restricting* initiatives deployed against populist parties in contemporary Europe. The profound democratic dilemmas posed by party bans means they rarely occur in liberal democracies. When they do, they usually target clearly extremist anti-system parties (Bourne 2018), which typically have much less ambiguous positions on liberal democracy than most populist parties (see Chapter 1).[1] Theoretically though, party bans provide a very direct way to *curb the ability of a populist party to implement illiberal or anti-democratic policies*; that is, bans prevent parties reaching power through elections (Bourne 2018). Where they result in dissolution or the confiscation of property, party bans will have a major impact on a party's *organizational and material resources* (ibid.).

One prominent example of a *rights-restricting* initiative is surveillance of the Alternative for Germany (AfD) by the *Bundesamt für Verfassungsschutz* (BfV, Federal Office for the Protection of the Constitution). The BfV is part of the German domestic intelligence service and in conjunction with 16 Lander equivalents, collects and publishes information about people and organizations which, among other things, threaten the 'free democratic basic order' in Germany. Under certain conditions, the BfV is authorized to suspend some fundamental rights, such as privacy and those relating to the collection of personal data, to use covert surveillance and paid informants, and monitor communications, including of those of elected parliamentarians. Der Flügel (The Wing), a faction within the AfD was classified as a suspect case in 2019, and in March 2020 the BfV publicly declared that Der Flügel was engaged in 'right-wing extremist activities' (Federal Minister of the Interior 2020: 16–17). In 2019, the AfD's official youth branch *Junge Alternative für Deutschland* was also classified as a subject for extended investigation. In early 2021, media reports claimed the BfV would classify the whole party as a suspected extremist organization (Diehl et al. 2021; Deutsche Welle, 2 March 2021).

---

[1] To my knowledge, only one of the 50-odd parties listed in Table 1.1, which shows populist parties with representation in European national parliaments in 2020, have ever been subject to party ban proceedings. Sinn Féin was banned in Northern Ireland between 1956 and 1974 when it was a very minor, and abstentionist adjunct to the Irish Republican Army, a very different position from that of the party today. Bale (2007) sees racism convictions leading to the dissolution of the Flemish Bloc in 2004 as a de facto party ban, but I discuss this below as an instance of judicial controls applying anti-racism legislation.

Following an AfD injunction, the Cologne Administrative Court in March 2022 authorized the BfV to publicly announce its classification of the AfD and its youth organization as a suspected extremist organization and subject it to further investigation (BfV 2021).

In another case, the Hungarian Supreme Court confirmed in 2009 a ban on the Hungarian Guard, a uniformed but unarmed 'militia' founded and chaired by the leader of right-wing populist party Movement for a Better Hungary (Jobbik) (Molnár 2016). The courts banned and dissolved the Hungarian Guard on the grounds that it violated human and minority rights guaranteed in the constitution (Póczik and Sárik 2019: 113). The group organized military-style marches with uniformed participants sporting symbols associated with the wartime authoritarian Arrow Cross regime (Molnár 2016: 64). Among its stated aims, the Hungarian Guard promised to contribute to 'national self-defence' and the 'maintenance on public order' and organized numerous marches intimidating Roma minorities (ibid.).

In contrast, there are many examples of *judicial controls* deployed against populist parties. In November 2004 the Flemish Block (VB) was found guilty of incitement to segregation and racism, a ruling which cut it off from state financing (Erk 2005; Brems 2006). In 2006, Daniel Féret, leader of the National Front in Belgium was convicted, jailed, and banned from contesting elections for ten years for inciting hatred because he distributed flyers stigmatizing North Africans (Jacobs and van Spanje 2020: 906). In October 2009, Forward Italy (FI) party founder and later Prime Minister Silvio Berlusconi's Fininvest company was fined €750 million for bribing a judge, with Berlusconi named as co-responsible (France24 2019). In October 2012 Berlusconi was convicted, sentenced to community service, and banned from public office for tax fraud, in a case involving his media company Mediaset (BBC News 2014). In June 2012, Finns Party parliamentarian and later party leader (2017–2021) Jussi Halla-aho, was convicted and fined for inciting hatred against an ethnic group in a blog post comparing Islam to paedophilia (yle.fi 2012). Around a year earlier Finns Party parliamentarian James Hirvissari was convicted for inciting hatred against an ethnic group in a blog post (yle.fi 2011). In July 2017, Umberto Bossi, founder of the Northern League, his son Renzo Bossi, and former party treasurer Francesco Belsito, were sentenced to jail for embezzling public funds (Deutsche Welle 2017). In August 2019, the Italian Court of Cassation found that in 2008–2010 the Northern League fraudulently claimed 49 million euros in election expenses (La Repubblica 2019). In April 2014, Slovenian Democratic Party leader Janez Janša was sentenced to two years in prison for bribery in connection to defence contracts (*Slovenian Times* 2015). In April

2012, founder of the National Front in France, Jean-Marie Le Pen was fined and convicted of dismissing crimes against humanity for stating the Nazi occupation of France was 'not particularly inhumane' (*Guardian* 2012). In April 2016, Le Pen was again fined and convicted of dismissing crimes against humanity for stating the Nazi gas chambers were only a 'detail of history' (Guaridan 2016). In June 2018 party leader Marine Le Pen and other National Rally members of the European Parliament were required to repay EU money misused to pay party staff carrying out non-parliamentary work (Politico.eu 2018). In January 2020 Alternative for Germany was fined €269,400 for illegally accepting free campaign material from a Swiss public relations agency (Deutsche Welle 2020). In September 2020, Party of Freedom leader Geert Wilders was convicted for insulting a group and incitement to discrimination for initiating a chant taken up by supporters calling for fewer Moroccans in the Netherlands (BBC News 2020). In August 2021 leader of the Austrian Freedom Party (FPÖ) Heinz-Christian Strache was found guilty of corruption, including providing favours for party donors, and sentenced to a 15-month suspended sentence (BBC News 2021). Beyond this list, there are many other cases, including those that made it to the courts but were dismissed. A number of these cases were launched by civil society actors, such as anti-racism and human rights NGOs, especially cases concerning hate speech and racism.

As discussed above, there are theoretical reasons to expect *rights-restrictions* and *judicial controls* will be a mixed blessing for populist parties. On the one hand, they *may diminish a party's material resources* by directly cutting off sources of funding or using up scarce resources in expensive legal proceedings. They may *diminish a party's human resources* by preventing some leaders from taking up public office, or weakening support for the leader internally. Rank-and-file members may prefer to distance themselves from a party subject to repressive IoPPs to avoid social and material costs for themselves. *Organizational resources may be depleted* if internal disputes arise about how to respond to threats, or actual experiences, of state repression. Corruption cases and or trials for racism or holocaust denial may tarnish reputations or *diminish moral resources*. Where resource depletion makes it difficult for a party to run an effective campaign or front appealing leaders and candidates, these IoPPs may *reduce support for populist parties*. To avoid such outcomes, they have *incentives to moderate*. On the other hand, repressive IoPPs may *boost party organizational resources:* Controversial trials may provide free publicity, strengthen 'issue ownership', or boost internal cohesion vis-à-vis an outside adversary. Repressive IoPPs may *increase support for populist parties* if they reinforce anti-establishment themes. Rather than inducing moderation, repressive IoPPs may *lead to radicalization* if those targeted decide to retreat from political engagement with the political mainstream.

At this stage, the empirical literature is still too underdeveloped to substantiate all these theoretical propositions or to show why repressive IoPPs may work differently in different contexts. Nevertheless, case studies charting the history, electoral ups and downs, and internal organizational features of populist parties provide many empirical illustrations that strengthen the plausibility of theory on these effects.

For example, the Alternative for Germany (AfD) responded to investigations and surveillance by the *Bundesamt für Verfassungsschutz* (BfV, Federal Office for the Protection of the Constitution) in a variety of different ways. In a strong indication that the AfD considered an official declaration classifying it as an extremist organization was detrimental, the party launched an injunction to prevent the BfV from publicly announcing the classification after media leaks indicated such a declaration was imminent (Global Freedom of Expression, 2021; Diehl et al. 2021; Deutsche Welle, 2 March 2021). At the same time, it adopted a series of measures to *present a more moderate* 'front stage' image. Der Flügel, the extremist faction named by the BfV, was formally dissolved in 2020, even though, as the BfV observed, 'functionaries and followers of Der Flügel [still] seek influence within the AfD to advance their political agenda' (BfV 2021). Another faction within the party, the Patriotic Platform, was also dissolved in the face of a threat of surveillance, as was the Lower Saxon branch of the party's youth organization (Heinze and Weisskircher 2021: 267–268). The party also created a 'list of incompatible organizations', used to restrict acceptance of new members from extremist organizations (ibid.: 268). In addition, as Heinze and Weisskircher observe, authorization of surveillance by the BfV exacerbated tensions within a party already marked by 'sharp intraparty conflict' (2021: 265). More specifically, surveillance *diminished organizational resources* by heightening tensions between 'Western neo-liberals' on the one hand, and 'Easterners', which included Der Flügel and many with 'strong personal and organizational ties to far-right groups', on the other (ibid.). As Heinze and Weisskircher further recount, following a close vote in the AfD executive committee, BfV scrutiny prompted the leader of the 'Western neo-liberals', Jörg Meuthen, to push for the revocation of Der Flügel leader Andreas Kalbitz's party membership, prompting 'hostile debates' among the party's two main factions (2021: 265, 269). Deep internal divides did not, however, appear to have hampered the party's ability to maintain its electoral success (ibid.: 264). In the 2021 federal elections, the AfD lost 2.3% of the vote and

11 seats, a small dent in its 2017 electoral breakthrough, when its vote share increased from 4.7 to 12.6%.

The ban of the Hungarian Guard in 2009, the unarmed militia of the right-wing party Jobbik, arguably led to the *diminution of an important organizational resource.* By various accounts, the Hungarian Guard contributed to Jobbik's electoral breakthrough in 2010, sparking considerable media attention and helping the party better 'exploit existing anti-Roma sentiments' (Varga 2014: 793; Póczik and Sárik 2019: 113). The Hungarian Guard also provided an important '"hook" to recruitment', contributing to the proliferation of local party cells, and helped Jobbik to integrate the diverse far-right scene (Krekó and Juhász 2018: 194–195). Varga suggests the ban provided additional *incentives for the party to moderate*, forcing it to focus more on economic aspects of its political programme (2014: 804). On the other hand, the Hungarian Guard was part of what led other parties, until recently, to ostracize Jobbik (Póczik and Sárik 2019: 106). In time, the relationship between the party and the far-right scene became an 'ambivalent relationship', something to be managed as the party began to focus on office ambitions and to moderate ideologically (Póczik and Sárik 2019: 118). While successor organizations emerged after the Hungarian Guard was banned, Jobbik leader Gábor Vona nevertheless allowed them 'to slowly, gradually fade away' (Krekó, and Juhász 2018: 198). In the short to medium term, the ban did not damage Jobbik's ability to breakthrough in the 2010 elections and win 16.7% or increase its vote share in 2014 to 20.2%.

There is some evidence that prosecutions for hate speech may *increase support for populist* parties or *boost their resources.* Van Spanje and de Vreese (2015) argue that a Court decision to prosecute the Dutch Party for Freedom (PVV) leader Geert Wilders for hate speech *increased its support.* In 2009, the Amsterdam Court of Appeal overturned a decision of the Public Prosecutors Service not to pursue Wilders in the courts for controversial statements about Islam, including equating it with fascism. The court decision launched a very public trial for hate speech which ended in Wilder's acquittal in June 2011. On the basis of a three-wave panel survey of Dutch voters questioned before and after the 2009 Amsterdam court ruling, the authors argued that the court ruling 'caused an across-the-board increase in probabilities for voting for the PVV' (ibid.: 125). That is, the court decision 'resulted in an immediate increase in support for the party by one to five percentage points among those who are moderately in favour of the assimilation of ethnic minorities in Dutch culture', which is in line with PVV policy (ibid.: 115). Moreover, the authors argue the decision to prosecute Wilders probably 'helped him in the electoral arena, both in the short run and in the long run' because indications of new support created a 'virtuous circle' whereby voters are more likely to support an increasingly important party they see as likely to be better able to deliver on policy goals (ibid.: 125). In this way, the authors argue, the Court decision 'contributed to the party's subsequent electoral lift-off', with support for the PVV at the 2010 election increasing nearly 10 percentage points to 15.5% and 24 seats (ibid.: 115).

In more recent work, Jacobs and van Spanje (2020) compare the effects of hate speech prosecutions on support for anti-immigration parties in Belgium (National Front), France (National Front/National Rally), Germany (National Democratic Party), and the Netherlands (Party for Freedom). The authors argue that decisions to prosecute a party and trial outcomes for hate speech increased visibility of anti-immigration politicians in the news (ibid.: 912). In other words, hate speech trials—especially those of Le Pen and Wilders—*boosted organizational resources* because they were 'highly mediatized and dominated the headlines for a protracted period' (ibid.: 916). This coverage 'gave rise to a reinforcing spiral of attention by enhancing the general newsworthiness of a political actor' (ibid.: 916). Despite expectations that this increased visibility would decrease support for the party by *depleting its moral resources*, analysis of opinion polls data showed 'no evidence that hate speech prosecution negatively affects electoral support' (ibid.: 914). Rather, in the Belgium and Dutch cases, the study found 'a positive effect of news visibility for the legal prosecution of an anti-immigrant politician on electoral support' (ibid.: 914). In the German and French cases, the relationship was indirect, since 'key events of the prosecution of anti-immigrant leaders for hate speech news are positively associated with general news visibility of these parties, which in turn is positively related to anti-immigration party support' (ibid.: 915).

While hate speech trials created publicity for the party, under Marine Le Pen, the National Front, renamed National Rally, sought at *least superficial moderation* or 'dédiabolisation' as part of a strategy to improve electoral fortunes (Ivaldi 2016: 226). The strategy involved an attempt to 'get away from the historical legacy of the French extreme right, avoiding in particular explicit references to anti-Semitism or Holocaust denial, which have been the principle causes for demonization in the past' (ibid.: 232). Jean-Marie Le Pen's controversial statements, including those leading to convictions for holocaust denial caused tensions in the party, as Marine Le Pen condemned and eventually expelled him from the party (ibid.: 232–233). On the other hand, as Zúquete observed in 2007, trouble with the courts fed into the missionary drive of the party's hard-core supporters, who saw the National Front as 'a besieged community undergoing terrible persecutions, sufferings and sacrifices' and whose actions were needed 'in order to keep alive the spirit of the "true France" and in the end, to redeem the mistakes and errors of the entire community' (ibid.: 42).

In the wake of corruption scandals, involving bribe-taking and military contracts, Slovenian Democratic Party (SDS) leader Janez Janša's not only spent time in prison, but his government also faced protests, vote loss, and a vote of no confidence leading to the fall of his government in 2013 (Deloy 2011: 2). As Deloy has argued, the scandal, which broke just before the 2008 elections, damaged Janša's standing—or *depleted a key human or moral resources*—but after 2011 the *scandal reduced support for the party* (Deloy 2011: 2; see also Haughton and Krašovec 2014). SDS vote share fell from 29.3 to 20.7% between 2008 and 2014 (–8.6%), after which it lost its ability to form a government. Nevertheless, Janša's imprisonment rallied at least some of the party faithful. For example, the leader's entry into prison was reportedly accompanied by a demonstration involving thousands of supporters (Brezar 2020). The sentence provided the perfect opportunity for the articulation of anti-elitist claims. Janša ran in the 2014 parliamentary elections (and won a seat) from prison, with a campaign 'organized almost exclusively around the supposed injustice inflicted on the leader by the Appeals Court's verdict' (Krašovec 2015: 272; Haughton and Krašovec 2014: 3). During the trial, which Janša and many supporters claimed was politically motivated, Janša disparaged the courts reportedly claiming: 'Normal citizens are practically powerless in courts where justice is meted out in such a manner' and that opinion polls showed 'the president of the party [was] trusted by more people than the administration of justice' (rtvslo.si). After the 2014 election, as Houghton and Krašovec point out, 'The party's poor showing in the election (20.7%) provoked it to claim the elections were not free and fair—and therefore also not legitimate—the first time any Slovenian party had made such a claim in twenty years of independence' (ibid.: 2014: 3). The Constitutional Court later quashed the sentence, and a new trial was ordered, but charges against Janša lapsed under the statute of limitations. The SDP has since been able to recover about half of its lost votes and Janša returned to government as prime minister in March 2020.

The emergence in 2012 of allegations that led to conviction of the Northern League's founder Umberto Bossi for embezzlement of public funds forced Bossi to resign, eventually opening the way for Matteo Salvini's transformation of the party from a regionalist to a nationalist party (Albertazzi and McDonnell 2015, 32; Vampa 2017: 41; Albertazzi et al. 2018: 646). The scandal *reduced organizational resources* by causing serious tensions within the party among those for and against Bossi and according to Albertazzi and

McDonnell *reduced support for the party*, by being 'the main cause of the party's poor subsequent performance' in the February 2013 general elections (2015: 37, 95). The Northern League was required to repay 49 million euros, an important *depletion on material resources*, although after complex organizational restructuring the party was able to set up a dual structure, minimizing the impact of debt on Salvini's operations (Zulianello 2021: 230–231).

In 2019, corruption scandals eventually leading to the conviction of former Austrian vice-chancellor and leader of the Austrian Freedom Party (FPÖ) Heinz-Christian Strache, led to the party's ejection from a coalition government (Eberl et al. 2020). In the subsequent snap general elections, the FPÖ saw *reduced support* of some 10% of its vote share. While corruption scandals involving the Freedom Party dominated the 2019 general election campaign, its *moral resources* were not damaged to the extent that its former coalition partner ruled out the possibility of renewing the governing formula (Eberl et al. 2020: 1358). Stache was later kicked out of the party.

In other cases, allegations of wrongdoing or convictions appear to have made little real impact. In 2004, the Belgian Court of Cassation confirmed rulings that Flemish Block (VB) advocated discrimination and incited hatred against immigrant ethnic minorities (Erk 2005; Brems 2006). Unable to prosecute a political party enjoying immunity from prosecution, the Courts ruled that organizations affiliated with it—three groups receiving state funding for the party, training its members, and producing radio and TV programmes—violated the 1981 Anti-Racism Act for supporting Flemish Block (Brems 2006). The three organizations were fined, but the Flemish Block dissolved itself and reformed as the new party, Flemish Interest (VB), just five days after the court decision against it (Erk 2005: 493). Lucardie et al. have argued that judicial threats were more difficult for the party to cope with than *ostracism* and indeed VB leader Filip Dewinter has reportedly 'emphasized that the high costs of convictions for racism overruled electoral gains' (Lucardie et al. 2021: 216). Lucardie at al. argue that Dewinter said a potential *reduction in material and organizational resources*—including 'financial costs of a trial and the fundamental threat of a ban on the party'—justified steps taken to adapt the party profile (ibid.: 217). Thus, at least *superficial moderation* or 'mainstreaming in terms of detoxifying a racist reputation' was an important response to the racism conviction (ibid.: 218). Seeking to rebrand itself as a Flemish nationalist party on the political right, the party 'cleansed' its statutes of 'more extreme positions' (Erk 2005; Lucardie et al. 2016: 212). The party encouraged members to change their behaviour, instructing local branches on 'how to avoid violations of the law against racism' (Lucardie et al. 2016:

212). Erk observed that the party, seeking to 'expand its appeal to voters who have so far been reluctant to vote for a party stigmatized as racist', also gave itself a 'cosmetic makeover': 'Party leaders are always well-dressed, they speak proper Dutch, they participate in family events, they tend to be courteous to their opponents in debates; and recently they have been careful to bring the spotlight to their new female members' (Erk 2005: 498). There were signs that moderation though was skin deep, as Lucardie et al. observe:

> The VB took care to avoid racist statements or actions under pressure of pending convictions. Yet hardcore members of the party were appeased as far as possible. Dewinter, with his base in Antwerp where a hardcore nationalist culture existed sometimes signaled to hardcore nationalists in and outside the party that mainstreaming was in this respect merely a veneer. The external pressure to moderate apparently did not lead to an internally supported change of strategy.
>
> **(2016: 219; see also Table 3.2)**

The longstanding battles of Forza Italia's founder Silvio Berlusconi with the courts shows corruption scandals do not necessarily lead to punishment at the polls. As McNally put it, 'Despite allegations for bribery, false accounting, false testimony, embezzlement, mafia connections and money laundering, Silvio Berlusconi led a long and successful career as an Italian politician' (McNally 2016: 6). Despite high-profile investigations and various rulings against him, Berlusconi was Italy's longest serving postwar prime minister and with his coalition partners was voted back into power on four occasions. One study explains the failure of voters to definitively remove Berlusconi out of government with the argument that 'when a voter believes corruption to be common, he [sic] is more likely to consider corrupt actions acceptable, and to be tolerant of corrupt politicians' (McNally 2016: 983). Similarly, Várnagy argued in relation to Hungary that while 'corruption issues surrounding Fidesz politicians has reached a critical level and even some of the party's less prominent politicians had begun to express concern about the party elite, it seems that most voters are already immune to the fact that politicians are corrupt' (2016: 129).

European Supranational Courts and the Empowerment of Domestic Oppositions

Since it was established in 1959, the European Court of Human Rights (ECtHR) has arguably become the most important source of *international checks and balances* aiming *to curb illiberal and anti-democratic policies of governments run by populist parties (and others)*. The ECtHR has consolidated its role as a body of international constitutional review, assessing whether states-party comply with the 1950 European Convention of Human Rights (ECHR). All 47 states-party to the ECHR now recognize the compulsory jurisdiction of the ECtHR. This permits individuals and groups to submit complaints against their government if they believe it has violated rights guaranteed in the Convention and when the litigant has first exhausted all domestic legal remedies.

The ECtHR has found that the Fidesz-led government in Hungary and the Law and Justice-led government in Poland have violated a wide range of Convention rights (see Appendix III for details). It ruled the governments have violated rights such as free expression; privacy and family life; torture and degrading treatment; freedom of assembly and association; freedom of thought, conscience, and religion; and the right to a fair trial. Among other things, ECtHR verdicts have ruled that key judicial reforms in both countries have undermined the independence of the judiciary and rights to a fair trial. This has included rulings dealing with premature termination of the mandates of senior judges and rulings confirming that judicial reforms in both countries compromised the status of courts. Strikingly, the ECtHR also ruled that the Polish Constitutional Court was not a 'tribunal established by law'. Rulings have also addressed government actions and laws affecting rights of religious and ethnic minorities and of asylum seekers; the rights of opposition parties to protest government action in and out of parliament; and the rights of NGOs and journalists to obtain information.

The Court of Justice of the EU (CJEU) provides another tool for challenging the actions of governing populist parties in the form of *international judicial controls*. As guardian of the EU treaties, the European Commission, a supranational executive appointed by the member states and the European Parliament, a body of directly elected representatives of EU citizens, may take a state to the CJEU if it thinks a member state has failed to fulfil an obligation under EU law. Member states may also take another state to court for this reason. A national court must ask the CJEU for a 'preliminary ruling' interpreting the EU Treaties and other EU institutional acts where this is necessary for a national court to rule in one of its own cases. The purpose of preliminary rulings is to ensure the uniform application of EU law by national courts.

There is now a long list of CJEU cases—both pending and completed— which aim *to curb illiberal and undemocratic policies of EU populist-led governments* using infringement and preliminary ruling proceedings (see Appendix IV). The European Commission has launched—and won—a series of cases challenging measures by the Fidesz-led government undermining autonomy of institutions empowered to constrain governmental power or attacking civil society organizations opposing the government. In its early rulings, the CJEU ruled that Hungary violated EU law with new rules on its Data Protection Commission and on a new lower retirement age for judges, prosecutors, and notaries, which had led to removal of some 10% of senior judges (Batory 2016: 692; Kosař and Šipulová 2018: 87; Scheppele et al. 2020: 42–43). These were soon followed by EU rulings against a higher education law targeting foreign universities and singling out Central European University, founded by Fidesz's political enemy George Soros. A Hungarian law affecting foreign-funded NGOs, some of which were forced to leave Hungary, and including Soros' Open Society Institute, was declared in violation with EU law. The CJEU also ruled against Hungarian asylum laws, introduced in the wake of the migration crisis, which restricted access and rights of asylum seekers. Other infringement procedures include cases initiated against 2020 laws reducing sanctions for racial and ethnic discrimination and further restricting access to asylum during the COVID pandemic, as well as a law limiting public access to content promoting LGBTQ+ identities to minors.

In Poland, the European Commission launched and won a series of infringement proceedings against various Law and Justice reforms undermining the independence of the judiciary. These included rules, following the Hungarian example, which lowered the retirement age of Supreme Court and Ordinary Court judges and rules for a new disciplinary committee effectively authorizing political interference in regulation of the judiciary. Other cases include infringement proceedings initiated against the so-called 'muzzle law', which among other things, prevented judges from asking the CJEU for preliminary rulings on matters relating to judicial independence, and a case regarding the Polish government's failure to act against so-called LGBTQ+ free zones established in several Law- and Justice- controlled regions.

Initially, the Commission's strategy focused on identifying violation of specific EU laws or treaty provisions with little direct link to democracy or the rule of law (see Appendix IV). This included directives on equal treatment in employment, free movement of services in the EU, asylum policy, and Article 63 TFEU on free movement of capital. Making a more direct link to rule of law and fundamental rights, many cases invoked provisions of the EU's Charter of Fundamental Rights, which EU institutions and the member states (when implementing EU law) are obliged to uphold. Fundamental Rights invoked included the right to a fair trial and effective remedy, academic freedom, freedom of association and expression, right to asylum, human dignity, respect for private life, and non-discrimination based on sexual orientation. Following a series of groundbreaking rulings, the CJEU developed a new doctrine permitting it to rule directly against acts of member states undermining independence of the judiciary. The key innovations concerned a reading of Article 19 (1) TEU, on member state obligation to ensure 'effective legal protection in the fields covered by Union law', together with Article 2 TEU on the EU's liberal democratic values and Article 4 (3) TEU on sincere cooperation in the attainment of the Union's objectives. The Court argued that these articles established a general obligation for member state governments to guarantee and respect the independence of their national courts and tribunals because this was necessary to guarantee the effectiveness of EU law (Pech and Platon 2018; Scheppele et al. 2020: 445). What made the case 'groundbreaking' was that the obligation applied regardless of whether reforms challenging judicial independence could be directly related to an EU law (on, for example, discrimination in employment) (Pech and Platon 2018). Applying the principle in a case on the independence of the Polish Supreme Court, the CJEU widened and deepened the principle of judicial independence, declaring the irremovability of judges a principle of cardinal importance in EU law (Pech and Kochenov 2021: 10).

As discussed above, *international checks and balances* by the ECtHRs and *international judicial controls* by the CJEU *may curb the ability of populist parties in government to implement illiberal or anti-democratic policies* when effectively enforced by domestic courts, lawmakers, executive agents, and administrators. They may also empower domestic opponents providing avenues to launch test cases, creating international pressure for domestic reforms, and authenticating complaints against the government with reference to internationally sanctioned standards. If they reveal inconsistencies in what governments do and say, the rulings of these supranational courts may *reduce moral resources* or the legitimacy of governing populist parties and *reduce their support*. On the other hand, *international checks and balances* and *international judicial controls* may be met by populist 'sovereignty counter-discourses', claiming the interventions are an illegitimate challenge by a 'corrupt' or 'self-interested' international elite to the will of a sovereign people. Populist backlash may *increase support for a government* and de-legitimize opponents by reinforcing nationalist and anti-establishment appeals.

The CJEU and the ECtHR are widely considered among the most effective of their kind (Helfer and Slaughter 1997; Keohane et al. 2000; Keller and Stone Sweet 2016; Kosař et al. 2020). Over the years, the rulings of both Courts have prompted legislative amendments, changes of domestic law, altered public policies and put core elements of constitutional and political systems under the spotlight. Their success is related, among other things, to reliance on 'vertical enforcement' (see above), which gives national courts a major role in ensuring compliance with the rulings of both courts. A committee of ministers from the member states monitors implementation of ECtHR judgments, but the ECtHR nevertheless relies heavily on domestic actors, particularly domestic courts and their willingness to 'translate ECtHRs rulings into day-to-day politics' (Kosař et al. 2020: 2). In addition, many states have incorporated the Convention into domestic law, which allows individuals to invoke it against their state for alleged violations of rights before domestic courts. For its part, the CJEU established the 'direct effect' of EU law in one of its earliest rulings. This allowed individuals to invoke EU treaty and secondary law before national courts to challenge the actions of others, including their own and other EU member governments. The enforcement of CJEU judgments through the domestic courts was soon supplemented by the doctrine that EU law was supreme over national law when these were in conflict. By accepting these doctrines and entering into a dialogue with the CJEU by way of preliminary rulings, national courts gave CJEU judgments 'roughly the same effect as judgments issued by domestic courts in the member states of the European Union' (Helfer and Slaughter 1997: 292). The ECtHR and CJEU also operate in favourable conditions.

As many scholars have observed, international courts work best in stable and consolidated liberal democracies where the rule of law is generally held in high regard (ibid.: 276–267, 330–331; Kosař et al. 2020: 1–2). Likewise, the effectiveness of the vertical mechanisms for enforcing ECtHR and CJEU rulings relies heavily on dialogue among supranational and relatively autonomous national courts and the voluntary participation of legal professions in a transnational 'community of law' (Helfer and Slaughter 1997: 333–334, 337; Keohane et al. 2000: 479; Moravcsik 2012: 104; Kosař et al. 2020: 3). Both conditions are now much shakier in Hungary and Poland than in the past. In these member states, the independence of the judiciary has been progressively weakened to the extent that many courts are now 'controlled' or 'captured' by the supporters of governing populist parties or led by 'fake' judges (Scheppele 2018; Sadurski 2019a and b; Pech et al. 2021). Both Fidesz and Law and Justice governments and captured courts in Hungary and Poland increasingly challenge the legitimacy of EU and ECHR law (Blauberger and Kelemen 2017; Kosař et al. 2020; Petrov 2020; Scheppele et al. 2020; Pech et al. 2021; Sajó 2021). As various scholars have observed, European human rights law and EU law have become a cleavage in disputes between established judges and many of those appointed by Fidesz and Law and Justice (Sadurski 2019a; Petrov 2020: 504; Ejchart-Dubois 2021; Pech and Kochenov 2021).

Regarding the ECtHR, another limitation is, as Kosař and Šipulová (2018) have argued, that ECtHR rulings often address symptoms rather than more fundamental underlying causes of human rights violations. For example, reflecting on the 2016 *Baka vs Hungary* ruling (see Appendix III), which dealt with the premature shortening of the term of a sitting Hungarian Supreme Court judge, the authors point out that the ECtHR lacks jurisdiction to rule on cases concerning separation of powers—the issue the heart of the *Baka* case—and therefore had to frame its judgment around narrower freedom of expression and fair trial violations. Faced with a similar case on political interference in disciplinary measures affecting Polish judges, the Court emphasized that its task was not to assess the overall legitimacy of judicial reforms, but to determine whether, and if so how, the changes affected applicant rights under the Convention (European Court of Human Rights 2021b).

Another problem is that supervision of compliance with ECtHR judgments 'does not seem strong enough to prevent minimalist compliance (Kosař and Šipulová 2018: 244). For example, in September 2020, some ten years after Hungarian Supreme Court judge Baka lost his position, and five years after the ECtHR ruling, the Council of Europe's Committee of Ministers (2021), which supervises execution of ECtHR judgments, acknowledged the limited impact of the ruling: The Committee 'noted with concern' that the Hungarian government had not taken any steps to strengthen judicial independence, safeguard against arbitrary removal of judges, or counter 'chilling effects' on judges' freedom of expression. More generally, the Court's ability to constrain illiberal and anti-democratic policies is limited by long time-delays between reforms and rulings, after which policy change becomes a fait accompli (Kosař et al. 2020: 244; Scheppele et al. 2020: 49).

Regarding the CJEU, rulings on politically sensitive issues appear to have had little immediate impact on the general trajectory of political reforms, even though Fidesz and Law and Justice often lose in court. Scholars have documented the many instances of 'creative compliance' in Hungary and Poland (Batory 2016). Creative compliance is action which 'creates the appearance of norm-conforming behaviour without giving up their original objective' (ibid.). For example, when Hungary lost the case against it for undermining independence of the Hungarian Data Protection Authority by abruptly terminating the Data Protection Commissioner's term of office, Hungary paid compensation but did not reinstate the Commissioner (ibid.). Hungary formally complied with the CJEU ruling against a law lowering the retirement age of judges. New rules allowed reinstatement of judges forced into retirement, but not the reinstatement of almost all of those in senior positions which had already been filled (with Fidesz appointees) (ibid.). Compensation was only offered to judges who didn't apply for reinstatement (ibid.: Scheppele et al. 2020: 42–43). The result was that the government got away with a 'major reshuffle of Hungary's judicial leadership to make it friendlier to the government' (Scheppele et al. 2020: 44). In 2013, Fidesz was willing to amend the Basic Law to address European Commission concerns about the role of the administration in the distribution of court cases, political campaign advertising, and a new tax affecting cases where court rulings created payment obligations for the state (Batory 2016: 693). These were small concessions scarcely addressing the bigger picture of successive constitutional reforms contributing to the systematic dismantling of the rule of law and checks on government power. By the time the CJEU ruled against the Hungarian University Law targeting the Central European University, the university had already moved parts of its operations to Vienna (Scheppele et al. 2020: 48). Similarly, when the CJEU declared Hungarian restrictions on foreign funding of NGOs in contravention of EU law, Hungary formally complied with the ruling, but Soros' Open Society Foundation and other prominent NGOs affected by the Hungarian restrictions had already left the country (ibid.).

In Poland, Law and Justice combined partial compliance with open defiance of the CJEU in what amounted to a serious escalation in the EU's rule of law crisis (Pech and Kochenov 2021: 25). Faced with infringement proceedings for new rules creating unequal retirement ages for male and female judges, Law and Justice changed those rules so that all judges had to retire at 65 years regardless of gender (Sadurski 2019a: 210). This was a 'politically easy and inexpensive' remedy for the Polish government, 'as it did not affect the central point of reforms, namely to subject judges to strong control by the executive and the MJ [minister of justice] in particular' (Sadurski 2019a: 210). Learning from the Hungarian experience, the CJEU began to use interim measures to try to prevent replacement of judges. For example, an interim measure applied to the Polish Law on the Supreme Court allowed 27 Supreme Court judges, and the first president of the Supreme Court (whose term of office is constitutionally guaranteed) to go back to work (Scheppele et al. 2020: 55–56; Pech and Kochenov 2021: 32). Law and Justice amended the law on the Supreme Court to comply with the interim order, although when the first president's term of office was up, her replacement was appointed in violation of the rules of procedure (Scheppele et al. 2020: 56). The CJEU also approved interim measures ordering the immediate suspension of disciplinary proceedings against judges by the Disciplinary Chamber of the Supreme Court (Pech and Kochenov 2021: 40). In December 2020, the Law and Justice government passed the so-called 'muzzle' law which sought to prevent Polish courts from requesting further preliminary rulings interpreting the meaning of EU law in relation to matters concerning judicial independence (ibid.: 68, 78; Pech et al. 2021: 59). The law was soon also subject to infringement proceedings and on 14 July 2021 an interim measure ordered its suspension, freezing all activities of the Disciplinary Chamber and repealing effects of its decisions (Ejchart-Dubois 2021). The 'captured' Polish Constitutional Court later ruled Poland did not have to comply with the order (Ejchart-Dubois 2021). Although the Polish government informed the European Commission it intended to 'dismantle the Disciplinary Chamber in its current form' after the CJEU ruled it incompatible with EU rules requiring the independence of judges, the Chamber continued to function (European Commission 2021). In a further escalation, the CJEU approved daily fines of €1 million for Poland's refusal to comply (Wanat 2021d). In the same month, the captured Polish Constitutional Court ruled that Article 19(1) TEU did not give the EU competence to rule on organization of the Polish judiciary, a ruling contravening the EU's foundational principle of the supremacy of EU law (Jaraczewski 2021).

Many scholars following these cases have reacted positively to the use of more robust measures to enforce CJEU judgments (Scheppele et al. 2020; Pech and Kochenov 2021; Pech et al. 2021). Pech et al. have argued, for instance, that CJEU judgments against judicial reforms and successive interim orders have had something of a 'containment effect' limiting the extent of reforms on judicial independence (2021: 3). On the other hand, these have 'not prevented Poland's abrupt descent into authoritarianism' (ibid.). As Scheppele et al. have argued, 'Despite ten years of EU attempts at reigning in Rule of Law violations and even as backsliding member states have lost cases at the Court of Justice, illiberal regimes inside the EU have become more consolidated: The EU has been losing through winning' (2020: 3).

More research is needed on the domestic effects of ECtHR and CJEU rulings. What is clear though, is that opportunities provided by the 'judicial mechanism' (Kolb 2007: 88) to form alliances with international courts have been used by civil society actors undertaking *adversarial* IoPPs, among others. A wide range of non-governmental actors have turned to ECtHRs in the face of democratic backsliding in Hungary and Poland, for example. As Bozóki and Hedegűs have observed for the Hungarian case, the number of ECtHR cases pursued by Hungarian citizens 'increased by a dramatic 1,177 per cent, from 436 to 5,569 between 2010 and 2016, while Hungary's share of total applications to the court rose from 0.71% to 10.41% in the same period' (2018: 1179). Similarly, the ECtHR has noted that there have been 38 applications lodged against Poland between 2018–2021 related to judicial reforms (European Court of Human Rights 2021b). Most of the Polish cases have been bought by individual judges personally affected by judicial reforms, although others have been bought by civil society actors, such as Advance Pharma, a pharmaceutical company complaining against a decision of the unlawfully constituted Supreme Court.

Strikingly, the EU's preliminary ruling procedure has been increasingly used as a vehicle of resistance by judges opposing their governments. As mentioned above, a national court must ask the CJEU for a 'preliminary ruling' interpreting the EU Treaties and other acts of EU institutions where this is necessary for national courts to rule in one their own cases. Pech and Kochenov have observed a 'new trend in EU constitutionalism, where national courts are increasingly turning to the Court of Justice, essentially to ask for help in resisting national measures which seek to undermine their own independence' (2021: 65). As of May 2021, the authors count no less than 37 requests for a preliminary ruling from Polish courts or chambers of courts 'not yet captured' by Law and Justice supporters (ibid.: 65). There was also a rise in preliminary ruling requests on judicial independence from other EU states, with an additional 11 referrals from Romanian courts and one each from Hungarian and Maltese courts decided or still pending as of early 2021 (ibid.: 65). The CJEU nevertheless has more limited jurisdiction under preliminary ruling proceedings. The role of the Court is to interpret EU law, leaving the referring court to rule on the matter at hand (ibid.: 74; Scheppele et al. 2020: 70). Like other rulings by supranational courts, the scope of preliminary rulings 'is limited to the issues posed by single cases' rather than systematic threats to the rule of law (ibid.).

Like other international initiatives—such as the initiation of the Commission's Rule of Law Framework, Article 7 TEU dialogue proceedings, and EU budget conditionality proceedings (see Chapters 5 and 6)—CJEU and ECtHR rulings have been widely publicized in Hungary and Poland and sometimes mobilized discursively to 'authenticate' opponents' criticisms of the government. In Poland, for example, many court proceedings were covered in national newspapers and flagged on social media by NGOs such as *Komitet Obrony Demokracji* (Committee for the Defence of Democracy with 233,957 Facebook followers), *Akcja Demokracja* (Action Democracy, with 147,573 Facebook followers), *Wolne Sądy* (Free Courts, with 87,406 Facebook followers). Appeals on the NGO's Facebook pages often referred to

European standards, linking these to Polish citizens' typically strong European identities. For example, a 2019 call by the Committee for Defence of Democracy (KOD) for demonstrations against the 'muzzle law' limiting the ability of Polish judges to make preliminary ruling requests to the CJEU (see above) stated 'We know that independent courts and civil liberties are very important values in the EU. And Poland is part of Europe' (Facebook Post, KODInternational, 18 December 2019). In 2018, activists from KOD, Action Democracy, Free Courts, and *Obywatele RP* (Citizens of the Republic of Poland) staged a demonstration in front of European Commission buildings, according to a KOD Facebook post 'to express gratitude for the decision on the shameful Act on the Supreme Court of Poland' (Facebook Post, 27 September 2018). While it is not clear how persuasive appeals to EU norms were for Polish citizens, they clearly contradicted Law and Justice claims framing judicial reforms as a remedy to defeat an 'elitist' 'caste' of 'heirs and followers of communist criminals' in the name of justice and democracy (Bojarski 2021: 1368).

On the other hand, *international checks and balances* and *international judicial controls* were met by populist 'sovereignty counter-discourses', claiming the interventions are an illegitimate challenge by an out of touch, 'corrupt', or 'self-interested' international elite to the will of a sovereign people. For example, Petrov has observed the rise of what he calls a 'genre of "Strasbourg bashing"' by populist parties attacking the ECtHR with the 'sovereigntist criticism of international institutions and critiques of the undemocratic nature of judicial review' (2020: 497). That is, populist parties portrayed the ECtHR as a 'foreign court which is not well-placed to assess domestic legal practices' and questioned whether unelected foreign judges should second-guess decisions of legitimate domestic parliaments' (ibid.). Marine Le Pen, for instance, has called for France to withdraw from the ECHR, claiming it 'posed visions that the people reject', while Party of Freedom's Gert Wilders claimed the democratic constitutional state was incompatible with the ECHR (ibid.: 499). After the ECtHR ruling in *Ilias and Ahmed vs Hungary* (see Appendix III), Hungarian Prime Minister Viktor Orbán described the ECtHR as a 'threat to the security of EU people and an invitation for migrants' (ibid.: 497; Michalopoulos 2017). Hungarian Secretary of State, Pál Völner, later reportedly claimed the ECtHR ruling was a 'Trojan horse used by 'international pro-migration forces' led by US billionaire George Soros to permit settlement of hundreds of thousands of migrants in Europe (Petrov 2020: 503). Although not always adverse to turning to the Court to pursue their own legal battles, Petrov observed populists often 'include international human rights courts in the "narrative of blame" which explains who is responsible for the current problems of the people' (ibid.: 478).

Similarly, populist governments deployed 'sovereignty counter-discourses' to delegitimize CJEU rulings and mobilized anti-elitist discourses in their critique of EU initiatives. For example, alongside its strategy of 'creative compliance' with successive infringement proceedings, the Fidesz government often responded defiantly in the face of infringement proceedings. Hungarian foreign minister Péter Szijjártó reacted to infringement proceedings against Hungary (and Poland and Czech Republic) for refusing to take a share of refugees as agreed among EU member states during the 2015 migration crisis, stating his government would 'not give in to blackmail' (Euractiv, 13 June 2017). It described Commission President Ursula von der Leyen's argument for launching infringement proceedings against Hungary's June 2021 LGBTQ+ legislation as 'based on false allegations' and 'biased political opinion' (Eder and von der Burchard 2021). Indeed, Fidesz increasingly expressed outright hostility to European institutions after it came to power, including a controversial poster campaign attacking European Commission President Jean-Claude Juncker (Arató 2020; Ágh 2021). 'Brussels' was pitched as one of the main external 'enemies'—alongside the International Monetary Fund, immigrants, and Hungarian-born billionaire émigré George Soros—from which Fidesz promised to protect Hungarians (Arató 2020: 113).

In an October 2021 speech in the European Parliament on the rule of law crisis in Poland, Polish Prime Minister Matheus Morawiecki described CJEU rulings as an attempt to limit Polish sovereignty through a 'creeping expansion of competencies' and a 'creeping revolution' (European Parliament 2021; see also Wanat 2021c; Herszenhorn, Bayer, and De La Baume 2021). No sovereign state could accept the CJEU's interpretation, the prime minister argued, because to do so would mean that the Union ceased to be a union of free, equal, and sovereign countries: 'If you want to make Europe into a nationless superstate, first gain the consent of all European countries and societies for this.' Law and Justice's coalition partners, United Poland, were less constrained: Polish Deputy Justice Minister Sebastian Kaleta described EU actions on the rule of law as an 'illegal usurpation' (Wanat 2021c). Like their Hungarian counterparts, a Law and Justice spokesperson also described infringement proceedings as politically motivated. Polish foreign affairs minister Jacek Czaputowicz, for example, argued 'The Commission and the ECJ are using this situation to strengthen their role in the European Union system, treating it as a chance to confirm their status' (Brzozowski 2019).

To conclude, this chapter has shown that like the party-based IoPPs discussed in Chapter 3, IoPPs relying on enforcement of the law affect populist parties in complex and sometimes contradictory ways. Enforcement—understood as the use, or threat, of coercion and institutional constraint—helps explain how *rights-restricting IoPPs, checks and balances,* and *judicial controls* by public authorities, as well as some kinds of *opposition politics* by political parties help populist parties achieve their goals or produce perverse effects. Some kinds of *opposition politics* initiatives by political parties and *adversarial* initiatives by civil societies do so indirectly, when these political actors find allies with the power to ensure enforcement.

Checks and balances by public authorities such as presidential vetoes and the rulings of international and domestic courts, and *opposition politics* such as parliamentary initiatives to block government initiatives may *curb the ability of populist parties in government to implement illiberal and anti-democratic policies*. The institutional apparatus authorizing these IoPP types may constrain governing populists and enable their opponents and are ultimately backed up by the use, or threat, of the coercive apparatus of the state. Where *adversarialism* by civil society actors takes the form of alliances with those able to initiate checks on executive power, such as political parties or the courts, the threat of coercion and institutional constraints may, indirectly, allow civil society initiatives to curb the ability of populist parties in government to implement illiberal and anti-democratic policies. On the other hand, such initiatives may also provoke a populist backlash, reinforcing anti-establishment themes *increasing support for populist parties*.

The chapter showed that there were theoretical reasons, and some empirical examples, supporting the argument that *rights-restrictions* and *judicial controls* could either contribute to the achievement of populist party goals or have perverse effects. On the one hand, these IoPP types may *diminish a party's material resources* by directly cutting off sources of funding or using up scarce resources in expensive legal proceedings. They may *diminish a party's human resources,* by ruling out some leaders from public office, or weakening support for the leader internally. Rank-and-file members may prefer to distance themselves from a party subject to repressive IoPPs to avoid social and material costs for themselves. These IoPP types might *diminish organizational resources* if internal disputes arise about how to respond to threats of, or actual experiences of, state repression, while corruption cases or trials for racism or holocaust denial may tarnish reputations or *diminish moral resources*. Where resource depletion makes it difficult for a party to run an effective campaign or front appealing leaders and candidates, IoPPs might *reduce support for populist parties*. To avoid such outcomes, they have incentives to *moderate ideologically* or in terms of their behaviour. On the other hand, repressive IoPPs may *boost party organizational resources*:

Controversial trials may provide free publicity, strengthen 'issue ownership' or boost internal cohesion vis-à-vis an outside adversary. Repressive IoPPs may *increase support for populist parties* if they reinforce anti-establishment themes and rather than inducing moderation, repressive IoPPs *may lead to radicalization* if those targeted decide to retreat from political engagement with the mainstream.

International checks and balances by the ECtHRs, and *international judicial controls* by the CJEU *may curb the ability of populist parties in government to implement illiberal or anti-democratic policies* when effectively enforced by domestic courts, lawmakers, executive agents, and administrators. They may also empower domestic opponents providing avenues to launch test cases, creating international pressure for domestic reforms, and authenticating complaints against the government with reference to internationally sanctioned standards. If they reveal inconsistencies in what governments do and say, the rulings of supranational courts may *diminish the moral resources,* or legitimacy, of governing populist parties and *reduce their support.* On the other hand, *international checks and balances* and *international judicial controls* may be met by populist 'sovereignty counter-discourses', claiming the interventions are an illegitimate challenge by an out-of-touch, 'corrupt' or 'self-interested' international elite to the will of a sovereign people. Populist backlash may *increase support for a government* and de-legitimize opponents by reinforcing nationalist and anti-establishment appeals.

This chapter has shown that an important way to understand how *rights-restricting* IoPPs, *judicial controls*, and *repressive* IoPPs work is through enforcement of the law. In the next chapter I examine how other kinds of IoPP work through leverage.

5
Leverage, International Sanctions, and Disruption

In this chapter I examine how initiatives opposing populist parties (IoPPs) work through leverage. This concept captures the way that mutual interdependence among states, and among citizens and governments, can be exploited by opponents to influence the policy choices of populist parties, particularly those in government. *International rights-restrictions*, such as financial or political sanctions rely on leverage, as do some kinds of *adversarial IoPPs* and *coercive confrontation* by civil society actors.

As it will be recalled, I argue that IoPPs are effective if they contribute to the achievement of one or more of the goals typically pursued by opponents of populist parties without producing perverse effects. I argue the main goals of those opposing populist parties are reducing support for populist parties among voters or sympathizers, diminishing their resources or inducing their moderation, as well as curbing illiberal and anti-democratic policies of governing populist parties. Perverse effects are increasing support for populist parties, boosting their resources, and radicalization.

In the first part of the chapter, I draw on theories and concepts from international relations, and the study of European integration and sociology to examine how IoPPs contribute to the achievement of opposition goals or produce perverse effects through leverage. Neo-liberal institutionalist theories of international relations and theories on the effectiveness of political conditionality in the context of EU enlargement provides the foundations for understanding how leverage works in the international arena (Nye and Keohane 1977; Keohane and Nye 1987; Moravcsik and Vachudova 2003; Schimmelfennig and Sedelmeier 2004 and 2020). More specifically, this literature tells us a great deal about the conditions under which *international rights-restricting IoPPs may curb the ability of populist parties in government to implement illiberal or anti-democratic policies*. In addition, research on international democracy-promotion initiatives, EU enlargement, sanctions, and international human rights law provide insights about domestic consequences of international IoPPs (Risse et al. 1999; Vachudova 2005 and 2008; Simmons 2009: 146; Levitsky and Way

2010: 47; Risse et al. 2013). These literatures direct attention to the way that *international rights-restricting* IoPPs may affect *support for and the resources of populist parties*, sometimes in a manner that *provides incentives for moderation*. Research on the political impact of social movements shows that civil society actors can exploit the dependence of governing elites on consent and political stability by orchestrating a form of society-based leverage or disruption to pursue their goals (Fox Piven and Cloward 1978; Andrews 2001; Kolb 2007; Tarrow 2011; Earl 2016). In this way, initiatives by civil society actors in the form of *coercive confrontation* and disruptive but non-violent forms of *adversarialism*, may also force governing populist parties to *curb illiberal and anti-democratic policies*.

The rest of the chapter explores the plausibility of these theoretical propositions, beginning with research on the challenges of using voting sanctions under Article 7 of the Treaty of the European Union and financial sanctions under EU Regulation 2020/2092 on a General Regime of Conditionality for the Protection of the Union Budget. In the last part I identify cases where the disruption of mass protests has led to the fall of populist party governments, changes in the policy agendas of governing populist parties, or difficulties conducting ordinary party business.

How IoPPs Work through Leverage

International sanctions and political conditionality

In international relations theory, 'leverage' is a concept used to explain outcomes in bargaining situations with reference to states' varying capabilities and vulnerabilities (Nye and Keohane 1977; Keohane and Nye 1987). Leverage is a useful concept because it draws on neo-liberal institutionalist theories, which assume international relations is based on many of the things the EU itself is about. That is, some states are seen as more powerful than others, but the integration of economies and political systems create 'complex interdependence' (Nye and Keohane 1977: 24–25; Keohane 2002: 14–15). Globalization, and more concretely, EU institutions and rules, build relationships of mutual dependence between people, firms, bureaucracies, associations, and states as they interact with others like them abroad. In other words, globalization and the EU provide opportunities and constraints that mean people and organizations gradually come to rely on each other to achieve at least some of their goals. In such a situation, it is not useful to deploy military force to achieve influence. It is more useful for states to create international institutions for mutual, positive sum, gain.

Leverage exploits this mutual interdependence, playing on the needs of states for continued cooperation to exercise power over others. It relies on *asymmetrical* power, where strong states can exploit the vulnerabilities of weaker ones (Nye and Keohane 1977: 10–11). Over the longer-term, leverage can help us understand why there might be limits to how far democratic backsliding in EU member states might go. As Vachudova has argued, the 'force of attraction of [EU] markets and institutions' can be conceived as 'passive leverage' (2005: 63). This amounts to a kind of a deep-rooted, structural influence of the EU over individual member states, which follows from the long-term costs of exclusion. It is a large part of what leads states to join the EU in the first place. For example, political elites in the small, post-communist states located not too far from Russia submitted themselves to the laborious process of joining the EU because of the 'tremendous economic and geopolitical benefits—particularly compared to the uncertain and potentially catastrophic costs of being left behind as others move forward' (Moravcsik and Vachudova 2003: 43; Vachudova 2005: 66–70). Non-membership has economic costs in terms of lost EU funds, as well as likely outflows of foreign direct investment, jobs, and expertise (Vachudova 2005: 70, 165; Kelemen 2020: 491). Not being a member means abiding by EU rules if you want to trade in practically the whole of Europe, without having a say in what those rules are (Vachudova 2005: 66, 75). The cover of the EU's weighty and well-established international trade rules help 'regulate relations with powerful neighbours' (Vachudova 2005: 66).

As we discuss EU responses to populism, it is worth keeping in mind that for most European states, long-term costs of exclusion create a power discrepancy favouring the EU as a whole when it can act coherently against individual states (Vachudova 2005: 67; see also Haughton 2014: 71, 80 on the case of Slovakia). Various commentators have argued along the lines of Schmidt and Bogdanowicz, that 'it is quite unrealistic' that a member state would be willing to risk its status as full member of the EU with provocations such as a 'straightforward refusal to follow the Court' (Schmidt and Bogdanowicz 2018: 1076; Kelemen 2020: 483). In the 2000s, this power discrepancy explained the EU's ability to influence change in both domestic institutions and a wide range of public policies in a manner that was both deep and unprecedented, even if selective and uneven (Moravcsik and Vachudova 2003; Schimmelfennig and Sedelmeier 2004; Vachudova 2005; Epstein and Sedelmeier 2008; Levitsky and Way 2010; on the limits to effectiveness, see: Grabbe 2001). Twenty years on, Vachudova argues, the longer-term, structural benefits of EU membership remain, even after the financial and other crises plaguing the EU (2016: 273; see also Haughton

2014: 71, 80). On the other hand, passive leverage relies on EU membership remaining attractive, which opinion polls on EU support suggest tends to fluctuate, and on an appreciation of material costs of EU-exit, which the UK experience suggests may not be a priority for voting publics (Levitsky and Way 2020: 41). Other powerful states—such as Russia or China—may deliberately seek to undermine EU leverage by courting would-be autocrats or deploying soft-power instruments such as international media and cultural exchanges to 'discredited Western democracies and democracy in general, while promoting their own models and norms' (Levitsky and Way 2010: 41; Diamond 2015: 151; Bugaric 2016: 85).

Of more immediate interest here is what Vachudova calls 'active leverage', or shorter-term, deliberate programmes of political conditionality (Vachudova 2005: 63). This works through rewards, or 'positive incentives' that encourage states to comply with international agreements and norms (Risse and Ropp 2013: 141). The conditions new members must fulfil are the most important example of rewards-based political conditionality. These conditions now require that a state is European, it respects liberal democratic values, and is committed to promoting them. New members must meet the 'Copenhagen criteria' requiring stable institutions guaranteeing democracy, the rule of law, human rights, and respect for the protection of minorities; a functioning market economy; and the ability to implement rules and obligations of membership. New members are now also required to develop good relations with their neighbours.

A second form of active leverage works through sanctions, or 'negative incentives' that punish states in retaliation for non-compliance of international norms or agreements (Guzman 2008: 33–34; Risse and Ropp 2013: 141). This kind of leverage captures important *international rights-restricting* IoPPs, such as EU voting sanctions for states which fail to live up to the EU's liberal democratic values or its new rules conditioning EU budget receipts on rule of law standards within member states (for more details see below). Understanding how 'active leverage' or 'negative incentives' works can, therefore, help us to understand how EU *international rights-restricting initiatives* may *curb the ability of populist parties in government to implement illiberal or anti-democratic policies*. That is, leverage theory suggests that, under certain conditions, states threatened or subject to international sanctions of this kind may be willing to avoid adopting illiberal and anti-democratic policies in the first place, or change them once adopted, if doing so allows them to retain benefits of international cooperation.

For this to happen, leverage theory leads us to expect, first, that states will be careful to choose their battles. Sanctions-based responses to populist parties may impose costs on both the target and sanctioning state and where action is collective, as in the EU, there may be differences among states in the value placed on a positive relationship with the targeted state (Guzman 2008: 47; Simmons 2009: 124–125). We can also expect some potential targets of EU sanctions will be more vulnerable to EU pressure than others. Vulnerability to leverage is rooted in the size and strength of a country's economy, with weak, small, and dependent states more vulnerable than larger ones with substantial military and economic power (Levitsky and Way 2010: 41; Risse and Ropp 2013: 20). Vulnerability to leverage may also be limited by countervailing economic or strategic interests, such as a state's strategic importance or possession of sought-after material resources (Levitsky and Way 2010: 41).

If a policy of sanctions (or rewards) can be agreed, effective leverage may depend on further conditions. As it will be recalled, leverage exploits mutual interdependence, playing on the needs of states for continued cooperation to exercise power over others. It relies on asymmetrical power, where strong states (or a group of states) can exploit the vulnerabilities of weaker ones. In their work on EU enlargement, Schimmelfennig and Sedelmeier identified five conditions that must be met for leverage to work (2004: 664–667, 2020). The strong need to get some things right. It must be *clear* what the strong want the weak to do. Demands must be *timely*, linking demands to consequences on a reasonably short time horizon. The strong must be *credible*; that is, the weak need to believe the strong will deliver on their promises or threats. The authors also argue that calculations of those in power in vulnerable states also matter. The weak need to think the *costs imposed* (*or rewards offered*) by the strong are important enough to respond to. Political elites in weak states need to think any changes the strong might demand have *low adaptation costs*, which won't fundamentally affect their hold on power.

This last point about *low adaptation costs* is particularly relevant for understanding obstacles for the working of *international rights-restricting* IoPPs. One lesson of the 2004 and 2007 EU enlargement processes was that despite possible economic advantages, autocratic governments had limited incentives to change their ways in exchange for EU membership (Schimmelfennig and Sedelmeier 2004: 669; Vachudova 2005: 72–73). Adaptation costs could be too high because the EU's rules requiring stable institutions guaranteeing democracy, rule of law, human rights, and respect for minorities 'would have required these governments to give up the very instruments on which their power rested' (Schimmelfennig and Sedelmeier 2004: 669). Schimmelfennig and Sedelmeier argue that similar costs apply for autocratizing states already in the EU, such that 'the influence of EU institutions on compliance decreases the more a government's hold on power depends on illiberal practices' (2020: 280–282; see also Blauberger and van Hüllen 2021: 8).

The optimal scenario for EU leverage appears to be when a state wants to join the EU and is well on the way to consolidating liberal democratic institutions (Schimmelfennig and Sedelmeier 2004; Vachudova 2005; Schimmelfennig and Sedelmeier 2020). Leverage does not guarantee that once a state joins the EU, it will remain a liberal democracy though. Power asymmetries are altered on entry into the EU. Decision-rules give new members more say over collective EU actions, more chances to strike bargains with potential opponents, and more veto powers (Moravcsik and Vachudova 2003: 52–53). Once EU membership is achieved, the size of EU rewards offered decline substantially (Sadurski 2004: 379; Epstein and Sedelmeier 2008: 797; Schimmelfennig and Sedelmeier 2020: 815). Nevertheless, so long as costs of withdrawing some benefit of EU cooperation remain, there is a possibility that states threatened or subject to EU sanctions may be willing to avoid adopting illiberal and anti-democratic policies in the first place, or to change them once adopted.

Leverage may not just affect bargaining outcomes in negotiations between states; it may indirectly affect governing populist parties by *decreasing support for populist parties* or *inducing moderation.* For governing parties, *international rights-restricting* initiatives, such as financial sanctions, may *decrease support* at home if voters or elites supporting the party 'perceive [they have] something to lose from international isolation' (Galtung 1967: 392, 395; Vachudova 2008; Simmons 2009: 146; Levitsky and Way 2010: 47). Such voters may turn against leaders whose behaviour seems to threaten their prosperity (Vachudova 2008: 872; Levitsky and Way 2010: 47). A government's failure to comply with an international agreement may generate opposition among domestic constituencies benefiting materially or in other ways from international cooperation (Keohane, Moravcsik, and Slaughter 2000: 476). As Levitsky and Way argue, this outcome is most likely where economic, political, social, and diplomatic links between those demanding democratic standards and those on the receiving end are dense, as is the case for the EU (2010, see also Galtung 1967: 396). This is because linkage means different kinds of domestic political actors have a stake in avoiding the costs of international isolation, including voters who expect integration with their neighbours to bring prosperity.

Some international IoPPs may help *reduce support for populist parties* by strengthening the opposition, particularly where that opposition is weak and fragmented. This can take the form of directly incentivizing collaboration among opposition parties, with rewards such as membership of international party federations or European parliament party groups (Spirova 2008; Levitsky and Way 2010: 111; von dem Berge and Poguntke 2013: 327). Less directly, international IoPPs may provide a 'focal point' helping opponents overcome their differences and concentrate their attention jointly on contesting governing parties. During the EU accession process, for example, various authors have argued that credible threats to a country's prospects of joining the EU provided a focal point helping unify fragmented and polarized oppositions in countries such as Slovakia, Romania, and Serbia (Vachudova 2008: 879; Levitsky and Way 2010: 95, 102, 111). In such cases, as Vachudova argued, '[a]ttacking ruling elites for forsaking the country's "return to Europe" and promising to move the country decisively towards EU membership formed an important part of an electoral platform that all opposition parties could agree on' (Vachudova 2005: 162–163). Pro-democracy campaigns, like human rights advocacy, may be particularly well suited to facilitate broader patterns of cooperation among opposition parties. As Risse and Sikkink argue, in some contexts claim-making of this nature is 'likely to serve as the main principled idea around which an opposition coalition can be formed' (Risse and Sikkink 1999: 25). Some domestic groups may participate in pro-democracy or human rights advocacy, not necessarily 'because they profoundly believe in human rights', but because they recognize such claims 'have more international support and legitimacy' and 'because it is an easier way to criticize the government' (Risse and Sikkink 1999: 26; Simmons 2009: 146).

International rights-restricting IoPPs may provide *incentives for populist parties to moderate* in order to avoid losing votes or becoming unattractive coalition partners. As Levitsky and Way have argued, international pariahs may become domestic pariahs where a party is held responsible for bringing about the international isolation of their country and where such isolation threatens access for national elites and the general public to the benefits of participation in the international system (2010: 96–97). During the EU accession process, for example, 'expectations of negative reactions from the European level should anti-democratic or hard-Eurosceptic parties—or both—be allowed to join the group of governing parties' could affect choice of coalition partners (Lewis 2008: 159; Vachudova 2008: 868–869; Haughton 2011: 10). Similarly, as Vachudova has argued, in hybrid democracies with a reasonable prospect of joining the EU and a pro-EU population, opposition parties had incentives to adopt more moderate policy positions to 'make their parties fit the increasingly attractive "pro-EU space" on the political spectrum' (2005: 163, 2008: 347). As in the pre-accession period, where incentives for moderation grew with 'increasing costs of illiberal rule'

(Pridham 2006: 347; Vachudova 2008: 865), EU voting or financial sanctions may likewise give incentives for all kinds of opposition parties to resist the temptation of engaging with illiberal populists on their own terms.

On the other hand, *international rights-restricting* initiatives such as sanctions may provoke a 'populist backlash' which may *increase support for populist parties*. In a manner analogous to populist backlash against initiatives involving international courts (see Chapter 4), international sanctions are often met by 'sovereignty counter-discourses', claiming that international initiatives are an 'illegitimate intervention in the internal affairs of the country' (Risse and Sikkink 1999: 223; Bermeo 2016: 15–16). Appeals to the illegitimacy of international sanctions can easily be expressed through the populist juxtaposition of 'the pure people' and an international 'corrupt elite' (Heinisch and Mazzoleni 2017: 108; Schlipphak and Treib 2017: 355). In the face of international sanctions, sovereignty counter-discourses may potentially build 'rally-round-the-flag' effects *increasing support for a populist-led government*. This is because 'citizens are more likely to follow the lead of their elites in situations framed as crisis' (Fallend and Heinisch 2016: 336; Schlipphak and Treib 2017: 354; Closa 2021: 4), and because 'governments can blame external sanctions for any hardship that voters experience and avoid scrutiny for failings of their own socio-economic policies' (Galtung 1967: 403; Sedelmeier 2017: 342). Sovereignty counter-discourses may also be used to 'de-certify', or 'invalidate' actors making appeals against it (McAdam, Tilly, and Tarrow 2001: 158), for example when civil society organizations funded by, or with close links to entities abroad, are 'framed and silenced as tools of foreign forces' (Bermeo 2016: 15). International IoPPs may also *boost the moral resources of populist parties* if they can 'present themselves as the only actors able to solve the problem' of unwanted international interventions, and if able to do so, strengthen 'citizen's confidence in their competence and trustworthiness' (Schlipphak and Treib 2017: 354–355).

Political disruption as social leverage

In addition to alliance building, discussed in the previous chapter, civil society actors may pursue their goals through a form of society-based leverage—or disruption. In this way, *coercive confrontation* by civil society actors and disruptive but non-violent forms of *adversarialism* may force governing populist parties to *curb illiberal and anti-democratic policies*. Disruption occurs when people 'withhold their accustomed cooperation' or 'cease to conform to accustomed institutional roles' (Fox Piven and Cloward 1978: 24).

It obstructs 'the normal operation of institutions' and 'the routine activities of opponents, bystanders, or authorities' (ibid.). As Fox Pivan and Cloward put it, with disruption 'Factories are shut down when workers walk out or sit down; welfare bureaucracies are thrown into chaos when crowds demand relief; landlords may be bankrupted when tenants refuse to pay rent' (ibid.). Online acts of sabotage, such as 'denial of service' protests disrupt the normal operation of institutions (Tarrow 2011: 101, 104). 'Flash activism'—such as rapidly assembled, massively supported participation in online petitions— 'may have the disruptive capacities of a flash flood' (Earl 2016: 275–384). Disruption may lead to political crisis and threaten lives and property. It gives urgency to the demands of opponents and may discredit incumbents (Kolb 2007: 76). It can usher in new governments deemed able to end chaos and may even result in regime change (ibid.). Disruption not only 'challenges authorities', it 'emboldens supporters, and keeps the public interested and amused' (Tarrow 2011: 101, 104).

Disruption is a way for civil society actors to address power imbalances. It is a form of 'negative sanction', or 'the withdrawal of a crucial contribution on which others depend, and it is therefore a natural resource for exerting power over others' (Fox Piven and Cloward 1978: 24). If it 'jeopardizes something the government values—for example a certain reputation, social peace, or their continued electoral success', protestors are more likely to extract concessions 'in exchange for restoring order' (Kolb 2007: 74). As Tarrow puts it, disruption may be 'the strongest weapon of social movements', giving 'weak actors leverage against powerful opponents' (Tarrow 2011: 103; see also Earl 2016: 376, for leverage provided by online forms of 'flash activism'). As a consequence, 'Elite reaction is ultimately focused in a self-interested way on ending protest' (Fox Piven, and Cloward 1978: 30; Andrews 2001: 74), and this can include *curbing illiberal and anti-democratic policies a populist party in government* would otherwise pursue. In rare cases, disruption it may lead to the removal of governing elites.

The effectiveness of disruption may depend on whether cooperation withheld by those causing disruption is crucial, whether those affected have something they can exchange to quell it, and whether the disruptors can protect themselves adequately from reprisals (Fox Piven and Cloward 1978: 25). Disruption is harder for political elites to ignore in highly competitive contexts, or political crises, when their hold on power is uncertain (Fox Piven and Cloward 1978: 28; Kolb 2007: 74; Earl 2016: 382). Similarly, 'when the disrupted institutions are central to economic production or the stability of social life, it becomes imperative that normal operations be restored if the regime is to maintain support among its constituents' (Fox Piven and

Cloward 1978: 29). On the other hand, disruptive acts may be ignored or repressed, if 'the disruptive group has little political leverage in its own right' or if the 'disrupted institution is not central to the society as a whole', especially during periods of political stability (ibid.: 26–27; Kolb 2007: 74). Furthermore, the longer-term impact of concessions made in response to disruption can be precarious, if once turmoil subsides, concessions may be withdrawn, diluted, or poorly implemented (Fox Piven and Cloward 1978: 34; Andrews 2001: 74; Kolb 2007: 76).

EU Voting and Financial Sanctions

International rights-restricting IoPPs are undertaken by public authorities, usually other states, or international organizations. They are an 'intolerant' mode of engagement, suspending rights and entitlements a government would usually receive by virtue of an international agreement or membership of an international organization. This kind of exceptional treatment includes denying rights which would usually be granted to state representatives in international institutions (including expulsion, or suspension of voting rights), or the application of sanctions preventing access to public goods (like funds), which a state would otherwise have a right to receive.

The first real test of political sanctions by EU member states against another occurred when the right-wing populist Freedom Party of Austria (FPÖ) joined a coalition government with the Austrian People's Party (ÖVP) after 1999 elections. Acting outside the EU framework, 14 members of the EU launched diplomatic sanctions, suspending bilateral official contacts at the political level with the Austrian government, refusing support for Austrians seeking jobs in international organizations, and downgrading access for Austrian ambassadors in EU capitals (Merlingen et al. 2001; Sadurski 2010; Bugaric 2016: 82). The sanctioning member states argued the FPÖ was an affront to EU values promoting human rights and democracy, and against racism and xenophobia, although may also have reflected domestic party political strategies to prevent similar taboo-breaking coalitions from taking root at home (Merlingen et al. 2001: 65). The sanctions were short-lived. Investigation by a group of top-level academic and political leaders cleared the ÖVP–FPÖ government of undermining European values, and in September 2000 sanctions were lifted unconditionally. For a long time, the Austrian sanctions were a cautionary tale, a warning that confrontational strategies could be counterproductive (Kochenov and Pech 2016: 1068; Closa 2021: 78).

The EU treaties don't provide for the expulsion of a member state, but there are provisions permitting sanctions that come quite close to it. Article 7 (2–4) of the Treaty on European Union (TEU) allows EU members to suspend certain rights, including voting rights in the Council if the other member states judge that there has been a 'serious and persistent breach' in the EU's fundamental liberal democratic values listed in Article 2 TEU. The Council is the main EU body channelling state interests in the EU decision process, so voting sanctions would seriously limit the influence of a sanctioned state. While a preventive, dialogue-based procedure written into Article 7(1) has been triggered (see Chapter 6), the sanctions procedure in Article 7 (2–4) has not been invoked. As former Commission President José Manuel Barroso (2012) famously described it, Article 7 sanctions are a 'nuclear option'. This alludes to the perception that Article 7 sanctions are a devastating weapon which could not even be contemplated unless things got very bad. As Besselink put this thought: 'The main use of Article 7 was that actually using it was unthinkable' (2017: 134).

In January 2021, EU Regulation 2020/2092 on a General Regime of Conditionality for the Protection of the Union Budget came into force. It tied EU funds to respect for the rule of law, allowing budget allocations to be suspended in part or full if this condition were not met. The Regulation links respect for the rule of law to the principles of sound financial management and protecting the union budget. As such, sanctions are framed in the regulation as a measure to guarantee that independent courts can effectively prosecute fraud, tax evasion, corruption, and conflicts of interest that might arise when a state spends EU money. It is a new form of active leverage, allowing the EU to exploit the dependence of a good number of its members on EU financial transfers.

Public debates on the new regulation made it clear that attacks on judicial independence in the EU's backsliding states, particularly in Hungary and Poland, were the main target. In February 2022 the CJEU ruled on the compatibility of the regulation with EU law. In April 2022, the Commission announced that it would trigger proceedings against Hungary, the first and so far only country to be subject to the mechanism. In December 2022 the EU Council suspended allocation of €6.3 billion of EU funds to Hungary due to 'breaches of the principles of the rule of law in Hungary, concerning public procurement, the effectiveness of prosecutorial action and the fight against corruption' (Council of the EU 2022a). The member states did not consider satisfactory Hungary's response to remedial actions proposed by the Commission regarding these issues. Similarly, the Council also approved 27 'super milestones' requiring institutional reforms to strengthen the rule of law, fulfilment of which would give Hungary access to €5.8 billion in EU COVID Recovery and Resilience grants (Council of the EU 2022b). The Commission also delayed approving release of EU COVID Recovery and Resilience grants to Poland, with negotiations centred on the country's compliance with CJEU judgments on judicial reforms (Kosc 2021; Zalan 2021; Gijs 2022).

As discussed above, leverage theory suggests that, under certain conditions, states threatened or subject to international sanctions of this kind may be willing to *curb illiberal and anti-democratic policies* if doing so allows them to retain benefits of cooperation. Leverage theory also provides insights into why, in the face of the now clear cases of democratic backsliding in Hungary and Poland, *international rights-restricting* IoPPs can be difficult to use. In addition to *timely* responses, leverage theory emphasizes the importance of *clear* demands on the part of sanctioners, an intrinsically challenging condition where vaguely formulated principles of liberal democracy are at stake. Leverage theory also directs our attention to potentially *high costs* for those targeted by EU sanctions, but also for those choosing to wield them. *Credibility* is also important. It proposes that if the likely targets of EU sanctions recognize the obstacles facing sanctioners, targeted states may have good reasons to discount the probability that sanctions will be used. They may calculate that demands to *curb illiberal and anti-democratic policies* can be taken lightly.

Clarity: As mentioned above, Article 7 (2–4) TEU provides for voting sanctions in the case of a 'serious and persistent breach' in the EU's fundamental liberal democratic values spelled out in Article 2 TEU. Article 2 states that the EU is founded on respect for human dignity, freedom, democracy, equality, the rule of law and human rights, including rights of minorities. In the member states, the article adds, the principles of pluralism, non-discrimination, tolerance, justice, solidarity, and equality between women and men prevail. In practice though, it can be difficult to work out precisely which governmental acts breach liberal democratic values, and when they amount to a serious and persistent breach. The practical meaning of these principles, and the best way to resolve conflicts between them, are the stuff of centuries of philosophical debate. A lesson of the 2004 and 2007 'eastward enlargement' of the EU was that leverage worked better for detailed market regulations than for much vaguer political conditionality (Sadurski 2004; Pridham 2006: 349; Grabbe 2014: 45; Schimmelfennig and Sedelmeier 2020). The EU does not have a 'democratic acquis', or clear rules on what kinds of institutions or policies states should adopt, or a comprehensive view of liberal democracy driving its political criteria (Grabbe 2001: 1025; Pridham 2006: 349; Grabbe 2014: 45–46). This meant that despite the 'magnetic attraction of the

EU' and the opportunity for 'enormous political influence' of the accession process, there were inconsistencies and gaps in what the EU required in terms of democratic reforms (Grabbe 2001: 1014, 1028; 2014).

Regulation 2020/2092 on the EU rule of law budget conditionality provides more clarity about how targeted states might change their policies to maintain the benefits of cooperation. The regulation includes a definition of the 'rule of law' (Article 2), indicators of 'breaches of the principles of the rule of law' (Article 3) and a more detailed list of 'conditions' triggering sanctions (Article 4). The regulation is littered with references to the most up-to-date case-law of the CJEU, and the European Commission is instructed to take account of relevant information from specialist EU and Council of Europe bodies, including the Venice Commission.

Making judgements about democratic quality are harder when likely targets use a strategy of 'autocratic legalism' to disarm and confuse critics (see Chapter 1) (Scheppele 2018; Sajó 2021). This happens when a government outwardly follows the letter of the law, steering clear of overt ruptures with known liberal democratic institutions and rules, or obvious human rights violations. Autocratic legalism allows governments to deliberately exploit the wide variety of practical ways in which 'freedom', 'democracy', or 'pluralism' can be organized to muddle debates about the implications of political reforms (Grabbe 2014: 46; Scheppele 2018). Already in 2013, for example, Scheppele observed that when the Fidesz government introduced constitutional reforms 'defenders could say that there was some law just like it somewhere in Europe' and this 'made it hard for European control bodies, with their checklist approach, to work out what Fidesz was doing' (2013: 561). In this manner Hungary was able to create what Scheppele called a 'Frankenstate':

> When Fidesz restricted competencies of the constitutional court, it argued to European bodies expressing concern that not all European bodies *had* constitutional courts so Europe could not insist on particular competencies of a particular court. When Fidesz brought the media under control, it noted that other countries in Europe had powerful media councils, too. When it changed the electoral laws, it justified each individual piece of what it did by pointing to some other unquestioned democracy that had done the same (gerrymandering, ending second-round runoffs, limiting campaign advertising).
>
> **(2013: 561)**

Following the Hungarian model, Law and Justice in Poland have also 'claimed that all of its judicial reforms borrowed the laws on the judiciary from some other (unnamed) member state of the European Union' (ibid.: 553).

Credibility: As the 'nuclear weapon' metaphor discussed above suggests, likely targets of Article 7 voting sanctions have grounds for thinking there is little chance it will ever be used against them. In addition to high costs for sanctioners (see below), the sanctions procedure makes agreement difficult (Sedelmeier 2017: 340; Kelemen 2020: 489). Even if one-third of member states or the European Commission trigger the sanctions procedure, all the member states must ultimately agree (minus the targeted state) that a 'serious and persistent breach' of EU values has occurred. This gives EU governments the deciding vote and even minimal disagreement in the Council can thwart a sanctions vote. The unanimity rule allows two or more backsliding states to gang up and block any vote against one of them. Populist-led governments in Poland, Hungary, and Czech Republic openly declared their opposition to the use of Article 7 sanctions, limiting the chance that a vote to trigger Article 7 sanctions would succeed (Dimitrov 2018; Dimitrov, Vladisavljevic, and Luca 2018; Closa 2021: 511). More generally, Closa points to caution among governments about EU interventions in domestic constitutional issues and an eagerness by several governments 'to assert the autonomy of democratically elected governments' (2021: 511, see also Sedelmeier 2017: 340; Kelemen 2020: 483). A decision by some national governments to sanction one of their fellows sits uneasily with practices of accommodation and consensus in the EU's intergovernmental bodies. As Kelemens has argued, 'EU governance is heavily influenced by norms of respect for national sovereignty', but also 'mutual trust, and the assumption that member states will respect the duty of "sincere cooperation" (TEU Article 4(3)) in fulfilling their EU obligations' (2020: 485; see also Jenne and Mudde 2012: 150; Sedelmeier 2017: 340).

Credibility issues are less acute for EU budget conditionality rules, which make it easier to suspend EU funding than to agree on Article 7 sanctions. Under Regulation 2020/2092, the European Commission alone is responsible for investigating and initiating the sanctions procedure and triggers preliminary talks about remedies to address underlying problems. Member states in the Council still have the final say but make their decision using standard EU qualified majority voting rules. Poland and Hungary, or other small groups of states with rule of law issues, will thus find it harder to block a decision. Additionally, as Blauberger and van Hüllen put it, Regulation 2020/2092 is a 'smart', not 'nuclear', weapon (2021: 8). It is possible to suspend payments outright, funds can be reduced or redirected, or embargos placed on new commitments. Sanctions can be lifted partially or fully depending on progress with compliance.

It is worth noting that in the past, EU financial measures intended for other purposes have been instrumentalized to pursue rule of law objectives, with some success. EU budget rules allow the EU to suspend funds where they suspect financial irregularities (Uitz 2020: 14). The EU suspended Cohesion Fund payments of €495 million to Hungary in 2012 due to its failure to follow state budget deficit rules (Goldner Lang 2019: 12). Hungary quickly took steps to correct its excessive deficit and the payment suspension was soon lifted (Goldner Lang 2019: 12). In August 2020, the European Commission refused to make small grants of between €5,000 and €25,000 to fund transnational municipality twinning partnerships involving six Polish local governments that had made anti-LGBTQ+ pledges (Wanat 2020). In an escalation of the conflict, the Commission warned in July 2021 that it would withhold some Structural Funds payments because of the anti-LGBTQ+ declarations (Wanat 2021a; Wanat and Tamma 2021). Following the threats, several of the Law and Justice party-led regions who had made anti-LBGTQ+ resolutions in 2019 and 2020 dropped them (Kosc 2021). (These declarations were later subject to an infringement proceeding for violation of EU law, see Appendix IV.) On the other hand, Bulgaria lost €520 million in EU funds in 2008 due to suspected fraud and the EU's refusal to accredit government agencies responsible for distributing EU funds (Lacatus and Sedelmeier 2020: 1241). In conjunction with the Cooperation and Verification Mechanism, which monitors judicial and anti-corruption reforms in Bulgaria, financial pressure led, according to Spendzharova and Vachudova, to only 'superficial domestic institutional changes addressing the EU's recommendations to combat corruption and improve the rule of law' and did not produce 'convincing results' (2012: 49; see also Lacatus and Sedelmeier 2020: 1241).

Timing is another potential problem for Article 7 sanctions, not least because treaty provisions have no deadlines for the conclusion of different stages of the decision process. The slow pace of proceedings against Poland and Hungary under Article 7(1) suggest that delays are likely for sanctions proceeding too (see Chapter 6). *Timing* is much improved in relation to new budget conditionality rules (Blauberger and van Hüllen 2021: 8). There are relatively short time limits built in at each step of the procedure, which are likely to prevent open-ended talks. On the other hand, the European Commission is the sole gatekeeper, excluding member states or the European Parliament from the trigger procedure.

High costs of sanctions: Suspending the treaty rights of a member state under Article 7 is a sizeable sanction for those targeted, but may also be costly for the sanctioners (Schimmelfennig and Sedelmeier 2020: 820). For the sanctioned, a ban on voting in the Council would undo what Vachudova described as the political benefits of EU membership, namely the benefits of 'voice' in the formation of rules which would have to be implemented to maintain access to the EU market (2005: 66, 75). Suspending voting rights falls short of expulsion, but in analogous situations the states subject to such sanctions have withdrawn from the sanctioning body (Besselink 2017: 130). Such an eventuality is likely to be highly divisive for the EU, provoking profound crisis. In addition, as Scheppele et al. have written, sanctioning states with business interests in targeted states 'will essentially be sanctioning their own enterprises' (2020: 35). The authors argue, 'If mutual interpenetration of economies make any military conflict too costly to pursue, the same surely applies to economic warfare of any kind' (ibid.).

Although the Commission is directed in Regulation 2020/2092 to propose sanctions proportionate to the degree of rule of law deficiencies, in the Hungarian and Polish cases, 'the sanctioning potential is immense' (Blauberger and van Hüllen 2021: 12). Financial sanctions may affect both the main EU budget, which for 2021–2027 amounts to €1074.3 billion, and the €750 billion of loans and grants under the EU's COVID Recovery and Resilience Facility (RRF). The two most likely candidates for financial sanctions are the largest recipients of EU funds. Poland gets most EU funds overall, while Hungary is the largest recipient per capita (Kelemen 2020: 490; Lacny 2021: 80–81). In 2019, EU funds for Poland amounted to 3% of its GDP, while for Hungary the figure was 4.55% of GDP (Kelemen 2020: 498; Lacny 2021: 80). At stake for Hungary after the December 2022 Council Decision to suspend Cohesion Funds and hold back COVID RRF allocations is around 2% of its 2021 GDP (Nguyen, 2022). According to Nguyen (2022) the impact of this sanction is likely to be considerable at a time of low growth and high inflation and when the Hungarian government must pay high interest rates to borrow internationally. Similarly, as Boras has argued for the Polish case, high inflation, energy crisis, high interest rates on Polish national bonds, and the war with Russia on its doorstep mean the 'Law and Justice Party cannot afford further economic deterioration'. '[C]ollapse of the credibility of Poland on the financial markets', was another threat, according to Boras (2022).

Not all member states are as vulnerable to financial sanctions as Poland and Hungary, though many states at the lower end of 'democratic quality' scale in the EU (see Table 1.2) receive more from the EU budget than they pay in. As Haughton has observed, 'politicians in these net recipient states tend to see the EU as a "cash cow" to be milked' (2014: 80). Yet, 'It is not just the prosaic issue of money, but more deeply seated vulnerabilities [of these relatively poor states] that are key' (Haughton 2014: 80).

It is notable that the threat of being cut out of the EU budget is exacerbated, in the Polish case, by other kinds of financial sanctions related to the rule of law. Under Article 260 of the Treaty on the Functioning of the EU (TFEU) the CJEU has the right to fine a member state which does not follow its rulings. The imposition of such fines is very rare, but if applied at the maximum level, could be 'immensely costly', such that it would probably not be 'feasible for a member state to "pay its way" out of an infringement on a prolonged basis' (Schmidt and Bogdanowicz 2018: 1074). Poland was hit by several EU fines for non-compliance. In 2017, when the Polish government publicly refused to comply with a Court order to stop illegal logging in Białowieża forest, the CJEU authorized fines of at least €100,000 a day (Schmidt and Bogdanowicz 2018: 1074; Pech and Kochenov 2021: 26). The Polish government soon complied with the court ruling (Sadurski 2019b: 209; Scheppele, Vladimirovich Kochenov, and Grabowska-Moroz 2020: 57; Pech and Kochenov 2021). In September 2021, in a case involving Poland and the Czech Republic, the CJEU ordered Poland to pay €500,000 a day for refusing to temporarily stop extraction of lignite at the Turów mine (Court of Justice of the EU 2021). In another case, the CJEU ordered Poland to pay daily fines of €1 million for failing to comply with a decision to temporarily halt some of the powers of the Disciplinary Chamber of the Polish Supreme Court (see Chapter 4) (European Commission 2021; Wanat 2021d).

High adaptation costs: Despite the intrinsic vagueness of liberal democratic principles stated in Article 2 TEU, we can make an educated guess about the kinds of changes Hungary and Poland might need to make to avoid voting or financial sanctions linked to a breach of EU values. The preventative, talks-based procedure written into Article 7(1) TEU (see Chapter 6) has been launched against Poland and Hungary to determine whether there is 'a clear risk of a serious breach' of EU values. The European Commission initiated proceedings against Poland, focusing mainly on reforms enhancing control of the Law and Justice party over the judiciary (European Commission 2017). The European Parliament, which launched proceedings against Hungary, had broader concerns. These included the functioning of the constitutional and electoral system, independence of the judiciary, corruption and conflict of interests, privacy and data protection, freedom of expression, academic freedom, freedom of religion and of association, the right to equal treatment, the rights of persons belonging to minorities, fundamental rights of migrants, asylum seekers and refugees, and economic and social rights (European Parliament 2018). The political conditions for release of EU funds repeat many of the same themes. Many are classic forms of what Bermeo has called 'executive aggrandizement', where governments 'weaken checks on executive power one by one, undertaking a series of institutional changes that hamper the power of opposition forces to challenge executive preferences'

(Bermeo 2016). Undoing some or all these reforms is highly likely to loosen the grip of Fidesz or Law and Justice parties on political power.

At the time of publication, it is too soon to say what the outcome of financial sanctions—or the threat of them—will be. Evaluations are mixed. For example, Boras points to several fundamental reforms undertaken by the Law and Justice government to 'secure its share of COVID-19 recovery funds' (2022: 1). Most importantly, in December 2022, the Law and Justice party introduced legislation to reform the judiciary to address EU concerns, such that, if implemented, 'Polish judges would not be punished for referring to ECJ jurisdiction or for refusing to adjudicate in panels with peers whose nominations violate the European standards of judicial independence' (ibid.: 2). Boras argues that this was the 'single most important step towards getting Poland's politicized judicial system back on track' (ibid.: 2), and could mean that 'the system of intimidation of judges and prosecutors ... would inevitably start to crumble' (ibid.: 3). Significantly, Judge Igor Tuleya, suspended under controversial disciplinary proceedings for a verdict critical of the government and a well-known symbol of opposition to the government's judicial reforms, was permitted to return work in the Warsaw district court (ibid.: 1). On the other hand, Scheppele, Kelemans and Morijn argue that 'Hungary has already tried to pass off cynical and ineffective "reforms" as serious responses to the Commission's first checklist of anti-corruption measures' (2022: 3). In addition, the authors argue 'by approving this plan with milestones that Hungary must meet to receive cash' EU authorities anticipate 'that satisfying them would be enough to trust Hungary with EU money ... though none of these conditions would by themselves address the fact that Hungary is not a democracy any longer' (ibid.: 3).

As discussed above, *international rights-restricting IoPPs* may have domestic consequences, including *decreasing support for populist parties* at home if sanctions create costs for government supporters or voters, or if it empowers the opposition. They may also provide incentives for populist parties in opposition *to moderate* if sanctions heighten the cost of illiberal and anti-democratic policy stances. On the other hand, if governing parties can successfully mount a populist backlash challenging the legitimacy of international interventions, IoPPs may *boost moral resources* such as legitimacy and *increase support for a governing populist party*.

It is an open question whether *international rights-restricting IoPPs* available to sanction Hungary and Poland have had—or would have—significant domestic consequences. Haughton's (2014) argument about the politicization of EU membership and access to EU funds in post-communist states suggests domestic actors and citizens will not be indifferent. The author argues that 'the EU has played a role as a reference point and a weapon to be invoked in domestic competition, particularly to lambast opponents for their incompetence, especially when it comes to the ability to access and manage EU funds' (ibid.: 84). This is because 'for such relatively poor states, money matters: hence the most potent impact of the EU on party politics tends to be in disputes, allegations and accusations surrounding the management and disbursement of European funds—all useful ammunition in highlighting a politician's, a party's or government's (in)competence' (ibid.: 84).

Several examples from the EU accession process show that international censure can have significant domestic consequences, although effects are less significant for states already part of the EU. The impact of the EU's decision at the 1997 Luxembourg European Council Summit to exclude Slovakia from formal EU accession negotiations following deterioration in democratic standards under Prime Minister Vladimír Mečiar is widely cited (Vachudova 2008: 871–872; Haughton and Rybář 2009: 554; Levitsky and Way 2010: 96). As Houghton and Rybář observe, in Slovakia '[t]he European debate that preceded entry initially revolved largely round who was responsible for the "No" issued at Luxembourg in 1997, and then about the conduct of negotiations' (ibid. 2009: 554). The EU action appears to have *reduced support* for Mečiar's party, Movement for a Democratic Slovakia (HZDS). As Vachudova argued, delaying Slovakia's EU accession significantly 'limited Mečiar's electoral appeal [and] transformed Slovakia's regional standing into a major campaign issue' in the 1998 Slovak national elections (2008: 871–872; see also Levitsky and Way 2010: 96). Similarly, in the 2002 election 'the prospect of EU membership provided an important source of electoral support' for parties opposing Mečiar's party, while 'Mečiar's perceived inability to advance EU membership appears to have limited his appeal' (Levitsky and Way 2010: 97). In that election the vote share of HZDS declined by nearly a third compared to 1998. On the other hand, the limits of international censure beyond the enlargement process can be observed in the Austrian case. European sanctions against the Austrian People's Party (ÖVP)–Freedom Party of Austria (FPÖ) coalition in 2000 are widely seen as a failure, not least because they *increased support for* the ÖVP–FPÖ government (Merlingen et al. 2001: 73).

It is notable that in the face of heightened conflict over the rule of law in Hungary and Poland, European integration has become a salient issue in recent electoral contests in both countries (Arató 2020; Szczerbiak 2020; Ágh 2021). There is some evidence that EU interventions, including the threat of sanctions, affected at least some of those opposing ruling populist parties. In Hungary, for example, it can be argued that pro-EU positions counterposing

Fidesz leader Viktor Orban's increasingly sharp critiques of the EU became a 'focal' point uniting Hungary's weak and fragmented opposition (Arató 2020; Ágh 2021). Against the two-thirds majority of parliamentary seats held by Fidesz and its coalition partner the Christian Democratic People's Party (KDNP) stand a diverse set of opposition parties including the right-wing nationalists of Jobbik (19.1% of votes, 2018), the Hungarian social democrats (MSZP, 11.95% votes, 2019), the greens of Politics Can Be Different (LMP, 7.1% of votes, 2018) and the social liberals of Democratic Coalition (DK, 5.4% of votes, 2018). As Ágh has argued, Hungary's opposition parties 'become more and more intensely pro-EU and their attitude towards the EU has been the main issue of their electoral and political cooperation by the late 2010s' (2021: 26). The 2019 European Parliament elections were a turning point in this regard: Against a background of limited cooperation among opposition parties and the Orbán regime's declared 'freedom fight' against the EU, the pro-EU opposition parties 'declared their own freedom fight against the Orbán regime in the spirit of Federative Europe' (ibid.: 25). Opposition parties mobilized, among other things, around a rejection of 'the hostile discourse and steps taken by the Hungarian government towards the EU' (MSZP) and claims that Hungary had to choose between Orbán and the EU (DK) (Arató 2020: 119–120; Ágh 2021: 26). The new-found cooperation among the previously fragmented opposition may have strengthened the opposition but did not reduce Fidesz's vote share in EP elections. Cooperation among opposition parties intensified subsequently though, and in October 2019 municipal elections, opposition parties defeated Fidesz in the capital city, Budapest, and many larger cities (Ágh 2021: 25). Opposition parties now govern 'large parts of the country through the municipal governments of "urban Hungary" in coalition' (Henley 2021; Ágh 2021: 25). In the April 2022 elections opposition parties competed on a joint ticket with a common candidate for prime minister (Péter Márki-Zay), although this was still not sufficient to defeat Fidesz.

Part of the explanation for *ideological moderation* of the Hungarian right-wing populist party Jobbik may also lie in the effects of international censure. Jobbik, founded as an extreme-right, anti-semitic and xenophobic hard Eurosceptic party, was for a long time an international pariah, complicating its inclusion in anti-Fidesz coalitions. As noted in Chapter 3, when Fidesz coopted more and more of Jobbik's signature policies, the two parties effectively 'changed places' (Pytlas 2016; Arató 2020: 114; Kim 2021: 143–158). Jobbik party leader Gábor Vona led a change of course towards the political centre, dropping anti-Semitic and xenophobic rhetoric and its Euroscepticism. Part of the explanation for moderation may be incentives created by Jobbik's status as an international pariah, which according to Enyedi and

Róna (2018) was an obstacle to Jobbik's office ambitions. As late as 2018, the authors argued that 'Jobbik is still an unlikely challenger in competition for office, as the international community is very unlikely to tolerate a Jobbik government' (ibid.: 265, 267). However over time the party became an integral part of the anti-Fidesz coalition and collaborated closely with other opposition parties.

In Poland, Europe has provided a focal point for opposition parties and civil society actors mobilizing against the government, although the impact of pro-European frames is less clear. Szczerbiak observes that during the 2019 European Parliament elections, 'seen as the first stage of the country's autumn first-order parliamentary campaign', the main opposition parties joined together to form the European Coalition (2020: 189). 'Europe' provided the glue binding this ideologically eclectic group of parties: As Szczerbiak observed, the European Coalition's campaign message was to 'frame the election as a "great choice" … between returning Poland to the European mainstream politics and a Law and Justice government which, it said, had undermined the country's international standing and thereby threatened its access to EU funds, and ultimately membership of the Union' (ibid.). Law and Justice were able, according to Szczerbiak, to dampen electoral effects of this message by avoiding overtly Eurosceptic rhetoric and insisting Poland's EU membership was not in doubt, both of which helped land a 'stunning victory' for the party in the European Parliament and subsequent 2019 national elections (ibid.: 179, 192). It is not clear this strategy will be successful in the future. Boras (2022) has argued that the willingness of Law and Justice to engage with EU demands for reform in exchange for EU COVID Recovery Funds is driven by the fear that the issue may weaken its support in upcoming elections.

Many of the Law and Justice's civil society opponents have also come together around positive reference to Europe (Karolewski 2016; Hall 2019). For example, the Committee for the Protection of Democracy (KOD), framed the 'PiS government as a threat to Poland's EU membership and conducive to isolation of Warsaw in Europe' (Karolewski 2016: 264). Slogans such as 'We are Europe', and claims by KOD leader Mateusz Kijowski that anti-PIS demonstrations were for 'everyone loving Europe, democracy and liberty', showed a pro-Europeanism at odds with PiS government critiques of the EU as 'a source of illegitimate political pressure, exercised by institutions without democracy legitimacy' (ibid.: 263). According to Closa, 'by appealing to pro-European sentiments, this strategy diminished the government's ability to mobilize a rally-round-the-flag response, and at the same time increased the legitimacy of the EU's actions' (2021: 8).

Fidesz and Law and Justice have responded to these initiatives in a variety of different registers, including the populist one. EU-initiated *international rights-restricting* IoPPs discussed here produced a 'populist backlash', although more research is needed to understand its effect on support for Hungarian and Polish governing parties and their *moral resources*, or legitimacy. IoPPs were met by populist 'sovereignty counter-discourses', claiming that EU interventions were an illegitimate challenge by an out-of-touch, 'corrupt', or 'self-interested' international elite to the will of a sovereign people. After coming to government in 2010, Fidesz's EU policy evolved from a pragmatic Europeanist orientation to a pronounced Euroscepticism (Arató 2020; Ágh 2021). As Arató has argued, once in government, Fidesz 'did not merely strenuously represent Hungarian interests, but expressed outright hostility to European institutions, passing through a phase of "soft Euroscepticism" between 2010–2014 to a hard Euroscepticism after 2014' (Arató 2020: 113). 'Brussels' was pitched as one of the main external 'enemies'—alongside the International Monetary Fund, immigrants, and Hungarian-born billionaire émigré George Soros—from which Fidesz promised to protect Hungarians (Arató 2020: 113). Eurosceptical campaigns often focused on immigration policies, including a national consultation titled 'Let's Stop Brussels', and a controversial poster campaign linking then European Commission President Jean-Claude Juncker and George Soros to anti-immigration messages (Deutsche Welle 2019). For its part, Law and Justice maintained its traditional soft-Euroscepticism, combining critiques of EU institutions with a 'stress on its strong commitment to continued membership of the Union as a core element of Polish foreign policy' (Szczerbiak 2020: 188). For example, Law and Justice 'accused the Commission of bias and double standards' and claimed the 'Commission was motivated by the fact that Warsaw had been robust in promoting Polish interests and values, and in opposing socially liberal and multicultural policies supported by the EU political establishment' (ibid.: 182).

Specifically, regarding *international rights-restricting* IoPPs discussed here, Poland and Hungary initially threatened to veto the EU budget and COVID Recovery Fund, if the Rule of Law Budget Conditionality Regulation was approved. When the law was approved nevertheless, they challenged the legality of Regulation 2020/2092 in the CJEU (but lost). The new Regulation was met by populist 'sovereignty counter-discourses', claiming EU interventions were an illegitimate challenge by an out-of-touch, 'corrupt', or 'self-interested' international elite to the will of a sovereign people. For example, Hungarian Justice Minister Judit Varga described those supporting the new budget rule of law mechanism as 'the Brussels elite and the left-liberal media', adding 'We say no to blackmailing with the rule of law!' (Bayer 2021). Similarly, Law and Justice leader Jarosław Kacznsky described the regulation as 'threats and blackmail' (Euroactiv 2020). Like Fidesz leader Viktor Orbán in other contexts, Kacznsky compared the EU's budget conditionality mechanism to Soviet rule, arguing that like the 'example of the Polish People's Republic', 'We're on the right side of history, and those who want to take away our sovereignty based on their own whims are headed for a fail' (Euroactiv 2020). At another point, Polish Prime Minister Matheus Morawiecki responded to Commission threats to link Poland's access to COVID Recovery Funds to compliance with ECJ rulings saying 'We don't want to have "a master and customer" relationship with the European Commission … Poland doesn't have any master. This is not a vassal relationship. Poland is not going to ask for it, because we have the full right' (Wannat and Tamma 2021).

Upheaval and Tumult in the Public Sphere

Coercive confrontation is a type of intolerant IoPP undertaken by civil society actors. It involves violence, understood as a form of contentious claim-making which 'inflicts physical damage on persons and/or objects' (Tarrow et al. 2001: 105–107; Tilly 2003: 3). Civil society actors also undertake a*dversarial* IoPPs, a tolerant mode of engagement with populist parties which use non-coercive means of public protest observing norms of civility. In practice these types of engagement are sometimes difficult to distinguish and may be used interchangeably during a single protest. Violent forms of protest are often highly disruptive, as are some kinds of non-violent *adversarial* opposition, such as demonstrations, boycotts, civil disobedience, and strikes (Cress and Snow 2000: 1078; Andrews 2001, 74; Tarrow 2011: 101). As discussed above, c*oercive confrontation* and disruptive but non-violent forms of *adversarialism* are a form of leverage jeopardizing social peace that may force governing populist parties to *curb illiberal and anti-democratic policies*, sometimes by removing them from power.

Perhaps the best illustration of the power of disruption is the forced resignation of governing populists in the wake of large-scale anti-government protests. There are several examples. In February 2013, for example, Janez Janša's Slovenian Democratic Party was removed from power in a no-confidence vote after a wave of protests against government austerity policies engulfed the country (Fink-Hafner 2013: 221; Fink-Hafner and Krasovec 2014). Mass protests were triggered when the mayor of Malibor, Slovenia's second-largest city, introduced speed cameras in what was seen as an unscrupulous local government money-making scheme in the midst of economic crisis (Bucik 2013; Kirn 2018). Protestors occupied public spaces in largely peaceful protests, although some protests responded to police repression with violence and damage to property (Bucik 2013; Kirn 2018). Protest spread across the whole country, including to the capital Ljubljana, and was supported by trade unions in a general strike supported by some 20,000 workers in fourteen cities (Kirn 2018). Protesters mobilized resentment against the whole political class following a wave of corruption scandals, but Prime Minister Janša was a major focus of demands for a change of leadership. Responding to the 'unprecedented protests' Janša's party lost support of coalition partners (Fink-Hafner and Krasovec 2014: 281). The party subsequently lost 5.6% of its vote share (from 26.3% to 20.7% of the vote) and Janša and his party were not able to return to government again until March 2020.

In Bulgaria, the minority government of the Citizens for European Development of Bulgaria (GERB) led by Prime Minister Boyko Borissov resigned in the wake of major protests against the government in the capital Sofia and other major cities (Spirova and Sharenkova-Toshkova 2021). The protests were initially provoked by high winter energy prices but evolved into anti-government protests (Rone 2017). As Rone observes:

> The protests reached their peak on February 17 [2013] when hundreds of thousands of people mobilized in more than 35 cities throughout the country. Over 30,000 took to the streets in Varna alone … Residents of Blagoevgrad blocked the international E79 highway which caused transport chaos and a traffic jam of over 20 kilometers. People all over the country chanted slogans like 'Mafia' and 'Resignation' and there were numerous posters with messages such as 'Electricity + Unemployment = Genocide' … After provocations on the part of some protestors, the police attacked them and a number of people were injured. On the morning of February 20, the 36-year-old alpinist Plamen Goranov set himself on fire in front of the municipality of Varna, demanding the resignation of the mayor. Hours after his self-immolation, Prime Minister Boiko Borisov resigned. Even after his resignation, a wave of self-immolations followed, the number of cases from February 2013 to May 2015 reaching 30.
>
> (ibid.: 149–150; see also Drezov 2013; Kolarova and Spirova 2014)

After these events GERB saw its vote share fall by 9.2% (from 39.7% to 30.5%) and lost 19 of its 116 seats, although Borisov and the party returned to government soon afterwards. Kolarova and Spirova (2014) argue that by resigning, GERB had been able to dissociate itself from its incumbency status.

Just short of a decade later, in 2020, a new wave of large anti-government protests over corruption took place, lasting some five months. Triggered by an exposé of state favours for oligarchs, and a raid on the offices of the president, protestors began gathering in the capital Sofia every evening from July 2020 for several months in demonstrations sometimes numbering 10,000 (Oliver 2020). Protestors clashed with police, including demonstrations where protestors threw 'eggs, tomatoes, water bottles and garbage' and later rocks and fire crackers at police, with dozens of people hospitalized (Dzhambazova 2020). Demands centred on resignation of chief prosecutor Ivan Geshev and Borisov's GERB government, and there were calls for systematic changes to deal with corruption, mafia associations with power-holders, judicial reforms, and free speech (Oliver et al. 2020; Yotova 2020). The protests shook the party system, creating a long period of political instability and fuelled support for a series of new anti-corruption parties. GERB saw a dramatic loss in its vote share of 10.3% (from 32.7% in 2017 to 22.4% in November 2021, but with a slight rise in 2022 to 24.5%). GERB was not able to form a government again until 2023, even though it was the largest party after several elections.

In March 2018, protests following the murder of journalist Ján Kuciak, who was investigating allegations of fraud and corruption linked to the ruling Social Democracy – Direction (SMER-SD), led to the resignation of long-standing SMER leader and Prime Minister Robert Fico, among others (Bútorová and Bútorová 2019: 83–84, 94; Láštic 2019: 244). By various accounts 'the killings led to the biggest protests in the country since the end of communism in 1989, as tens of thousands of people demanded a government shake-up or early elections' (Bútorová and Bútorová 2019: 83–84; Lastic 2019: 348). Non-violent rallies took place in several waves, in and outside of Slovakia. Calls for the resignation of Fico, who seemed unable to 'explain how two of his closest advisors at the Office of the Government had professional and personal ties with Italian organized crime', were 'vocalized by public protest, the media and also by president Kiska, the parliamentary opposition and also junior coalition partner Most-Hid' (Lastic 2019: 2478). Although it did not initially lead to the fall of the government, SMER-SD experienced a considerable drop in mayoral seats in 2018 local elections and the SMER-SD candidate for president lost to liberal, environmental lawyer Zuzana Čaputová in the 2019 elections. In the 2020 general elections, the party lost 10% of its vote share (from 28.3% in 2016 to 18.3% in 2020) opening the way for a new OĽaNO-led government after the 2020 elections.

The effects of disruption can fall short of forcing populists from power but still be consequential. In 2014, mass protests in Hungary, described as the largest mobilization since Fidesz came to power and since the transition to democracy, led the government to abandon a proposed law taxing Internet usage (Ferrari 2019: 70–71, 75). Protesters organized on Facebook and marched in the centre of Budapest, but also targeted Fidesz party headquarters, among other things 'throwing old pieces of IT equipment—modems, routers, keyboards and even monitors against the building' (Ferrari 2019: 75). In Poland, mass protests and a women's strike under the banner of the Black Protests led, at least temporarily, to the Law and Justice government abandoning attempts to tighten abortion law in 2016 (Bielinka-Kowalewska 2017; Hall 2019; Gwiazda 2021: 589). However, when the captured Constitutional Tribunal ruled that one of three exceptions to the ban on abortion was unconstitutional, renewed mass protests from October 2020 did not prevent the 'near-total' abortion ban in Poland from coming into effect (Motak et al. 2021: 604). In the midst of July 2017 mass protests in the wake of the Law and Justice government's hastily enacted Law on the Supreme Court, the Polish President Andrzej Duda vetoed two of the three legislative pillars of the government's judicial reforms weakening the autonomy of the Polish courts (Bojarski 2021: 1373). A 'Chain of Lights' protest, beginning in front of the Supreme Court in Warsaw had grown 'into hundreds of local protests in front of the court building, grouping thousands of people throughout Poland for several days' (Bojarski 2021: 1373). An amended version of the disputed laws vetoed by the president, which dealt with the National Council of the Judiciary and Supreme Court, were passed a few months later, only to be challenged in the CJEU (see Chapter 4) (Bojarski 2021: 1373).

To conclude, this chapter has shown that leverage, understood as exploitation of mutual interdependence among states, and among citizens and governments, can be used by opponents to influence the policy choices of populist parties, particularly those in government. In the international arena, leverage theory shows how states subject to, or threatened, with *international rights-restricting* IoPPs, such as voting or financial sanctions, may *curb illiberal and anti-democratic policies* if doing so allows governing populist parties to retain benefits of cooperation. In relation to Article 7 TEU voting sanctions, or financial sanctions under EU Regulation 2020/2092, leverage theory provides insights into why in the face of democratic backsliding in Hungary and Poland *international rights-restricting* initiatives have been difficult to mobilize, and why voting sanctions are less likely to be used than financial sanctions. The liberal democratic values protected by Article 7 TEU are abstract, allowing delays and uncertainty as member states sort through obfuscating 'democratic double talk' by Fidesz and Law and Justice. New rules on financial sanctions, though, can rely on recently developed, clearer EU case law on rule of law violations. Article 7 voting sanctions fall short of expulsion but is not dissimilar to this and as Brexit showed, a contentious break is costly for the whole EU. Costs of withholding EU funds are lower, and much lower for the EU as a whole compared to net recipients like Poland and Hungary. High costs for the sanctioners—and unanimity (minus targeted state) decision rules—make the threat of Council voting sanctions less than credible, especially where Hungary and Poland have each other's back. Rules are less demanding for financial sanctions, which helps explain why they have been used against Hungary. At the same time, the EU faces strong resistance in Hungary and Poland because to meet EU liberal democratic standards, populist governments must dismantle parts of the political edifice keeping them in power.

It has also shown that in theory at least, *international rights-restricting IoPPs* may have domestic consequences, including *decreasing support for populist parties* at home if sanctions create costs for government supporters or voters, or if it empowers the opposition. These initiatives may also provide incentives for populist parties in opposition *to moderate* if sanctions heighten the cost of illiberal and anti-democratic policy stances. On the other hand, if governing parties can successfully mount a populist backlash challenging the legitimacy of international interventions, IoPPs may *boost moral resources* and *increase support for a governing populist party.*

Social leverage obtained through disruption helps us to understand how *coercive confrontation* by civil society actors and disruptive but non-violent forms of *adversarialism* may force governing populist parties to *curb illiberal and anti-democratic policies*. In some cases, mass disruptive protests have forced populist governments to drop or delay such policies, and occasionally protests have forced populist parties from power altogether.

This chapter has shown that an important way to understand how *international rights-restricting IoPPs, coercive confrontation*, and disruptive forms of adversarialism work is through the leverage, or the exploitation of mutual dependence. In the next chapter I examine how other kinds of IoPP work through persuasion.

6
Persuasion, Talk, and New Ideas

In this chapter I examine how initiatives opposing populist parties (IoPPs) work through persuasion. In a democracy, talk and new ideas are the most straightforward and arguably the most legitimate tools to oppose populist parties. They are often high on the list of proposed responses to populist parties (Mudde and Rovira Kaltwasser 2017: 118; Zielonka 2018: 116; Mounk 2018: 18, 208–214; Ziblatt and Levitsky 2018: 78). Persuasion can be challenging though. We seem to live in a 'post-truth' era, often believe what we want to hear in online 'echo chambers', and the populist style is often anti-intellectual. Talk and new ideas can fall flat, dismissed as 'fake news'. Lies and corruption can be overlooked. If it deepens suspicion of fellow citizens or foreign detractors, denigration or critique may simply increase support for populist parties or boost internal solidarity.

Despite difficulties, understanding how IoPPs work through persuasion can tell us a great deal about how those opposing populist parties may achieve their goals. Persuasion is integral for understanding how IoPPs based on *public* and *political persuasion* by, respectively, public authorities and political parties might be effective, including the effects of demonizing discourses and international dialogue. Persuasion also helps us understand additional ways in which *coercive confrontation* and *adversarial* IoPPs based on protest and dispute by civil society actors may help populists' opponents reach their goals.

As it will be recalled, I argue that IoPPs are effective if they contribute to the achievement of one or more of the goals typically pursued by opponents of populist parties without producing perverse effects. The main goals of those opposing populist parties are reducing support for populist parties among voters or sympathizers, diminishing their resources or inducing the moderation of populist parties, as well as curbing illiberal and anti-democratic policies of populist parties. Perverse effects are increasing support for populist parties, boosting their resources and radicalization.

In the first part of the chapter, I draw on theories and concepts from sociology, party politics, and the study of European integration and international relations to examine how IoPPs contribute to the achievement of opposition goals or produce perverse effects by reframing the terms of public debate, stigmatizing and shaming populist party leaders and their supporters. The sociological literature on collective action frames provides theories and concepts for understanding how persuasive IoPPs by different kinds of political actors can *reduce support for populist parties* or *curb their ability to implement illiberal and anti-democratic policies* (Benford and Snow 2000; Gamson 2007; Givan et al. 2010; Tarrow 2010, 2011; Rochon 2018). Together with the insights of resource mobilization theory discussed in previous chapters, studies on voting and party politics help us understand how stigmatizing forms of *public persuasion* by public authorities and *political persuasion* by political parties may either positively or negatively affect *support for and resources of political parties* and *induce either moderation or radicalization* (van Heerden and van der Brug 2017: 37; van Spanje and Azrout 2019; Schwörer and Fernández-García 2021: 3). Studies on international norms show how *public persuasion* by other states and international organizations may through the 'mobilization of shame' persuade governing populist parties to *curb illiberal or anti-democratic policies* or *undermine their moral resources* (Keck and Sikkink 1998; Risse and Sikkink 1999; Risse and Ropp 2013). This literature also provides concepts and theories for understanding how these international IoPPs may, on the contrary, provoke a populist backlash *increasing populist party support* or *boosting their moral resources.*

These arguments must, of necessity, draw largely from theoretical work. Empirical studies examining the effects of persuasion against populism are few and far between. Yet by weaving theoretical knowledge with a careful reading of studies on anti-populism, demonization, accounts of civil society mobilization against governing populist parties and dialogue in the EU on the rule of law, the chapter shows that persuasion can plausibly be considered one of the main tools through which the opponents of populist parties may achieve their goals.

How IoPPs Work through Persuasion

Framing and stigmatization

'Frames' are ideational constructions articulating theories about the world and how it works. They provide a framework which organizes experience and guides action, rendering some events or occurrences more meaningful than others, and in terms of collective action, mobilizing supporters and demobilizing antagonists (Benford and Snow 2000: 614). Framing theory conceives of political actors as 'signifying agents actively engaged in the production and maintenance of meaning for constituents, antagonists, and bystanders' (Benford and Snow 2000: 613; Cress and Snow 2000). As students of protest and social movements have observed, the development of 'diagnostic', 'prognostic', and 'motivational' frames which resonate with other ideas prevalent in the political community are crucial for persuading others to accept new political ideas (Benford and Snow 2000). Diagnostic framing is seen as particularly important for attaining desired outcomes because it 'problematizes and focuses attention on an issue, helps shape how the issue is perceived', and 'identifies who or what is culpable, thereby identifying the targets or sources of the outcomes sought' (ibid.: 617). Prognostic framing 'stipulates specific remedies or goals' which political actors work towards as well as 'the means or tactics for achieving these objectives' (ibid.). Motivational framing 'provides a "call to arms" or rationale for engaging in ameliorative collective action, including the construction of appropriate vocabularies of motive' (ibid.).

Such frames will be effective if they are 'resonant', or in other words credible and salient (ibid.: 620). Credible frames are *consistent* (there is a congruence between articulated beliefs, claims, and actions); *empirically credible* (adherents believe there is a 'fit between the framings and the events in the world'); and are articulated by *speakers credible to adherents* (due to 'status and/or perceived expertise ... and/or the organizations they represent') (ibid.: 620–621). Frames are salient if they are *central* to the beliefs, values, and ideas of those they are addressed to; are *experientially commensurate* (congruent 'with the personal, everyday experiences of those they are addressed to'); and have *narrative fidelity* (resonate with the 'extant [but evolving] stock of meanings, beliefs, ideological, practices, values, myths, narratives' within a community) (ibid.: 622, 629; Gamson 2007: 254–256).

The diffusion of new frames may alter the way people think about a particular topic and potentially their values and behaviour (Rochon 2018). New frames can be *directly* 'transmitted through interpersonal contacts, organizational linkages or networks' which facilitate learning, borrowing and adaptation of new ideas (Givan et al. 2010: 2; Tarrow 2010, 2011: 192–193). Relational diffusion of this type may change behaviour when others 'emulate' actions they learn from those with whom they have 'preexisting relationships of trust, intimacy or regular communication' (Tarrow 2010: 209). *Indirect* forms of diffusion are channelled through the traditional mass media and online communication networks. They may alter behaviour through 'demonstration effects', whereby people exposed to new ways of interpreting the world 'imitate' the actions of others who seem to be similar to them or to be experiencing similar things (Givan et al. 2010; Tarrow 2010).

The role of media organizations in the diffusion of new frames often make them important allies for those opposing populist parties. Indeed, as Gamson argues 'the mass media arena is *the* major site of contests over meaning because the players in the policy process *assume* its pervasive influence— whether it is justified or not' (2007: 243; see also Koopmans 2005). By supplying the 'oxygen of publicity', media attention can attract 'sympathy, support, and goodwill' from bystanders (Gamson 2007: 249). In addition, media attention sometimes 'creates power' giving certain political actors 'standing' because '[b]eing visible and quoted defines for other journalists and a broader public who really matters' (ibid.: 251).

Widely disseminated and resonant frames may help all kinds of political actors opposing populist parties to achieve their goals, including those articulated through *public persuasion* by public authorities and *political persuasion* by political parties. However, they are particularly important for understanding how civil society actors, through *coercive confrontation* and *adversarial* IoPPs may do so. Over and above the ability to build alliances (see Chapter 4) and the exploitation of the leverage that disruption may give (see Chapter 5), the diffusion of new frames is one of the most important ways for civil society actors to achieve their goals (e.g., Benford and Snow 2000; Gamson 2007; Tarrow 2010 and 2011). This is especially so for civil society groups, such as social movements, whose capacity to 'realize their general aims has been considered low', not least because they typically 'dwarf' states and political parties 'in terms of size, resources, and power' (della Porta and Diani 2006: 239; Amenta and Caren 2007: 462). Through the kinds of protest actions typical of *coercive confrontational* and *adversarial* IoPPs, civil society actors can send signals, or communicate a 'particular kind of information about urgent societal problems' to elites (Hutter and Vliegenthart 2018; Hutter, Kriesi, and Lorenzini 2018: 237). The signal sent is more likely to be heard—and receive media attention—if it is articulated in large protests, involves authoritative or famous people, and using tactics that are spectacular, novel, disruptive, conflictual, and/or violent (Gamson and Meyer 1996; Taylor and van Dyke 2007; Rucht 2013: 257–258; Roggeband and Klandermans 2017: 187–190). Technological advances permit activists to address the public in a manner which is faster, targeting larger audiences and over longer distances. They may also permit activists to circumvent 'the filters and biases inherent to conventional and mostly commercially-oriented mass media ... [with] journalists as gatekeepers' (Rucht 2013: 261–263).

All kinds of opponents able to disseminate resonant critical frames *may reduce support for populist parties* if they can change public preferences, or perceptions of the pros and cons of an issue, or its perceived salience (Giugni

2004: 191). Civil society actors may be able to do this directly or by changing the perception of other powerful actors such as political parties or governing elites on the question of what the public wants (Burstein 1999). Less organized online interactions that reach viral circulation 'may also shape public opinion, or at least issue salience as a component of public opinion' (Earl 2016: 386). Over the longer term, civil society and other actors can help change cultural values, as the long history of campaigns on issues such as slavery; race, gender, and sexuality; peace and war; climate change; and immigration attest (Earl 2003; Rochon 2018). As Rochon has observed, cultural changes such as these may take place in different domains: At the level of shared beliefs, values, and meanings held by individuals; the web of symbols, and the meanings they signify in language, rituals, and institutional rules; and broader social identities encompassing world views, social practices, and beliefs of entire communities (2018, see also Earl 2003: 510).

If they can change public opinion, opponents may alter the policy agendas of governing populist parties and so *curb implementation of illiberal or antidemocratic politics*. In a democracy, as various authors observe, governments will 'often do what their citizens want, and they are especially likely to do so when an issue is important to the public and its wishes are clear' (Burstein 1999: 15; Burstein and Linton 2002; Giugni 2004: 189, 198–213, 228). Even in hybrid democracies, where democratic quality is lower than in consolidated democracies, governing populist parties must remain responsive to public opinion if they are to stay in power beyond the next election (Levitsky and Way 2010).

Civil society actors may be able to make governing elites accommodate their demands if they can persuade those with institutional positions of authority to 'see some benefit in aiding the group the challenger represents' (Amenta 2005: 31; Amenta and Caren 2007: 473). As Amenta and co-authors argue, governing elected officials and state bureaucrats may be persuaded to accommodate the demands of civil society groups if they 'see a challenger as potentially facilitating or disrupting their own goals' (see Amenta 2005; Amenta and Caren 2007: 473). Relevant goals include 'improving electoral prospects by augmenting or cementing new electoral coalitions or gaining in public opinion, acting on political beliefs, and increasing support for missions of governmental bureaucrats, among others' (Amenta 2005: 31; Amenta and Caren 2007: 473). Different strategies may be more effective in different contexts: 'If the political regime is supportive and the domestic bureaucrats are professionalized and supportive, limited protest based mainly on evidence of mobilization is likely to be sufficient' to influence public policy (Amenta and Caren 2007: 474). In this context, '[m]embers of a reform-oriented regime are likely to use the evidence of mobilization and modest protest as a confirmation of the beneficiary group's relative importance in an electoral coalition', while '[d]omestic bureaucrats are likely to portray the mobilization as indicating the need for the augmentation or greater enforcement of its program' (ibid.). On the other hand, influencing 'public policy is likely to be more difficult if neither a supportive regime nor administrative authority exists' (ibid.). In this context, 'limited protest ... [is] likely to be ignored or have a limited effect' (ibid.).

The adoption of stigmatizing frames is a discursive strategy often deployed in the polarized political environments typically inhabited by populist parties. As Irvin Goffman (1963) argued in his seminal work on the topic, stigma creates 'spoiled' identities. Stigma is a 'deeply discrediting' attribute, whereby individuals or groups are 'disqualified from full social acceptance' (ibid.: 9, 13). Various scholars working on stigmatization in the form of demonizing discourses have argued that stigmatizion may *reduce support for political parties, diminish their resources*, and *induce moderation* (van Heerden and van der Brug 2017: 37; van Spanje and Azrout 2019; Schwörer and Fernández-García 2021: 3). Demonizing discourses frame a political actor as the personification of evil and aim to persuade others that a group is 'abnormal' and 'dangerous' (van Heerden and van der Brug 2017; van Spanje and Azrout 2019: 288–290; Schwörer and Fernández-García 2021). In the twenty-first century labelling a party as Nazi, fascist, racist, or anti-Semitic is widely seen as a form of demonization, though it is a matter of debate whether labelling a party as populist is also a form of demonization (compare van Heerden and van der Brug 2017: 37; van Spanje and Azrout 2019: 293–294 with Stavrakakis 2014, 2018; Miró 2019; Hamdaoui 2021a, 2021b). As Boykoff points out, there can also be 'bi-level demonization' which links 'dissidents to a demonized group or individual from the international arena' (2007: 293). In this type of demonization, an 'external foe is depicted as deserving of punishment, and the linking of domestic dissidents to the external demon ... makes the domestic dissident more vulnerable to state repression' (ibid.).

In a society where democratic principles are valued, stigmatizing frames demonizing a party *may reduce its support* by creating doubts about its democratic credentials. As van Heerden and van der Brug argue, stigmatizing frames are a form of negative campaigning signalling that the targeted 'party must be regarded as a dangerous political outcast that threatens democracy' (2017: 37). In other words, a party's electoral attractiveness may decline because when 'a party is labelled "neo-Nazi" or "fascist," its viability as an option in a democracy is clearly in question' (van Spanje and Azrout 2019: 291).

Stigmatizing frames are, arguably, specifically designed to *diminish a party's moral resources*, or legitimacy, which may in turn, affect a party's ability to get media coverage, generate public attention, or access influential allies or other resources (Edwards et al. 2018). Stigmatizing frames may also *diminish a party's human resources* insofar as they increase social or material costs for individuals or groups associating with the party (Klandermans 1984: 586; McCarthy and Zald 2002: 536). Stigmatization can also undermine a *party's material resources* if it is difficult to attract members and supporters able to make substantial financial donations (Art 2007: 341, 344). Stigmatization thus makes social actors 'appear less respectable and less viable, and therefore less worthy of support' (Boykoff 2007: 297). It challenges 'solidarity maintenance efforts, complicates recruitment, and makes the mobilization of support from bystander publics much more difficult' (ibid.). It may also put a group 'on the defensive, on the ever-unfolding path of self-explanation, justificatory back-tracking, and damage control' (ibid.).

Negative effects of stigmatization on party support and organizational resources may, in turn, provide *incentives for moderation* to 'overcome the stigma relation' (ibid.). This can include 'channelling' forms of mobilization into more moderate action repertoire (Earl 2003; Davenport 2004; Tilly 2004; Boykoff 2007; Davenport 2007; Earl 2011). It may also prompt those targeted by stigmatizing frames to moderate ideologically through what has sometimes been called 'de-demonization' strategies (e.g., Ivaldi 2016). As Ignazi has observed, radicals have strong incentives to at least pay 'homage' to democratic rules in order to 'avoid stigmatization from other political actors and from the public at large' (2003: 200). This is not only because 'democracy is almost universally accepted as an ideal type of regime', but also because it allows them to 'exploit the rules of the game to their own advantage' (ibid.).

Efforts to persuade populist parties or their supporters through stigmatization may misfire though. Negative forms of *public* and *political persuasion*, where public authorities and political parties label populists or their supporters as 'Nazis' or 'fascists'—or in the case of US presidential candidate Hilary Clinton's infamous misstep, 'a basket of deplorables'—may *increase support for populist parties* by reinforcing the anti-elitism central to populist appeals. Likewise, *coercive confrontation* and *adversarial* IoPPs by civil society actors mobilizing stigmatizing frames may reinforce anti-elitist appeals, especially if populists can effectively use counter-frames presenting opponents as political or cultural 'enemies' (such as 'liberal cosmopolitan elites', or 'cultural Marxists'). As Rovira Kaltwasser has argued, when populists' 'opponents are tempted to use moral language, and present themselves as the "good democrats" and portray the populists as "bad autocrats" … populist forces might become stronger, since they will have proof that the establishment acts in an arrogant manner and has no interest in considering the demands that are allegedly being raised by the people' (2019: 89). Stigmatizing frames used in media campaigns may help create a unifying 'underdog mythology of being prosecuted by powerful media elites' (Fallend and Heinisch 2016: 332). Like repressive IoPPs discussed in Chapter 4, stigmatizing frames may inadvertently *bolster organizational resources* by creating a unifying sense that the party and its supporters are a 'community under siege' (Levite and Tarrow 1983: 298; Zúquete 2007: 36–47), or produce 'sectarian closure' (Levite and Tarrow 1983). It may also sharpen a sense of injury and victimhood among supporters, adding to a sense of distance from, and distrust of, the political mainstream (van Spanje and van der Brug 2007: 1023; Fallend and Heinisch 2016: 332; Rovira Kaltwasser 2019: 89). In these ways, stigmatizing frames *may induce radicalization* if it provides reasons for supporters to 'retreat and go underground', opening the possibility that 'the apathetic become politicized, the reformers become radicalized, and the revolutionaries redouble their efforts' (Lichbach 1987: 269; Davenport 2004; Tilly 2004; Koopmans 2005: 159; van Donselaar 2017).

Shaming and negotiations abroad

Especially since the end of the Cold War, the idea that legitimate rule is linked to basic human rights provisions and at least minimally to the occurrence of regular, reasonably free elections to select political leaders has become widespread (Levitsky and Way 2010; Bermeo 2016; Levitsky and Way 2020). To be sure, appeals to such international democracy norms have often been shallow, inconsistent, and are now increasingly shaky as the liberal international order falters (Diamond 2015: 151; Levitsky and Way 2020; Sajó 2021: 198–204). Yet, honouring democracy norms is still seen as a requirement for accessing some benefits of international cooperation. In Europe, the EU and Council of Europe are focal points of a dense set of rules and institutions which regulate, monitor, interpret, and enforce international agreements promoting liberal democracy and human rights. Over time, the EU has sought to build an international identity as a community of liberal democracies, even as a decades-long debate about the EU's democratic deficit makes it rather easy to pick holes in the EU's self-presentation as a bastion of liberal democracy.

As discussed in the previous chapter, 'material' leverage such as EU voting sanctions limiting access to the benefits of international cooperation and financial sanctions limiting EU budget receipts can, under certain conditions, be used to promote international democracy norms and pressure states to curb illiberal and anti-democratic policies. What various scholars have called 'moral' or 'social' leverage provides an alternative way to achieve these goals (Keck and Sikkink 1998; Risse and Sikkink 1999; Risse and Ropp 2013; Friman 2015). While material leverage works through rational calculations, incentives, costs and benefits, moral or social leverage involves 'mobilization of shame' (Keck and Sikkink 1998: 23–24; Risse and Ropp 2013: 12, 20–21). The mobilization of shame works by holding norm-violating behaviour up to the light of international scrutiny and showing a gap between commitments and practice. Shaming works through a 'process of persuasion, since it convinces leaders that their behaviour is inconsistent with an identity to which they aspire' (Risse and Sikkink 1999: 13, 15). It 'constructs categories of "us" and "them"', reaffirming the identities of an in-group, but denouncing an out-group of '[n]orm violating states … as pariah states which do not belong to the "civilized community" of states' (ibid.: 8, 13, 15). The effectiveness of social leverage clearly depends on whether the targets of shaming value 'the good opinion of others', 'aspire to belong to a normative community of nations', and are 'trying to raise their status in the international system' (Keck and Sikkink 1998: 23–24; Risse and Ropp 2013: 20–21).

Even when these conditions are not fully met, shaming may lead to a form of 'rhetorical entrapment', which occurs where a government's public commitments to an international norm 'opens space' for others 'to catch the government in its own rhetoric', such that it 'becomes very hard for the government to deny the validity of human rights norms' (Risse and Sikkink 1999: 15). Even where governments adapt to international norms for instrumental reasons, the 'more they "talk the talk" … the more they entangle themselves in a moral discourse which they cannot escape in the long run' (ibid.). That is, where opponents challenge a government's arguments and validity claims regarding adherence to an international norm, governments may find they 'become entangled in … the logic of argumentative rationality [which] slowly but surely takes over' (ibid.).

Importantly, even where political actors 'accept the validity and significance of norms in their discursive practices', they may still disagree about 'whether certain behaviour is covered by a norm' (ibid.: 13). When this occurs, 'principled beliefs' embedded in international norms may 'carry the day when they persuade actors in potentially winning coalitions to interpret their material and political interests and preferences in light of the idea and to accept its social obligations as appropriate' (ibid.: 14). 'Winning coalitions' in this context are formed through 'argumentative consensus', and when '[p]eople become convinced and persuaded to change their instrumental interests, or to see their interests in new ways, following the principled ideas' (ibid.: 14). As Risse and Ropp argue, 'arguing, persuasion and learning' have 'an advantage over coercion or the manipulation of incentive structures in that it induces actors into voluntary compliance with costly rules' and is 'longer-lasting' (2013: 14). Over time, international norms may become 'internalized', becoming taken-for-granted 'standard operating procedure' (Risse and Sikkink 1999: 16–17).

It could be argued that governing European populist parties are relatively vulnerable to processes of 'rhetorical entrapment' when challenged by international actors. This is because the 'ideology of democracy' is so central to populist claim-making (Canovan 2002: 38); so much so that even populist-run competitive authoritarian regimes seek to maintain a democratic façade (Levitsky and Way 2010; Scheppele 2018). As Risse and Sikkink observe, it may be difficult for all but the most closed authoritarian regimes to dismiss international interventions out of hand: Refusals to comply with human rights norms, for instance, 'almost never take the form of an open rejection of human rights, but is mostly expressed in terms of reference to an allegedly more valid international norm, [such as] national sovereignty' (1999: 24). When confronted by international criticisms about democratic standards, populist elites may thus find themselves under pressure to enter into dialogue with opposition groups about the meaning of democracy, thereby (re)igniting the broader 'ideological contest between populist and liberal understandings of democracy' (Canovan 2002: 38). Indeed, as various scholars have hinted, international democracy norms may be part of the reason why many populist-led, and even semi-authoritarian states take pains to present themselves as law-abiding democrats (Scheppele 2013; Bermeo 2016: 15; (Scheppele 2018; Lührmann, Tannenberg, and Lindberg 2018: 1108; Sajó 2021).

Of course, these claims must be carefully made. The pressures and incentives favouring the emergence of new democracies have always been inconsistent, selective, and sometimes superficial. Large, rich, and militarily powerful states—such as the USA, China, and Russia—have always been harder to persuade (Levitsky and Way 2010: 41; Risse and Ropp 2013: 20). Other interests often trump democratic norms. A state's strategic location, valued security and economic relationships, or their control of vital natural resources, may shield them from pressure to democratize. In addition, states like China and Russia appear to be actively 'pushing back against democratic norms' using the 'soft power' of international media, educational institutes, and exchange programmes (Diamond 2015: 151).

The effectiveness of pressure to adopt international norms is likely to be higher in democracies than autocracies (Risse and Sikkink 1999: 289; Risse and Ropp 2013: 17). In established democracies, as Risse and Ropp argue in relation to international human rights norms, respect for such norms 'constitutes an institutionalized logic of appropriateness' (2013: 17). Democracies also commit fewer human rights violations and so when challenged, the costs of adapting to international norms are lower. Similarly, as Sedelmeier has argued in relation to EU appeals to international democracy norms, dialogue with member states is more likely to be effective when the act of accommodating EU positions has low adaptation costs which don't threaten an incumbent's hold on power (2017: 344). Dialogue relating to international democracy norms is also likely to be more effective when EU interlocutors are considered legitimate, or when support for the EU is high enough among the public and the main political parties to counteract a domestic backlash (2017: 344).

Furthermore, as Risse and Sikkink observe, a core difference between the responsiveness of democracies and authoritarian regimes to international norms is that 'domestic mobilization' of the kind permitted in a democracy can more effectively create pressure for change at home (1999: 288). International initiatives promoting democracy norms may thus empower domestic opponents in various ways, helping them *curb illiberal and anti-democratic policies of governing populist parties* from below. Publicity given to the claims of populist opponents by international IoPPs—like analogous cases of new international human rights treaties or judgments by international courts—may increase the salience of the issues raised and help keep them on the political agenda at home (Keohane et al. 2000: 467; Simmons 2009: 134). Similarly, international IoPPs, such as joint statements by the leaders of liberal democratic states, may help 'authenticate' the claims of opponents criticizing the government (Finnemore and Sikkink 1998: 893; Simmons 2009: 4, 130, 147). Where governments have been able to limit access to negative information, international IoPPs such as publicized statements by international democracy monitoring bodies, transnational advocacy coalitions, the European Parliament, or other states, may provide alternative, authoritative sources of information. During the EU enlargement process, as Vachudova has argued, authoritative voices from the EU helped rebalance 'information asymmetries', thereby 'circumvent[ing] attempts by the government to monopolise information', and under some conditions helped 'opposition actors to make a stronger case against the illiberal rulers' (2005: 139, 164; see also Earl 2016). Currently, the role of international actors in rebalancing information asymmetries may take on a new significance where populist-led governments have limited media freedoms, which according to the World Press Freedom Index (2021) includes governments led by Fidesz in Hungary and Law and Justice in Poland. As Simmons has argued, governments that fail to meet their publicly ratified commitments may face 'inconsistency costs', which 'risk loss of a degree of domestic legitimacy' or *moral resources*, and which may, under certain conditions, '*erode their domestic support*' (my italics 2009: 145).

Similarly, collaboration within transnational advocacy coalitions may help tilt the balance of influence in the direction of national oppositions, NGOs, and social movements with limited political influence at home. Transnational advocacy coalitions allow domestic oppositions to tap into a broader network's 'access, leverage and information (and often money)' (Keck and Sikkink 1998: 12–13; Risse and Sikkink 1999: 18, 25). Activists create and participate in transnational networks because they believe it will 'further their organizational missions—by sharing information, attaining greater visibility, gaining access to wider publics, multiplying channels of institutional access' (Keck and Sikkink 1998: 14, 25). Through participation in transnational advocacy networks in the field of human rights, for instance, opposition groups may be able to 'convince international human rights organizations, donor institutions and/or great powers to pressure norm-violating states' (Risse and Sikkink 1999: 18). In this way, 'international contacts can amplify the demands of domestic groups, pry open space for new issues and then echo these demands back to the domestic arena' (Keck and Sikkink 1998: 13; Risse and Sikkink 1999: 18, 25). It may also add to what Tarrow, Tilly, and McAdam call 'certification' or the selective 'validation of actors, their performances and claims by external actors', seen as necessary for a political actor's very 'rights to exist, act, make claims and/or draw routinely on government-controlled resources' (2011: 146).

On the other hand, *public persuasion* by other states, international organizations, or transnational NGOs may provoke a 'populist backlash' which *increases support for populist parties*. As discussed above, where international actors criticize a state government, they will often be met by 'sovereignty counter-discourses', insisting that international norms invoked are incompatible with domestic norms (Risse and Ropp 2013: 21; Risse and Sikkink 2013: 290–291). Such sovereignty counter-discourses easily resonate with populist appeals to the sovereignty of the people, claiming international initiatives are an 'illegitimate intervention in the internal affairs of the country' and opposing the 'suggestion that its national practices in this area are subject to international jurisdiction' (Risse and Sikkink 1999: 223; Bermeo 2016: 15–16). Appeals to the illegitimacy of international IoPPs can easily be expressed through the populist juxtaposition of 'the pure people' and 'corrupt elite', with the latter often turned outwards to incorporate international actors (Heinisch and Mazzoleni 2017: 108; Schlipphak and Treib 2017: 355).

Defending Democracy, the Anti-Populist Frame, and Demonization

Public persuasion by authorities such as heads of state, prime ministers, or government officials, and *political persuasion* by political parties, is speech or symbolic action aiming to persuade populist parties and their supporters to change their views or behaviour. *Coercive confrontation* and *adversarial* IoPPs by civil society actors may also pursue such goals. *Coercive confrontation* includes acts such as war or insurgency, which primarily pursue goals through physical force, but political violence is also an act of communication symbolically conveying meaning with the aim of changing the views or behaviour of targets and bystanders. *Adversarial* IoPPs, a tolerant mode of engagement with populist parties, uses non-coercive means of public protest in the form of speech and symbolic actions to the same ends.

Polarizing explicitly 'anti-populist' frames provide a potent illustration of these persuasive IoPPs. As Stavrakakis and others have argued, anti-populism is a rhetorical strategy generating a caricature of the populist as the 'enemy' and which seeks to delegitimize, discredit, stigmatize, and demonize populists (2018; 53, see also Stavrakakis 2014; Miró 2019; Hamdaoui 2021a, 2021b). In other words, anti-populism defines populism as abnormal or deviant, typically with reference to a reified conception of the liberal democratic status quo and European integration. Anti-populism has been described as a defining mode of opposition to populist parties in Greece, deployed by representatives of public authorities both at home and abroad, and other Greek political parties and civil society actors such as journalists and academics (Stavrakakis 2014, 2018; see also Tsatsanis 2021). Primary targets were the left-wing Coalition of the Radical Left (SYRIZA) and the right-wing Independent Greeks, both of which rose to prominence following the 2010 economic crisis and later jointly led the government between 2015 and 2019 (ibid.). Miró (2019) has observed that anti-populist discourses and similar processes of demonization and delegitimization by leading public figures, political parties, and civil society actors like the mass media accompanied the rise of Podemos in Spain. In Italy, the Sardine, a social movement emerging in 2019 and principally mobilizing against Matteo Salvini's League, explicitly positioned itself as an anti-populist movement (Caruso and De Blasio 2021; Hamdaoui 2021a).

As discussed above, initiatives opposing populist parties through persuasion may *decrease support for populist parties* if the diffusion of resonant critical ideational frames turns public opinion against a populist party or decreases the salience of their signature policies. More specifically, critical frames may do this if they present populists as a political problem, or the cause of, rather than the cure for, social ills (diagnostic framing); specify alternative and more attractive strategies to deal with these problems (prognostic framing); and articulate attractive identities for those who take a stand against populist parties (motivational framing). In addition, plausible signs that public opinion is turning against them may lead governing populist parties to accommodate those opposing them *by curbing illiberal and anti-democratic policies*. In addition, stigmatizing frames, such as demonizing discourses, may *reduce support for a populist party* by creating doubts about its democratic credentials, *diminish party moral, human, and material resources* by making support for the party unattractive, and thereby *create incentives for moderation*. Alternatively, stigmatizing frames *may increase support for populist parties* by reinforcing anti-elitist appeals, *boost resources* by strengthening a sense of common identity against an external foe, or provide *incentives for radicalization* by fostering a sense of separation from the political mainstream.

Several studies on anti-populist frames show they contain the above-mentioned elements of effective ideational frames. In the context of the 2010 financial crisis and deep economic recession in Greece, for example, anti-populist *diagnostic frames* portrayed populists as 'the greatest enemy of Greece', as 'plague' and 'havoc', as actors 'turning people against themselves' and threatening to turn the Greek economic crisis into 'national tragedy' (Stavrakakis 2014: 509). In the press, populists were commonly described with adjectives such as 'extreme, vulgar, dangerous, cheap, fanatical, clientelist, catastrophic, unbearable, lumpen, irresponsible, savage, total, unscrupulous' (Stavrakakis 2018: 54). In Spain, as Miró argues, anti-populist frames branded Podemos as, among other things, 'lepenists', 'dangerous for democracy', 'full of freaks', and a 'threat to the Welfare State' (2019: 121). A long list of senior political figures depicted the party as a 'peril to Spain', as harbouring 'autocratic temptations', and in some cases of being linked to the Basque nationalist terrorist group Euskadi Ta Askatasuna (ibid.). Spanish

Socialist Workers Party Prime Minister Pedro Sánchez, which later governed with Podemos, previously rejected pacts with the party, claiming Podemos' 'populism was rooted in Venezuela, which meant a path towards "rationing lists, a lack of democracy, and greater inequality"' (ibid.).

Anti-populist *prognostic frames* typically contrasted supposedly 'moderate', 'professional', or 'rational' personnel running existing national and international bodies with 'incompetent', 'simplistic', and 'extremist' populists (Stavrakakis 2014; Ostiguy 2017; Moffitt 2018; Stavrakakis 2018; Hamdaoui 2021a, 2021b). At its most extreme, as Stavrakakis argues for Greece, anti-populists downgraded populists to 'subhumans, to bare life: cavemen, Neanderthals and troglodytes' (2014: 510). In a similar vein Hamdaoui observed that anti-populists claimed 'populist leaders are incompetent or malignant demagogues that will lead countries to disaster by implementing oversimplistic measures and granting too much decision-making power to laypersons. Indeed, for anti-populists, political and economic issues are too intricate and should be handled by experts rather than the common people or "unprepared" populist leaders' (Hamdaoui 2021a).

Anti-populist *motivational* frames appealed to pro-European identities, often defining populism as a threat to the claimed achievements of the whole postwar European project in terms of peace, democracy, and human rights (Stavrakakis 2014: 510). Anti-populism has also been linked to political and social identities. As Moffit and Ostiguy have argued, anti-populism denigrates populist style, or 'ways of being or acting politically', as 'uncivilised' (Moffitt 2016, 2018; Ostiguy 2017: 79). Similarly, Hamdaoui observes a 'stylistic anti-populism' defined as a self-conscious performance of 'codes, behaviour, mannerisms and a specific rhetoric', 'made of formal and pro-institutional language' and 'a technical or intellectual approach to politics' which 'encourages respect towards political elites and favours composure over exuberance' (Hamdaoui 2021a: 2).

More detailed research is needed on the effects of anti-populist frames for party support and adoption of illiberal and anti-democratic policies by governing populists. Nevertheless, specialists in the field have suggested that by 'vilifying the opponent and reducing them to the "inferior" other', anti-populism may *reduce support for populist parties* because it 'strip[s] them of any morally redeemable quality in the contest of electoral politics' (Stavrakakis 2018: 53). It may also do so by 'reformulating existing social identities' and 'perceived interests' (Miró 2019: 117). Specialists have observed broader implications of anti-populist frames: Stavrakakis, for example, argued that by discrediting and denouncing 'whoever diverges from the dominant neoliberal administration of the crisis' as an 'irresponsible populist, an enemy of European values', anti-populism 'sabotaged' egalitarian political projects of the left and helped usher in an era of austerity politics (2014: 508–509; Stavrakakis 2018: 52). Similarly, Miró argued that in Spain after the financial crisis, 'anti-populism appeared as a master political logic, which, in a two-fold move, delegitimized ... anti-austerity demands as being populist while at the same time consolidating the precrisis neoliberal model of development' (2019: 128).

We know more about the effects of demonizing frames targeting radical right populists. More-or-less overt links to the fascist past marginalized the extreme right in Europe for decades after the Second World War (Kitschelt and McGann 1997; Ignazi 2003; Rydgren 2007). Despite the apparent rejection of biological theories of racism and overt anti-democratic positions by most of the contemporary radical right (ibid.), several studies show that demonizating frames denigrating the radical right as Nazis, fascists, or racists *reduced support for radical right populist parties* by *undermining moral resources*, or legitimacy. Van Heeden and van der Brug's research on demonization of the Dutch Freedom Party (PVV), showed that demonization produced a loss of votes when the party emerged (2017: 43). They also observe that demonizing frames become less effective over time, especially after a boost in party legitimacy obtained through cooperation with a governing coalition of mainstream parties (ibid.). As the authors explain, this may be because 'political newcomers are most vulnerable to elite cues suggesting that a party is legitimate', but also because 'it becomes harder for the political establishment to convincingly dismiss the party leadership as Nazis' when 'the party has attracted a loyal core of supporters', 'party officials have become entrenched in legislative bodies', and when 'the political establishment has already cooperated with [it]' (ibid.: 38). In another study on the PVV, van Spanje and Azrout show that for those holding anti-immigrant attitudes, exposure to demonizing frames reported in the media 'lowered voters' perceived legitimacy of the PVV', which in turn, 'decreased their propensity to vote for that party' (2019: 283, 297). The study suggested that demonization might be particularly successful in undermining party legitimacy and thus voter support where voters were 'in two minds' about a party (ibid.: 288). That is, demonizing frames were likely to be more successful in relation to those who may support a radical right populist party's opposition to immigration but 'subscribe to anti-prejudice, pro-democracy and anti-violence norms, deeming e.g., neo-Nazism and fascism unacceptable' (ibid. 2019: 288).

Elsewhere, mobilization around critical pro-democracy and related anti-corruption frames helped shift public opinion in a way that not only *reduced support for governing populists* but ended in their downfall. In Slovakia, for example, the murder of journalist Ján Kuciak led to protests by a group of young activists under the slogan 'For a Decent Slovakia' (Bútorová and Bútora 2019: 83–84, 94; Láštic 2019: 348). Kuciak had been investigating allegations of fraud and corruption linked to the ruling Social Democracy – Direction (SMER) party, and the scandal led to the resignation of long-standing party leader Robert Fico as prime minister in 2018 (Bútorová and Bútora 2019: 83–84, 94). Support for the party plummeted from 28.3% to 18.3% when SMER faced the electorate in 2020, leading to a doubling of support for the anti-corruption Ordinary People and Independent Personalities (OĽaNO), whose leader soon formed a new government.

In Bulgaria, a corruption scandal involving state favours for oligarchs, and a raid on the offices of the presidency, triggered large protests demanding the resignation of the government led by Boris Boyko's Citizens for the European Development of Bulgaria (GERB). In addition to calling for judicial reforms and free speech, protestors framed both governmental and broader system change as the solution to deal with corruption (Oliver, von der Burchard, and de la Baume 2020; Yotova 2020). GERB was forced out of government in 2021. Three successive election campaigns in that year centred on the issue of corruption. GERB lost many votes, falling from 32.7% votes and 95 seats in 2017 to 22.4% votes and 59 seats in November 2021, although started to recover again in 2022 and 2023 elections.

In October 2021, Andrej Babiš' Action of Dissatisfied Citizens (ANO) party was forced from government by a self-styled 'democratic bloc' of opposition parties in a campaign airing the various corruption scandals dogging the billionaire prime minister (Euronews 2021a; Hutt 2021). A European Commission audit on agricultural subsidies found Babiš had breached conflict of interest laws through his control of agri-food conglomerate Agrofert, a company to which Babiš had allocated EU funds. In addition, the Pandora Papers, produced by an international consortium of journalists, alleged just before the 2021 elections that Babiš had deposited money in a secret shell company to buy a €19 million chateau in France (Euronews 2021b; Mortkowitz 2021). ANO's small 2.5% loss in vote share and its six fewer parliamentary seats allowed opposition parties to form a new government. Although Babiš was later acquitted of alleged EU subsidies fraud by a Czech court in 2023, a planned political comeback in presidential elections of that year did not succeed (Preussen 2023).

It is also worth briefly mentioning other prominent examples of civil society mobilization deploying pro-democracy frames against populist governments, even though outcomes of mobilization are less clear. Indeed, the profound ambiguity of populist orientation to democracy noted in Chapter 1 makes claims and counterclaims about democratic credentials a field ripe for 'framing contests'. In Poland, a movement organizing under the banner of the Committee for Defence of Democracy (KOD) emerged soon after Law and Justice (PiS) won power in 2015. Triggered by new laws on the Constitutional Court, a new appointment system for positions in public television and radio, and police reforms, KOD was behind the organization of mass protests all over the country on these and other issues such as new abortion legislation and women's rights (Karolewski 2016: 259; Bielinka-Kowalewska 2017; Hall 2019; Bojarski 2021). Political parties, such as the main centre-left opposition party Civic Platform, actively participated in the movement and its activities (Karolewski 2016: 260). KOD deployed a *diagnostic frame* defining its goal as a 'struggle against an authoritarian government which [sic] main goal is to demolish democracy in Poland' (ibid.: 261). Rejecting PiS's claimed democratic credentials, KOD described the government as 'Polish authoritarianism with a democratic window-dressing' and attacked it with slogans such as 'demokratura' and 'portmanteau of democracy' (ibid.). As the movement's name hints, KOD deployed a *prognostic frame* calling for restoration of Polish democracy, claiming for itself the role of representing 'the true will of the people' (ibid.). *Motivational frames* emphasized attractive identities such as the movement's affinity with the communist-era resistance movement, and by pursuing alliances and support from EU institutions, an affinity with Poles' strongly pro-European identities (ibid.)

Along with other organizations and groups, KOD became an important focal point of opposition to PiS. This and other opposition activity did not make a serious dent in PiS electoral support. Nevertheless, as mentioned in Chapter 4, disruptive mass protests organized by KOD on abortion laws and some judicial reforms *curbed the ability of populist parties to implement illiberal and arguably anti-democratic policies*, at least temporarily (Bielinka-Kowalewska 2017; Hall 2019; Bojarski 2021; Gwiazda 2021: 589; Ilonszki and Dudzińska 2021: 611). More generally, commentators argued that KOD and other pro-democracy groups have played a 'key role in the rebirth of the culture of protest in Poland', an achievement 'with no parallel over the preceding 20 years' (Karolewski 2016: 264; Bielinka-Kowalewska 2017: 4, 6–7). It has provided formative experiences for new generations, building new identities (Hall 2019: 1497; Radiukiewicz 2019: 367), and as some have argued, developed an internationalization strategy helping legitimize interventions by international actors such as the EU (Karolewski 2016: 259–263; Closa 2021: 8; Bojarski 2021).

In Hungary, civil society mobilization has been progressively constrained by increasing cooptation of civil society by Fidesz, as well as actions undermining critical organizations (Molnár 2016; Ilonszki and Dudzińska 2021). Yet civil society opponents have not stood still, intermittently organizing anti-government protests around controversial new laws. Results have been mixed but have not made a dent in the high level of support for Fidesz in the country. Large anti-government protests included a 2011 trade-union led movement of servicemen and women linking loss of early retirement benefits to calls for 'a restoration of rule of law and democratic government' (Hungarian Social Movement) (Boris and Vári 2015: 184); large protests under the banner of press freedom against a new media law in 2012 (Milla) (Petócz 2015); and student-led protests against education budget cuts in 2012 with slogans including 'Free country, Free university' (HaHa) (Zontea 2015). A successful 2014 Internet tax movement employing mass rallies forced the government to drop its plans, although according to Ferrari the success of this movement lay in sidestepping constitutional issues (Ferrari 2019: 74). Another successful campaign, the 2017 'NOlympia' referendum mobilizing around anti-government themes such as corruption and neglect of public services, led Fidesz to drop its Olympic bid and helped launch a new but not particularly successful movement party (Kim 2021: 137; Ágh 2021: 34). In 2017, large numbers gathered under the banner of academic freedom and freedom of association to protest so-called 'Stop Soros' Laws, which included new rules hampering foreign-funded NGOs and eventually forced Central European University to move part of its operations abroad. After the 2018 elections delivering a new governing majority to Fidesz, large crowds demonstrated in Budapest under the slogan 'We are the Majority' (Kim 2021: 141–142). Protests against the 2018 so-called 'Slave law', which increased permissible overtime, did not change government policy, but as Varnagy argues, offered an important 'platform for opposition to act as a unified force, making their collaboration more credible at upcoming municipal elections' (Vágó 2019; Várnagy 2020: 179).

In a study of the radical right Republikaner (REP) in Germany, Art argued that stigmatizing frames demonizing the party as Nazis, combined with *ostracism* by mainstream parties, *reduced support for the REP* and led to its demise (2007: 341). Among other things, Art explains the REP's poor electoral performance with reference to the effects of stigmatization on the diminution of various kinds of party resources. Repeated labelling of the REP as a Nazi party *diminished its moral resources*, especially in a country with a political culture highly critical of the Nazi past (ibid.: 337). High costs of associating with the stigmatized party reduced *the party's human resources*. These included social costs such as negative reactions from friends, limited chances of ascending to leadership positions in voluntary associations, as well as fears that joining the REP or publicly supporting it would have material costs, such as a negative effect on professional lives or damage to property (ibid.: 340–341). According to the author, this made it difficult to recruit good candidates for elections or to retain members with sufficient education and skills to 'build and maintain a fledgling political organisation' (ibid.: 341). Stigmatization also diminished the *party's material resources*, making it difficult to attract members and supporters able to make substantial financial donations (ibid.: 341, 344). In more recent work, Art pointed to the heavy personal toll of stigmatization on former Alternative for Germany (AfD) party leader Frauke Petry (2018: 83). This included difficulty finding an apartment, having her van set on fire and her kids bullied at school, as well as struggling to get hotel reservations for party business (ibid.).

On the other hand, stigmatizing frames may *boost the organizational resource* of party unity where it leads 'to a stronger sense of solidarity and group-think among activists' (van Spanje and van der Brug 2007: 1023). In relation to the National Front under Jean-Marie Le Pen, for example, Zúquete observed the role of outsider status on the strengthening of internal party identity: 'The National Front sees itself as a besieged community undergoing terrible persecutions, sufferings, and sacrifices in order to keep alive the spirit of the "true France" and in the end, to redeem the mistakes and errors of the entire community' (2007: 42). Integration of party members is built at least in part around a shared experience of being outsiders because 'a person who joins the National Front experiences a gradual process of stigmatization from the rest of society' (ibid.). This creates a 'dynamic of outsiderhood', Zúquete argues, which is 'essential to understanding the missionary nature of the community of true believers of the National Front' (ibid.: 105). This community 'see themselves as different and set apart not only from militants of other parties but also from that "passive France" still resistant to the Front's message yet whom the militants are duty bound to convert' (ibid.). This helps sustain a 'deep rooted' notion 'among the militants, of being a community under siege that endures pain, sacrifices and persecutions in order to realize their mission' (ibid.). Similarly, Zulianello has argued that being a *'leghista'*, or member or sympathizer of the (Northern) League in Italy, 'often has negative repercussions on private life, social relationships and even personal finance' (2021: 234). Costs of association with the party may be 'compensated', according to one interviewee, by development of a 'microcosm, where the affections, in some cases even colleagues, friends … the personal world is built within the boundaries of *leghismo*' (ibid.: 234). As discussed earlier, Sijsterman (2021) makes a similar point about stigmatization in the case of the *ostracized* Flemish Interest (VB).

Recognizing the costs of demonizating discourses, many radical right parties with vote- or office-seeking ambitions have pursued ostensibly *moderating de-demonization strategies*. As Rydgren observed, in the 1980s many radical right parties sought to end electoral marginalization by adopting a more moderate master frame pioneered by the leader of the French National Front, Jean-Marie Le Pen (2005: 413). The new 'ethnopluralist' master frame favoured separation grounded on a non-hierarchical conception of race relations and proposed 'that different ethnicities are not necessarily superior or inferior, only different and incompatible' (Rydgren 2005: 427). In so doing, they dropped stigmatized ideas of 'biological racism' and anti-Semitism, as well as clear-cut anti-democratic critiques, or anything that could be associated with Nazism or fascism.

Where radical right parties struggled to shake such associations, they had incentives to take further steps. In 2011, for instance, when Marine Le Pen took over leadership of the French National Front, the party adopted an explicit *'dédiabolisation'* strategy and even changed the party name to National Rally to improve electoral fortunes (Ivaldi 2016: 226). This strategy sought to move the party 'away from the historical legacy of the French extreme right' and involved avoiding 'explicit references to anti-Semitism or Holocaust denial, which have been the principle causes for demonization in the past' (ibid.: 232). In 2015, Marine Le Pen famously expelled her father when he made statements diminishing the crimes of the Holocaust as a 'detail of the Second World War' (ibid.). The new leadership also sought to 'break ties with the nationalist milieu and extreme right groups' (ibid.: 232). Even if, as Ivaldi argued, moderation was superficial, it appeared to meet with some success, probably 'helping the French radical right to broaden its support base ... sett[ing] new historical records' in successive electoral contests (ibid.: 226).

The Sweden Democrats (SD) made a similar journey from the 1990s. As Hellström and Nilsson have argued, mainstream parties, the media, and civil society long framed the Sweden Democrats (SD) as the 'devil in disguise', and routinely reminded voters of the party's neo-Nazi origins (2010: 64; see also Widfeldt 2016).). De-demonization led to the expulsion of extremists, a leadership takeover by moderates, a clampdown on compromising behaviour (such as wearing of military uniforms and use of Nazi chants), and use of 'non-racist and non-extremist language' (Widfeldt 2016). According to Widfeldt, 'throwing off the burdensome SD baggage from the 1980s and

1990s', when the party was more closely linked to the neo-Nazi milieu, was an imporant part of the party's electoral breakthrough in 2010. At this point, the author argues, the SD became a party voters 'could vote for without feeling guilty' (ibid.: 215).

EU Dialogue on the Rule of Law

International dialogue is another form of *public persuasion*, typically involving discussions between governing populist parties on the one hand, and the governments of other states or officials of international organizations on the other. This has long been the EU's preferred method for dealing with democratic backsliding by member states (Kochenov and Pech 2016: 1066; Closa 2019, 2021). Indeed, Sedelmeier has argued that 'short of treaty changes, EU institutions will have to rely primarily on political safeguards based on dialogue, persuasion, and shaming' to influence such governments (2017: 349).

There have been several notable initiatives, some more successful than others. In 2012, as Sedelmeier (2017) relates, the EU was able to apply effective social pressure to *curb illiberal and undemocratic policies* in Romania. In this case, former European Commission President José Manuel Barroso and European Council President Herman van Rompuy persuaded Romania's Social Democratic Party leader Victor Ponta to reverse measures undermining the rule of law. These measures included changes Ponta's government made to a law affecting the conduct of referenda, amendments which had made it easier to impeach his political rival, President Traian Băsescu. Following dialogue with the EU, Ponta accepted a list of recommendations to restore the rule of law.

Soon after, in 2014, the European Commission launched a new dialogue-based Rule of Law Framework. The initiative was essentially an 'early warning tool', or a procedure for talks with a member state seemingly on its way to Article 7 TEU voting sanctions (see Chapter 5). Creation of the Rule of Law framework reflected Commission preferences for non-confrontational strategies drawing on the authority of the EU's established rule book (Kochenov and Pech 2016: 1066; Closa 2019, 2021). It pursues 'compliance through engagement' by first trying to persuade member states to comply with EU law (Closa 2019: 697, 702). If this fails, the Commission may then use stronger enforcement powers, depending on whether or not it has support from other key players, especially the member states (Kochenov and Pech 2016: 1066; Closa 2019: 697, 701). While Hungary was at first glance an obvious candidate for talks, only Poland was targeted. By some accounts this was due to political connections between Fidesz and the European People's Party leadership in the Commission, but others have argued that the Commission preferred engaging with Hungary through the Court of Justice of the EU (see Chapter 4 and Appendix IV) (Kochenov and Pech 2016: 1068; Closa 2019: 709; Kelemen 2020: 487–488).

The Commission issued four non-binding Rule of Law Recommendations to Poland. These addressed measures deemed incompatible with the Polish Constitution and basic European standards on judicial independence and EU law (Kochenov and Pech 2016: 1069; Pech et al. 2021: 5). More specifically, recommendations challenged unlawful appointment of individuals to the Constitutional Court, including its president; a deliberate refusal to publish or fully implement several critical Constitutional Court rulings; media reforms; and judicial reforms affecting the Supreme Court, ordinary courts, the National Council of the Judiciary, and the National School of the Judiciary. According to various specialists, the Polish government was unwilling to engage sincerely in dialogue (Kochenov and Pech 2016: 1066–1067; Scheppele et al. 2020: 36). Leading figures in Poland—from President Andrzej Duda and Law and Justice leader Jaroslav Kaczyński downwards—publicly challenged the legitimacy of the Commission to even hold talks (Closa 2019: 707, 2021: 10). As Closa observed, once the process began, Polish authorities refused to respond to the first Rule of Law Opinions, delayed responses to recommendations, ignored official requests to attend meetings in Brussels, adopted a confrontational stance, and ultimately failed to address issues (2019: 698). Unsatisfied with the result of dialogue, on 20 December 2017 the Commission initiated proceedings under Article 7(1) TEU against Poland.

Article 7 TEU is best known for the possibility of voting sanctions (see Chapter 5), but so far, it has only been used for dialogue. Article 7(1) is activated if either one-third of member states, the European Parliament, or the Commission think there is a 'clear risk of a serious breach' of EU values. While Article 7 TEU was for a long time dismissed as an almost unusable 'nuclear option', developments in Hungary and Poland eventually led the European Commission and European Parliament to drop caution and launch proceedings. In December 2017, the European Commission triggered the dialogue procedure against the Law and Justice government in Poland and in September 2018, the European Parliament launched one against the Fidesz-led government in Hungary. The procedure is often called a 'preventive mechanism', but its outcome is more like a public telling-off. If the European Parliament and four-fifths of EU governments agree, the procedure could end in a declaration that there is indeed a 'clear risk' that Fidesz- and/or Law and

Justice-led governments are in 'serious breach' of EU values and in delivery of recommendations on how to fix this.

So far, dialogue has proceeded at a snail's pace. As of 1 January 2023, only five hearings have been held, five for Hungary and five for Poland (Pech and Jaraczewski 2023: 10). Hearings with Poland were held in the General Affairs Council on 26 June, 18 September, and 11 December 2018, but suspended to prevent interference in the Polish parliament elections of October 2019 (Pech et al. 2021: 43). Hearings with Hungary were held under the Finnish presidency in September and December 2019. Hearings were suspended in 2020 due to the COVID-19 pandemic, so that during the whole of 2020 the Council spent a total of one hour on a confidential discussion about the state of play in Poland and Hungary (Pech et al. 2021: 20). According to Pech et al. the Romanian government, when holding the Council presidency, 'actively sought to prevent the organization of a new hearing at a time where it was itself engaged in a severe process of rule of law backsliding' (ibid.). In June 2021 and December 2021 the General Affairs Council held further hearings, and in February 2022 it held a hearing on the rule of law in Poland.

As discussed above, where other states subject norm-violating behaviour of a state to international scrutiny, *public persuasion* through international dialogue may work through the 'mobilization of shame'. Under certain conditions, shining a light in an international forum on inconsistencies between a government's claimed commitment to democratic principles and practices, and casting doubt on its worthiness as a member of the community of states, may persuade an autocratizing state to *curb illiberal or democratic policies*. International dialogue may also empower domestic opponents by keeping critical views of the government on the political agenda, providing alternative information which may balance 'information asymmetries', or authenticate claims of opponents critical of the government.

By various accounts, conditions in Romania in 2012 were better suited to persuasion through the mobilization of shame than in Hungary and Poland. EU influence was successful in Romania, according to Sedelmeier, because 'it was not prohibitively costly for Ponta's government to comply with the EU's demands' due to the unpopularity of the man targeted by the government's problematic measures (2017: 344). That is, President Băsescu was likely to lose upcoming presidential elections whether the measure were retained or not (ibid.). As such, the rule of law breaches were not essential for Ponta to hold on to power (ibid.). Moreover, the risk of a domestic backlash was mitigated by the EU's 'high legitimacy both within the broader public and main political parties, including Ponta's [party]' (ibid.). EU legitimacy also made the government more susceptible to 'shaming' by its international partners (ibid.). These conditions, Sedelmeier argues, are 'manifestly absent in the case of the Fidesz government in Hungary and arguably—albeit less unfavourable—in the case of the PiS government in Poland' (ibid.: 349).

Most accounts of both the Commission's Rule of Law Framework and Article 7(1) talks emphasize failure, measured by an inability to halt rapid, progressive decline in the quality of democracy in the targeted states (see Table 1.2). Some critics have argued that the Commission's 'naïve' 'faith in dialogue' was more than ineffective, it was counterproductive (Pech et al. 2021: 21). At heart, as Pech et al. argue, the problem is that 'dialogue with bad faith actors who are deliberately undermining the rule of law does not work ... Authoritarian minded national authorities have indeed learned they can beat the EU by creating new irreversible facts on the ground while pretending to be interested in further "dialogue"' (2021: 39; see also Scheppele et al. 2020: 37). Throughout the short-lived Rule of Law Framework dialogue, for example, the Polish government 'speeded up political capture of the Constitutional Tribunal and then went on to politically capture the public media, the civil service, prosecutors office, ordinary courts, and finally the Supreme Court' (Kochenov and Pech 2016: 1067; Scheppele et al. 2020: 37–38; Pech et al. 2021: 21). In the EU, dialogue, as Scheppele put it, is 'designed for "normal" times when slowing down a critical process made a friendly settlement possible or when having useful metrics for comparison across Member States would allow the Commission to better plan for the future' (Scheppele et al. 2020: 36).

Moreover, in line with the Council's traditional 'preference for secrecy and deferential attitudes when it comes to assessing one of its member's record' (Closa 2021: 10–12; Pech et al. 2021: 19), dialogue seems to be organized to minimize shame. As Pech et al. point out, discussions in the Council take place without written documents prepared in advance and no minutes are taken (2021: 19). Working methods seem to favour the targeted party, the authors argue: The Council implemented Article 7(1) requirements to 'hear' the targeted member states through a form of 'peer review', where dialogue departs from a 'partial selection of topics for discussion without any public explanations' and 'lacks transparency' (ibid.). There are limited opportunities for fact-checking 'misleading' or 'factually inaccurate statements' or 'involvement of relevant external stakeholders with expertise on the matters under discussion' (Pech et al. 2021: 19).

Domestic effects should not be discounted though, even if more research is needed to better understand how EU rule of law dialogues—and indeed other international initiatives—affect populist party governments. Sedelmeier has observed that EU initiatives 'keep cases open on the agenda' and thereby 'sustain social pressure as a resource for domestic actors working to overturn illiberal governmental practices' (2017: 347). Along these lines, as Closa has also observed: 'Despite encountering criticism, engagement has permitted the Commission to amplify its concerns to a wider EU audience, including national governments, and to raise awareness about the situation in Hungary and Poland what [*sic*, which] appears to be a precondition for government mobilization' (2021: 9). Scheppele et al. also concede that 'the Commission's Rule of Law Framework did make the rule of law issues in Poland visible in the EU each time the Commission issued another formal (and public) warning to the country' (2020: 38). Indeed, reporting of EU and other international initiatives by Polish dailies such as *Wyborcza* and *Rzeczpospolita*, for example, have helped keep opposition to the Law and Justice party on the political agenda in the country. These newspapers regularly covered the EU's rule of law dialogues and Article 7 proceedings, the many EU infringement proceedings, ECtHRs rulings, critiques of Law and Justice reforms from the European Parliament, the Council of Europe, Venice Commission, the Organization for Security and Cooperation in Europe, the Office for Democratic Institutions and Human Rights, international leaders etc.[1] On social media, Polish opposition NGOs like the *Komitet Obrony Demokracji* (Committee for the Defence of Democracy with 233,957 Facebook followers), *Akcja Demokracja* (Action Democracy, with 147.573 Facebook followers), *Wolne Sądy* (Free Courts, with 87.406 Facebook followers) follow, publicize, and comment on EU initiatives closely. Such appeals to international standards articulated by authoritative external actors may persuade some supporters to disregard, or at least doubt, populist party claims. Indeed, as Sedelemeier has argued, conditions in Poland are, at least in theory, propitious for a positive influence of EU actions on domestic opposition to Law and Justice. That is, the author argues, when a target government is Eurosceptic (as in the case of Fidesz or PiS [Law and Justice]), but the EU enjoys significant support among the public (as in Poland), greater publicity and a more transparent process that explicitly specifies the concerns of EU institutions is more promising, as it provides additional legitimacy to the arguments of the domestic opposition' (Sedelmeier 2017: 346).

At the same time, both Law and Justice and Fidesz often responded to these initiatives in the populist register. Hungary challenged (and lost) a case in the CJEU against the European Parliament vote triggering Article

---

[1] A survey of newspaper coverage of opposition initiatives by Dr Aleksandra Moroska-Bonkiewicz and Dr Katarzyna Domagała from the University of Wroclaw seen by the author substantiates this point.

7(1) TEU. Fidesz also claimed the European Parliament's Sargentini report, which spelled out the case against Hungary, was factually incorrect (De La Baume and Herszenhorn 2018; Varga 2021). In a speech in the European Parliament prior to its Article 7(1) vote Fidesz Prime Minister Victor Orbán invoked 'sovereignty' counter-discourses, pitching the procedure as an illegitimate intervention into the internal affairs of the country (Plenary, 11 September 2018). Orbán linked invocation of Article 7(1) to Hungary's tough stance on immigration, suggesting the country was being unfairly condemned because Hungarians had decided not to be 'a country of immigrants'. Orbán also claimed opponents sought to exclude a government led by a party winning a majority of votes, and in anti-elitist tones, suggested MEPs thought they knew better than Hungarians themselves what was in their interests. The Sargentini report was described as an insult and lacking respect for Hungarians. Orbán also described invocation of Article 7(1) as *ultra vires* and an 'abuse of power', alluding to political forces unfairly taking revenge because they could not win their support through other means. Claiming the mantle of the 'true democrat', Orbán reminded the chamber that, unlike many MEPs, Hungarians had shed blood for freedom and democracy and promised to stand up to EU opponents in an electoral contest where the people of Europe could decide on the future of Europe and restore democracy to European politics. Taking a more explicitly anti-elitist tone Hungarian Justice Minister Judit Varga described the EP's role in Article 7(1) proceedings as a 'witch hunt', and EP actions as 'conceited omnipotence', where it acted as 'a self-elected knight of the rule of law ... [which] wishes to become the prosecutor, judge, and executor' (Varga 2021).

In addition to challenging the legality of the EU's Rule of Law Framework (Closa 2019: 707, 2021: 10), Law and Justice often raised doubts about its democratic legitimacy. For example, Polish foreign minister Witold Waszczykowski remarked: 'An EU official, who came to office via political connections, writes to a democratically-elected government ... [Commission Vice-President] Mr Timmermans is not a legitimate partner for me' (Euroactiv 2016). After the launch of Article 7 proceedings against Poland, a statement from the Polish Ministry of Foreign Affairs said the government 'deplored' what it saw as an 'essentially political' decision (Tamma 2017). It claimed the Law and Justice-led government would continue with reforms because 'we owe it to our voters' (Tamma 2017). Authors of critical statements 'addressed to institutions outside of Poland are called by the ruling majority and dependent media as "traitors"' (Bojarski 2021: 1382).

On the other hand, there are some indications in the Polish case, at least, of a certain vulnerability to 'rhetorical entrapment', which according to Risse and Sikkink make it difficult for all but the most closed authoritarian regimes to dismiss international interventions out of hand (1999: 15). Indeed, rather than openly rejecting international democracy norms and EU values, the government often responds to EU rule of law initiatives claiming its actions are misunderstood. Law and Justice leaders have framed judicial reforms as pro-democracy moves which for the 'good of the nation and justice' would clean out an elitist 'caste' heir to 'communist criminals' (Bojarski 2021: 1368; Sadurski 2019b; Szczerbiak 2020). At one point, the Polish prime minister claimed: 'Our partners do not understand what the post-communist reality looks like. The justice system had a problem with self-cleansing', arguing that reforms were needed to democratize a judicial system that had never properly been dealt with after the fall of communism (Brzozowski 2018). After the launch of Article 7(1) proceedings against Poland, a statement from the Polish Ministry of Foreign Affairs claimed, among other things, that Poland had been subject to a 'campaign of negative information about reforms ... [which] is not based on facts' (Tamma 2017). It called on other member states to 'listen carefully to Polish arguments', 'without unnecessarily stigmatizing' Poland (ibid.). Similarly, in a 2021 EP speech on the rule of law crisis in Poland, Law and Justice Prime Minister Matheus Morawiecki called on other states not to name and shame, or to point fingers at those who can be easily blamed (Plenary, 19 October 2021).

To conclude, this chapter has shown how persuasion can be used by opponents to influence the policy choices of populist parties by reframing the terms of public debate, stigmatizing and shaming populist party leaders and their supporters. Initiatives opposing populist parties through persuasion may *decrease support for populist parties* if the diffusion of resonant critical ideational frames turns public opinion against a populist party or decreases the salience of their signature policies. They may do so if they present populists as a political problem, or the cause of, rather than the cure for, social ills (diagnostic framing); specify alternative and more attractive strategies to deal with these problems (prognostic framing); and articulate attractive identities for those who take a stand against populist parties (motivational framing). In addition, plausible signs that public opinion is turning against them may lead governing populist parties to accommodate oppositions *by curbing illiberal and anti-democratic policies.*

Stigmatizing frames, such as demonizing discourses, may *reduce support for a populist party* by creating doubts about its democratic credentials, *diminish a populist party's moral, human, and material resources* by making support for the party unattractive, and thereby *create incentives for moderation.* Alternatively, stigmatizing frames *may increase support for populist parties* by reinforcing anti-elitist appeals, *boost resources* by strengthening a sense of common identity against an external foe, or provide *incentives for radicalization* by fostering a sense of separation from the political mainstream.

Where other states subject the norm-violating behaviour of a state to international scrutiny, *public persuasion* through international dialogue may work through the 'mobilization of shame'. Under certain conditions, shining light in an international forum on inconsistencies between a government's claimed commitment to democratic principles and practices, and casting doubt on its worthiness as a member of the community of states, may persuade an autocratizing state to *curb illiberal or democratic policies*. International dialogue may also empower domestic opponents by keeping critical views of the government on the political agenda, providing alternative information which may balance 'information asymmetries', or authenticate critical claims of opponents.

In the next chapter I knit together arguments about the complex links between initiatives, processes of change, goals, and perverse effects discussed in this and preceding chapters to outline a 'bottom-up' theory of effective opposition to populist parties.

Conclusion

A 'Bottom-Up' Theory of Effective Opposition to Populist Parties

For some people, populist successes are alarming. Living in Europe's autocratizing states means living with democratic doubletalk, political manipulation, and a profound weakening of chances to control what those in government can do to their fellow citizens. Appeals to the ideal of the people governing themselves, of taking back control, may be seeds that lead to less-than liberal kinds of 'populist democracy', or outright authoritarianism. It is important to recognize though, that populist appeals can be hitched to a very wide variety of political projects, some authoritarian, others emancipatory and progressive, others still decidedly oriented towards the status quo. Populist parties may raise issues that other parties have ignored and pressure governments to adopt policies that benefit more people. They may inspire people who have not been active in politics to demand more rights and better treatment. Elites may in fact be corrupt. There may be a need for real democracy. On top of this, populism has a fluid public meaning which doesn't always coincide with scholarly definitions. Opponents may not always recognize the distinctions made in scholarly debates between populism and extremism, or between liberalism and democracy. In this complex situation, it makes most sense to speak of the ambiguity of populist orientations to liberal democracy.

Parties usually regarded as populist are key players in many European countries, and by extension, in the joint bodies sharing political power among European states. This means that opposition to populist parties now takes a very wide variety of forms. Contemporary modes of engagement with populist parties include old-style 'intolerant' rights-restrictions and ostracism, as well as a wide range of 'tolerant' strategies where public authorities, political parties, and civil society actors respond to populist parties using the tools of 'normal politics'. Opposition to populist parties also takes place in a Europeanized political field. The degree of interdependence between states in the EU makes it difficult to ignore the policies of populist governments, who may be governing partners. International organizations and networks of transnational actors monitor, and sometimes mobilize against, populist parties within states. These two facts of contemporary European politics—that populist parties are so successful that they are often part of the political mainstream, and that their opponents use many of the tactics routinely employed against all kinds of political rivals—are the context within what I call democratic defence as 'normal politics' plays out.

In Chapter 2, I developed a new typology to better capture this setting. Reviewing a wide range of theoretical and empirical literatures, I explored the effects of these initiatives opposing populist parties (IoPPs), aiming to identify the mechanisms, or processes by which populist parties might be affected by acts of opposition against them. This led me to identify four main ways in which opposition initiatives might affect populist parties: Opponents may be able to manipulate the strategic choices of populist parties and their supporters. They may enforce legal rules, deploying the coercive authority of the state and institutional routines to constrain what populist parties do. They can exploit mutual interdependence to leverage change. Opponents may persuade populist parties and their supporters to think or behave differently. Throughout, I sought to link initiatives and processes to goals and perverse effects. That is, I sought to identify how IoPPs curbed the ability of populist parties in government to implement illiberal or anti-democratic policies, reduced or increased support for populist parties, diminished or boosted their resources, or induced moderation or radicalization. In this final chapter I restate, clarify, and knit together arguments about the complex links between initiatives, processes of change, goals, and perverse effects to build a 'bottom-up' theory of effective opposition to populist parties.

What is an 'Effective' Initiative Opposing Populist Parties?

A long-standing method for evaluating the effectiveness of public policy interventions is to look at intended objectives or goals, and whether these have been met (Vedung 2012). In other words, effectiveness is evaluated according to a 'goal attainment model', which involves first identifying the goals of a political intervention, teasing out their actual meaning and perhaps rank order, and then finding ways to measure goal attainment. The next step is to examine which goals, if any, were achieved in practice, allowing for the possibility that goals may be achieved only to a certain degree, and that interventions may in fact be counterproductive. Applying such a model for studying the effectiveness of opposition to populism is attractive. It is parsimonious and intuitive. Many of the initiatives opposing populist parties discussed in the previous chapters are analogous to public policy interventions, with many initiatives undertaken by the same actors and using the same procedures as those who make policy decisions in other areas of public life.

There are several limitations facing a goal-attainment model for evaluating the effects of political interventions. One danger is that focusing on the parts misses the bigger picture (Vedung 2012: 388–392). This translates here into the critique that by focusing on short-to-medium term goals—namely, curbing populist policy influence, reducing support, diminishing resources, and inducing moderation—fails to address what might ultimately defeat populist parties wholesale. As I have already suggested in the Introduction, what might be a weakness in some cases is a strength for the case at hand. It is problematic from a normative point of view to pursue the complete marginalization of populist parties in European politics. Any goal of this nature could only with great difficulty overcome foundational liberal democratic commitments to pluralism and tolerance. European populist parties often articulate widespread and sometimes reasonable grievances with the status quo and pursue a variety of objectives which do not necessarily undermine the quality of democratic politics in a country. In addition, it is probably unrealistic to try to 'defeat' populism. Populist successes mean that they are so entrenched in European party systems that they seem to be here to stay, at least for the medium term. In this context, it is more useful to focus on partial successes, as well as the possibility for perverse effects.

Missing the wood for the trees may, arguably, be more of problem regarding possible perverse effects of initiatives opposing populist parties. Perverse effects can be defined narrowly or broadly. This book focuses on narrowly conceived perverse effects directly affecting populist parties themselves; that is, their policies, support, resources, ideological position, and political style. On the other hand, broadly defined perverse effects could include the role that opposition to populist parties may have in exacerbating the political and social polarization typically accompanying populist successes (Enyedi 2016: 16; Norris and Inglehart 2019: 54; Pappas 2019: 24; Rovira Kaltwasser 2019: 892). Responding to the grievances raised by, or taking on the policy agenda of, populist parties, may also shift the ideological centre of gravity of the entire political system, something many scholars have observed under the rubric 'contagion to the right' (Minkenberg 2003; Bale 2003; Akkerman, de Lange, and Roodouijn 2016: 16; van Spanje 2018: 153–154). Others write of a 'stylistic' co-optation, where 'a populist party can contaminate the other parties by influencing the style of leadership, the type of party discourse, and the relationship between leaders and followers' (Mény and Surel 2002a: 19;

Albertazzi, Bonansinga, and Vampa 2021: 58). Initiatives deploying the coercive power of the state in particular may decrease support for the liberal democratic system as a whole, especially among those already dissatisfied with the way democracy works (Lichbach 1987: 269; Berman 2008: 16; van Spanje 2018: 154). Failed international interventions may undermine self-confidence in the institutions attempting them, as many argue was the result of EU's 'traumatic' failed attempts to impose diplomatic sanctions against Austria in 2000 (Müller 2014b: 153; Kochenov and Pech 2016: 1068; Closa 2021: 78). This is a fruitful topic for future research.

Another problem with a goal-attainment model is that, as Vedung warns, identifying the goals of political interventions is not always straightforward (2012: 388–392). Goals may be vague, multiple, conflicting, or covert. This challenge is particularly acute when identifying the goals of initiatives opposing populist parties. Some of those acting to oppose populist parties may act instrumentally, designing strategies to achieve specific goals. Many others will be less well organized or less-experienced opponents. They may be unclear about what they want to achieve, or the likely consequences of their actions. In the foregoing discussion, I have dealt with this problem by inferring goals of opposition to populist parties from data and research obtained from various sources. These include the large literature on responses to populist parties, and to similar challengers such as extremist and anti-system parties; my previous research on party bans (Bourne 2018); and data on IoPPs collected with colleagues from the Carlsberg Foundation's *Challenges for Europe project on Populism and Democratic Defence in Europe*.[1]

Before I go on to summarize and order arguments about the links between initiatives, goals, and perverse effects identified in earlier chapters, it is important to restate that my argument is empirical rather than normative. The long tradition of philosophical debate on the virtues and perils of 'tolerating the intolerant' points to the need for deep normative reflection over the appropriateness of, and best modalities for, achieving these goals (Locke 1689; Popper 1966; Rawls 1971; Rummens and Abts 2010; Müller 2016a; Rijpkema 2018; Malkopoulou and Kirshner 2019).

From Initiatives to Goals

IoPPs may delimit the participation of populist parties in the public sphere and/or the impact of at least some of their ideas and actions on public policy.

---

[1] 'Challenges for Europe Programme', Carlsberg Foundation (CF20-008) *Populism and Democratic Defence In Europe*, 1 January 2020 to 31 December 2023.

In the preceding pages, I have shown that these ambitions can be broken down into four main goals: Curbing the ability of populist parties to implement anti-democratic and illiberal policies, reducing support for populist parties, diminishing populist party resources, or inducing moderation. Summarizing this discussion, we can see that while some IoPPs are better suited to achieving some goals over others, many goals can be achieved by multiple initiatives. In other words, achieving one goal does not exclude, or may even enhance, the possibility of achieving others.

Curb implementation of anti-democratic or illiberal policies by populists in government

IoPPs may constrain the ability of populist parties to implement anti-democratic or illiberal policies in three main ways: By excluding populists from the governing arena, blocking implementation of government policy created, or influenced by populist parties, or convincing them their interests are harmed by implementing such policies. *Rights-restricting* IoPPs, such as party bans, directly exclude a populist party from the political arena. Although contemporary cases are rare, party bans prevent a party from participating in elections, the only legitimate avenue to governmental power in a democracy (Bourne 2018). A much more common way to exclude a populist party from the governing arena is *ostracism*, which involves the refusal by other political parties to cooperate with it on principled grounds. *Governmental ostracism* (or cordon sanitaire) will exclude a party unable to win elections outright by excluding it from governing coalitions. This is often accompanied by *parliamentary ostracism*, where other parties limit an *ostracized* party's policy influence by refusing to support its parliamentary initiatives.

When a populist party is strong enough to form a government, their opponents may have access to a range of *checks and balances* designed to limit governmental powers. Depending on constitutional design, and the independence of alternative sites of political power, those opposing governing populist parties can, for instance, challenge the constitutionality of government laws and actions in the courts, use presidential powers or opposition majorities in parliamentary upper chambers to block or delay legislative initiatives. On rare occasions opponents may launch impeachment proceedings against government leaders. The powers of supervisory bodies, such as ombudsmen, electoral commissions, or media regulators may also constrain the ability governing populist parties to push through illiberal or anti-democratic activities. Where 'democratic backsliding' or 'autocratization' limit constraints on governing populists, the existence of at least some independent institutions may nevertheless allow *checks and balances* to constrain the policy agenda of governing populists. Political parties may also deploy the tools of normal *oppositional politics* against governing populist parties, such as using parliamentary procedures to defeat government bills or ultimately remove a government or key ministers through a vote of no confidence.

International *rights-restricting* IoPPs, such as Article 7 TEU voting sanctions or financial sanctions for rule of law deficiencies, exploit asymmetrical interdependence to pressure EU member governments to reverse illiberal or anti-democratic policies. International *judicial controls,* such as EU infringement proceedings addressing rule of law deficiencies, do so by building on the usual incentives for compliance with international law and the implementing role of national authorities. International *checks and balances,* such as the review of government acts by the European Court of Human Rights (see Appendix III), also challenge illiberal and anti-democratic policies by governing populists. *Public persuasion* by public figures such as presidents, prime ministers, leaders of other states and international organizations aim to persuade populists in government to change their policies through appeals to international norms.

Civil society actors may oppose illiberal and anti-democratic policies of populist parties in government, mostly by demonstrating their claims against illiberal or anti-democratic actions in the public sphere. On occasion this takes the form of *coercive confrontation,* involving claim making which causes physical damage to people or property. This includes physical attacks on leading populists, damage to their property, or physically obstructing demonstrations of support for governing populists. It can also take the form of non-coercive, or *adversarial* demonstrations of opposition to government policies, including marches, strikes, civil disobedience, art and satire, and information campaigns, using both traditional and social media. Opposition by civil society actors may curb illiberal and anti-democratic policies of governing populist parties if they can find influential allies such as courts or political parties, if they can leverage concessions from the government through disruption, or by influencing public opinion and convincing governors their interests are threatened by not accommodating opponents' demands.

Reduce support for populist parties

In a democracy, it almost goes without saying that opponents will try to reduce support for populist parties by encouraging people not to vote for populists. Reducing the vote share of a party weakens its influence in the political system more generally and its chances of forming or joining a coalition government. The main way IoPPs may reduce support is if they create disincentives to vote for populist parties; alienate their core voters; or cast doubts on their democratic credentials, competence, or ability to respond to grievances and needs of voters. *Ostracism*, or the decision of other parties to rule out cooperation with a populist party on principled grounds, may create disincentives for instrumentally minded voters to vote for the populist party. Such voters direct their votes to parties that can deliver their preferred policies, and there are few incentives to vote for a populist party that will never get into government. This may be especially so when mainstream parties *coopt* a populist party's signature policies. *Policy cooptation* may corrode the distinctiveness of a party's policy ideas, decreasing incentives for voters to choose it, at least where its policies are concerned. *Cooperation in government* may put voters off in other ways. Populist parties' anti-elitist claims may be less convincing when office ambitions make it part of the 'ruling elite', the compromises made with coalition partners may alienate core voters, and the challenges of office may expose a populist party's lack of governmental experience. International *rights-restricting* IoPPs, such as voting sanctions under Article 7 TEU, or financial sanctions under the EU's new budget conditionality mechanism, may undermine voter support for governing populist parties if voters think they have something to lose from sanctions.

Where voters hold generally positive views on democracy, IoPPs creating doubts about a populist party's democratic credentials may delegitimize a party to the extent that some people stop voting for it. IoPPs which may create such an impression include *rights-restrictions*, which signal that other parties, courts, or security services consider the party a potential threat to liberal democracy; *judicial controls*, which might authoritatively qualify party policies or important party figures as racist, corrupt, unconstitutional, illiberal, or anti-democratic; and forms of *public* and *political persuasion* and civil society *adversarialism* which repeatedly condemn populist parties with demonizing discourses. *Public persuasion* in the form of monitoring by international organizations, *judicial controls* in the form of rulings of supranational courts, and *adversarial* initiatives by transnational civil society groups may publicize gaps between words and deeds, helping party and civil society opponents discredit populist party claims. More generally, IoPPs taking the form of *public* and *political persuasion,* or civil society *coercive confrontation* or *adversarialism,* may help opponents win 'framing contests' (Gamson 2007). That is, such initiatives may succeed in convincing voters that populist parties were not responsive to their values and needs, or that they were wrong to accept populist theories about the causes of, and best remedies to deal with, the dissatisfactions in their lives.

Diminish populist party resources

A third, and related goal pursued by those opposing populist parties is the depletion of resources populist parties have to hand for pursuing their objectives in the political arena. First, IoPPs may affect a party's human resources such as the time, skills, experience, and knowledge of talented individuals, or the political weight a large membership brings (Edwards et al. 2018: 80). *Judicial controls* directly targeting populist leaders—such as a corruption trial, or *adversarial* media campaigns attacking their credibility—may undermine human resources by ruling out some leaders from public office or weakening support for the leader internally. Individuals will be less likely to associate with a party if they think it will bring legal problems or social stigmatization, which may result from *rights-restricting* initiatives like party bans or surveillance, *judicial controls* such as racism or corruption trials, *ostracism,* or *demonizing discourses* by any kind of opponent.

IoPPs may deplete material resources by limiting access to state funding or other material infrastructure such as property, office space, and equipment (Edwards et al. 2018: 80). This is perhaps clearest for *rights-restricting* IoPPs which lead to confiscation of a party's property or deny it access to state funding. Depletion of material resources may also follow *judicial controls,* like trials for misuse of public funding which require a party to relinquish or pay back money obtained illegally. *Ostracism* can create material costs because it denies a party access to the rewards of office. Organizational resources may be depleted if IoPPs undermine the ability of the party to maintain internal solidarity, recruit members, cultivate new leaders, run effective campaigns, or if they create dissatisfaction with the leader among rank-and-file members (Edwards et al. 2018). Such internal party tensions may result from IoPPs where parties must decide how to respond to legal problems following *rights-restricting* initiatives like party bans, surveillance, the denial of public funds, or *judicial controls* such as racism or corruption trials, as well as party initiatives such as *ostracism*. When other parties agree to *cooperate in government or parliament* with populist parties, internal tensions between moderates and hardliners can emerge or be exacerbated in response to the constraints of governing or compromises of coalition politics.

IoPPs undermining a populist party's legitimacy or authenticity, the sympathy of its supporters, or celebrity endorsement may deplete moral resources (Edwards et al. 2018: 83). *Rights-restrictions* and *judicial controls*, perhaps resulting in high-profile court cases and the jailing of dissidents, may tarnish reputations. Forms of *public and political persuasion* and *coercive confrontation* and *adversarialism* deploying *demonizing discourses* may deplete moral resources by portraying an actor as the personification of evil. All kinds of international IoPPs, whether voting or financial sanctions targeting the violation of democracy norms, or international monitoring and dialogue, may undermine the domestic legitimacy of governing populist parties by revealing inconsistencies between what populists say about their democratic credentials and international standards.

Induce moderation

The opponents of populist parties may create incentives to make populist parties 'moderate' political appeals and/or employ more conventional political behaviour. As discussed in more detail in Chapter 3, a party 'moderates' in ideological terms if it aligns its policy bids towards some kind of 'mean' policy position in comparison with other parties, including acceptance of core principles and values of the liberal democratic status quo (Akkerman and Rooduijn 2015: 1141; Akkerman et al. 2016). A second way of defining moderation refers to behaviour challenging informal rules of politics, including styles of speech or dress, modes of argumentation, or practices of representation (Jagers and Walgrave 2007; Moffitt 2016; Ostiguy 2017).

IoPPs may induce ideological or behavioural 'moderation' by creating rewards for parties which change their policy proposals and behaviour, or by creating costs for those that do not. IoPPs may also aim to persuade populist party leaders and supporters to observe and internalize liberal democratic values. Populist parties that want to, or do, *cooperate in government* have incentives to moderate their ideological positions and political behaviour to establish or maintain good relations with governing partners. In some circumstances, populist parties have incentives to respond to *policy-cooptation* by trying to differentiate their appeals from the copycats through moderating their positions. In contrast, the threat and application of various kinds of intolerant IoPPs may create costs for populist parties that do not moderate, including *rights-restricting* IoPPs which might lead to party bans or surveillance; *judicial controls*, which might result in fines or imprisonment of leaders; and *ostracism*, which might scare away voters. In the process of articulating claims opposing populist parties, and efforts to reframe public debates, civil society actors using both *coercive confrontation* and *adversarialism* may persuade populist parties and their supporters to adopt more moderate policy preferences and action repertoire. So too might the efforts of leading public figures and political parties using *public* or *political persuasion.* Opposition parties in countries subject to international *rights-restricting* IoPPs may have incentives to avoid pariah status by resisting the temptation to meet successful illiberal populists on their own terms.

From Initiatives to Perverse Effects

As understood here, perverse effects are negative, unintended consequences of opposition to populist parties. Like goals they are conceived narrowly as consequences of opposition directly affecting populist parties, rather than the broader political system or society as a whole. That is, perverse effects of IoPPs may increase rather than decrease support for populist parties, boost rather than diminish their resources, and induce radicalization instead of inducing ideological moderation.

Increase support for populist parties

In the rough and tumble of democratic competition for votes, populist parties may be able to turn opposition against them from a problem into an opportunity for winning votes and increasing support. The main ways populist parties can do this is to discredit opponents by framing IoPPs as 'evidence' supporting core anti-establishment themes and invoking a corresponding need to renew popular sovereignty. IoPPs may also increase support for populist parties if voters see them as a way to have policy preferences put on the governing agenda or provide an opportunity for populist parties to showcase competence and respectability.

Opposition initiated by public authorities and other political parties—the prototypical 'corrupt elite' of populist discourse—are particularly vulnerable to populist counter-discourses. *Rights-restricting* IoPPs, *checks and balances,* and *judicial controls,* all of which typically involve the courts, may be met by populist claims that 'actors who are neither elected nor controlled by "the people" have decided to censor the party which gives voice to the "silent majority"' (Rovira Kaltwasser 2019: 89). *Ostracism* may seem like a cartel-like closing of ranks by the political establishment as may coordination among *opposition parties* who may launch no-confidence motions or other initiatives to defeat populist policy or legislative initiatives. Initiatives based on *public* and *political persuasion*, such as stigmatizing and demonizing discourses may similarly misfire. Calling populists and their supporters 'Nazis', 'fascists', or racists may reinforce populist appeals with anti-elitist themes. Forms of *coercive confrontation* and *adversarialism* by civil society actors relying on such discourses may also do so, especially if opponents are framed as political or cultural 'enemies' like 'liberal cosmopolitan elites', or 'cultural Marxists'.

International IoPPs may provoke a vote-winning 'populist backlash', bolstering anti-elitist claims encompassing international actors, or increasing support for populists in government through nationalist 'rallying-round-the-flag'. IoPPs which may produce such an effect include *international rights-restricting* initiatives such as Article 7 TEU voting sanctions or EU rule of law financial sanctions; *international checks* on executive authority, such as rulings of the ECtHR; *international judicial controls* in the form of CJEU rulings, or *public persuasion* in the form of critiques from international bodies, or by leaders of other states. Where convincing, populist appeals rejecting international intervention as an assault on the sovereignty of the 'national' people by 'foreign' elites may increase support for populists in government among nationally minded citizens. Where successful, such 'rally-round-the-flag' effects make citizens more likely to trust populist leaders and allow governments to blame external forces for hardships otherwise attributable to the government. Such international IoPPs may also be used to delegitimize domestic opponents cooperating with political actors from abroad.

Various strategies of *forbearance* by political parties may also help populist parties increase their support. Voters have incentives to vote for a populist party if they think it will create or maintain pressure on other parties to *coopt* populist agendas voters approve of. Similarly, if other parties are willing to *cooperate* with populist parties, the latter may see an increase in support because it gives policy-oriented voters hope that their preferences might become government policy. If *cooperation in government* is successful, it may increase support for populist parties by providing evidence of their competence and respectability.

Boost populist party resources

IoPPs may boost populist parties' material, moral, and organizational resources by providing access to rewards of office, free publicity, and by strengthening internal solidarity. *Cooperation* with populists in government is likely to give populist parties access to a wide range of material resources that come with political office. *Cooperation in government* and *policy co-optation* may also boost the salience and respectability of issues that win votes for populist parties, thereby boosting their moral resources. If governing populist parties can mount a successful populist backlash against international interventions, IoPPs may also boost moral resources by strengthening citizen confidence in the government.

IoPPs which strengthen internal cohesion can be an organizational resource for populist parties. Repressive IoPPs, especially *rights-restrictions* like party bans and surveillance, and *judicial controls*, that result in harsh financial penalties or detention of leaders and members, may boost organizational resources such as internal solidarity by fostering a stronger sense of community. *Ostracism* may affect internal solidarity in a similar way, and also help the party avoid divisive issues or difficult compromises on radical policies. *Public* and *political persuasion* in the form of demonizing discourses, and negative framing by civil society organizations, whether in the form of *coercive confrontational* or *adversarial* IoPPs, may strengthen internal cohesion by sharpening a sense among supporters of injury and victimhood, as well as distance from, and distrust of, political elites. All IoPPs that generate controversy may potentially boost populist party organizational resources by providing 'free publicity', which may increase the salience of populist ideas on the political agenda or enhance the appeal of a populist party for certain audiences. This may be especially so with high profile court cases—such as party ban, racism and hate speech trials, or cases on the constitutionality of governing populists' signature policies—which may in addition, profitably enhance a party's 'issue ownership'.

Induce radicalization

IoPPs may lead to radicalization of populist parties' political appeals and/or adoption of less conventional political behaviour. They may do so by providing incentives for party leaders and members to withdraw from institutional politics, focusing appeals to members and supporters with more extreme policy ideas and unconventional political action repertoires. Radicalization can be conceived as the opposite of ideological moderation as defined above. That is, radicalization refers to a shift of parties' ideological position 'away from the mean towards the extremes of the political spectrum' (Akkerman and Rooduijn 2015: 1141), whether on the socio-economic or socio-cultural dimensions of political competition or in terms of support for the liberal democratic status quo. It may also take the form of more frequent and blatant use of extremist language and symbols, or increasing ties with extremist movements. Parties subject to *rights-restricting* measures, such as party bans or surveillance, like other repressive state responses to challengers may encourage parties to 'go underground' and open the possibility that the apathetic become politicized and the moderates radicalize. By taking office goals off the table, *ostracism* provides incentives for populist parties to retain radical policy positions to keep its core supporters on board, even if this does not exclude the possibility of moderation on some policy dimensions. If other parties try to *coopt* their signature policies, populist parties have incentives to differentiate their policy bids through radicalization to avoid losing votes. While ideological moderation sometimes results from *cooperation in government*, radicalization can also occur, especially when a party is able to adopt a strategy of 'one foot in and one foot out of government' (Zaslove 2012: 431).

Effective Opposition as Achieving Goals without Perverse Effects

With clearer ideas about the range of opposition initiatives, how they affect populist parties, goals typically pursued and possible perverse effects, the foundations of a theory of effective opposition to populist parties are now in place. This theory can be summarized with reference to a simple formula: Effective initiatives opposing populist parties achieve at least one of the goals of opposition without producing perverse effects.

As argued above, the scale of populist successes over the last few decades and the reasonable expectation that populism will remain entrenched in European party systems means their opponents cannot reasonably expect to 'defeat populism' in the short to medium term. It is therefore more useful to look at whether initiatives opposing populist parties achieve the less ambitious but still consequential goals also discussed above, and whether efforts to achieve these goals generate unanticipated, perverse effects. This approach is also more normatively attractive, given that European populist parties often articulate widely held and sometimes reasonable grievances with the status quo and pursue a variety of objectives, which do not necessarily undermine the quality of democratic politics in a country. In these conditions, aiming to 'defeat' populism could only with great difficulty overcome foundational liberal democratic commitments to pluralism and tolerance.

There are several other advantages to evaluating effective opposition with reference to the achievement of opposition goals. In the first place, it allows researchers to evaluate the effectiveness of both individual, perhaps small-scale, localized initiatives as well as clusters of initiatives involving different types of political actors or multiple countries. Using the theoretical tools I present in this book researchers can examine how initiatives produce either desired outcomes or perverse effects or both. In this way, my approach allows for the development of a more sophisticated understanding of the multiple and possibly contradictory effects of opposition to populist parties in varied contexts. Indeed, if we look at goal attainment alone, it is clear that goals may be related in complex ways (see Figure C.1).

Thus, IoPPs that reduce support for a populist party may keep a party from positions of influence, making it harder to implement illiberal and anti-democratic policies, but it may also diminish resources to campaign, especially where state funding and media access is based on vote share. IoPPs diminishing the resources a party has at hand may also make it harder to operate and campaign effectively, which may in turn reduce its support and make it harder to win enough power to implement illiberal and anti-democratic policies. IoPPs inducing moderation may mean populist parties no longer aim to implement illiberal or undemocratic policies, but it may also be a strategic response to reduced support or diminished resources. Yet moderation itself may reduce support among radical supporters or reduce human and organizational resources if supporters leave the party or mount divisive internal campaigns to reverse a new policy course. At the same time, IoPPs curbing the ability of a populist party to implement illiberal or anti-democratic policies may reduce a populist parties' support, for example, if voters feel their interests are damaged by international sanctions. They may also weaken populist party resources if curbs are obtained using initiatives that undermine the legitimacy of the government or empower the opposition. Curbing a governing populist party's ability to implement illiberal or anti-democratic policies may encourage populists

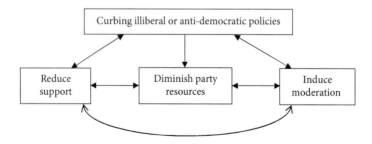

Figure C.1 Interaction of goals pursued by the opponents of populist parties

in opposition to moderate their policy stances to avoid losing votes or becoming unattractive coalition partners.

An additional advantage of a theory of effectiveness focusing on initiatives, goals, and perverse effects is that it allows for a flexible, 'bottom-up' research design. That is, the researcher can start with specific actions (IoPPs) and then look to theories spelled out here to find hypotheses on the broader consequences of these initiatives for the achievement of goals and generation of perverse effects. It involves first finding out what kinds of initiatives have been deployed in a particular country or against a particular populist party. The typology developed in Chapter 2 provides a starting point for such an endeavour, allowing the researcher to check whether initiatives undertaken elsewhere can be observed in the case or cases of interest. The next step is to work out whether initiatives contribute to achievement of goals or produce perverse effects. In what is an already complex theoretical argument, I have not spelled out in any detail how to measure goal attainment or perverse effects. Nevertheless, the wide range of empirical examples used throughout the book provide many ideas on how such measures might be developed. This includes observing trends in the democratic quality of governing populist party's policy outputs, or their compliance with the decisions of domestic or international tribunals; measuring changes in vote shares or a party's prominence in, or length of, government tenure; observing a populist party's evolving policy positions and public performances; or tracing changes in public opinion or other indicators of support, such as party membership.

A third step is to offer an account of how opponents achieved their goals, why they failed, or why initiatives were counterproductive. Theories discussed in Chapters 3 to 6 and the summary of arguments earlier in this chapter provide concepts and theoretical propositions to explain how IoPPs work through the manipulation of strategic choice, enforcement, leverage, and persuasion to achieve goals and produce perverse effects. These chapters also include theoretical accounts of the conditions under which IoPPs work best and when they might fail. Among other things, these discussions focus attention on the impact of a targeted party's organizational strength; institutional, political, and cultural opportunity structures; pre-existing democratic quality and 'resilience'; the calculations of governing populist parties about what needs to be done to stay in power; and clarity, credibility, timeliness, adaptation costs, and legitimacy of international interventions.

This bottom-up approach is well suited to capture the wide variety in patterns of opposition to populist parties in contemporary Europe. We already know that some kinds of initiatives are used in some countries, but not in others. Some initiatives can only really be used against populist parties in government, while others can only be used against those in opposition. Some initiatives may become more or less feasible over time or depend on the degree of political openness in a country. The bottom-up approach I outline here is designed to capture this reality. It allows researchers to study the effects of individual initiatives within one or more countries, as well as combinations of initiatives within one or several countries. Researchers can then use the approach to compare effectiveness across many countries, even though traditions of opposition vary. Depending on the topic of interest, researchers can pick and choose from the menu of concepts, theories, and hypotheses linking IoPPs with goal attainment and perverse effects.

The features of the bottom-up approach also permit, under certain conditions, insights developed with European populist parties in mind to travel to other regions of the world. The approach developed here assumes that opposition takes place in a democratic setting, although not necessarily within the high-quality, consolidated liberal democracies of the kind predominant in Europe. This suggests basic affinities between applicable theoretical constructs and political settings in the Americas, the region outside of Europe where populism has been most successful. Despite important differences in terms of democratic traditions, institutional structures and political culture, hypotheses about effects of opposition are plausible starting-points for analysing the effects of IoPPs in this part of the world. For example, the bottom-up approach I present here draws attention to constitutional constraints on the populist former president of the United States Donald Trump's ability to implement illiberal and anti-democratic policies. It invites questions about the impact of the horizontal separation of powers at the federal level as well as the distribution of political powers between federal and state governments, which provides alternative sites of power from which to mobilize opposition and block controversial policies. Similarly, Trump's personal legal problems, and investigations into his role in attacks on the US State Capitol Building on 6 January 2021 invites us to think about consequences for both Trump's leadership of the Republican Party and the effects of populist counter-discourses on support for Trump. The bottom-up approach I present here also assumes a degree of regional integration that is not matched elsewhere, even though regional organizations in places as diverse as Africa and the Americas pursue democratization and democracy protection agendas. Nevertheless, many of the theoretical constructs used to understand international IoPPs in the European case are drawn from the broader international relations literature. As such, they invite reflection on the ways in which the USA, as a global hegemon, promotes (or otherwise) liberal international orders; the impact of leverage and linkage on the quality of democracy within states; or the extent to which populist-led governments are willing to comply with international human rights law or to internationalize international democracy norms.

And finally, a bottom-up approach provides a way to address some of the fundamental methodological problems of establishing causality in the social world. In other words, a bottom-up approach makes it easier to connect political interventions more accurately—in our case, IoPPs—with outcomes of interest—in our case, achievement of goals pursued. It does so by providing a conceptual framework open to varying alternative explanations for outcomes observed. It also opens the possibility of observing *equifinality*, where outcomes may be achieved by different paths, or more specifically, how different IoPPs may combine in different ways to achieve the same goals or perverse effects in different contexts.

In sum, the approach was developed to study opposition to populist parties in Europe, an area of the world where populism has been highly successful in recent years, and where the level of regional integration facilitates a more substantial role for transnational and international actors. Yet populist successes in other parts of the world, particularly the USA and Latin America, raise the question of how well the model travels beyond the European case, where political systems vary, liberal democracy is less rooted, and regional integration is less substantial.

Practical Applications and Future Research

The ambition of this book is to provide a new way to study democratic defence in contemporary Europe. It can also be read as a manual or toolkit for those who disagree politically with populist parties. The preceding pages should have made it clear that even though opponents face democratic dilemmas and difficult choices, they are not powerless, even against the strongest, most successful populist parties. There are several more concrete lessons:

- Opposition to populist parties involves sorting through claims about who has the democratic high ground. Opposing populist parties in the name of democratic defence is complicated by the attractiveness of appeals to popular sovereignty, their electoral success, and by the fact that populist parties often mobilize genuine and reasonable grievances.
- There are many different ways to constrain populist parties or limit their influence without giving up commitments to political pluralism and liberal democratic principles. Populists can lose in fair elections or may

change following an orderly trial in the courts. They sometimes drop controversial policies in the wake of protests.
- Repressive and demonizing strategies are not necessarily ineffective, but they are harder to justify against populist parties who win many votes and are willing to participate in elections.
- Coercion, or the threat of coercion, is only one way to constrain populist parties or limit their influence. Opponents can structure the political environment to give populist parties incentives to change their behaviour. Populist parties and their supporters can also be persuaded to behave or think differently through dialogue or the dissemination of compelling political frames.
- A wide variety of political actors have the power to constrain populist parties, not just public authorities authorizing the use of coercion or political parties competing with populists in elections. Civil society can also effectively oppose populist parties, through strategies including disruption, shaming and stigmatization, and the dissemination of new ideas.
- International actors have a role to play in opposing populist parties as allies to domestic opponents, standard-setters, and as partners whose preferences are costly to ignore.
- In a context of democratic backsliding, the odds of constraining populist parties and limiting their influence are diminished but not extinguished. Hybrid democracies offer opportunities for opposition, even without a level playing field.
- Populist parties are likely to respond to opposition with countermeasures, including information campaigns, court challenges, and populist and sovereignty counter-discourses. These can have unintended consequences and need to be anticipated as much as possible when adopting one or other strategy of opposition.
- The choice and effectiveness of opposition initiatives are usually context dependent. In addition to the resilience of existing networks, political cultures of opposition and the varying resources of opponents, different strategies will work differently depending on the nature and resources of the populist party targeted. It matters if a populist party is in or out of government, how strong its popular support base is, and the extent to which a populist party is willing to work within liberal democratic institutions.

In many ways, this book is a leap in the dark. This is the first attempt to look at the big picture of opposition to populist parties in contemporary Europe.

I aimed to theorize how whole societies and international actors oppose populist parties. As I have shown here, we know something about some kinds of opposition—such as the impact of party-political strategies and recent EU responses to democratic backsliding. We have only scattered knowledge about civil society responses in different EU member states. It is less clear how all this fits together.

My approach here has been to draw together as much theory and empirical material as I could reasonably digest in a book project and to weave it together into a theory illustrated by plausible illustrations. While there are many finer points of theory, and many empirical examples I did not discuss, I am confident that the typology, mechanisms, and effects of initiatives on populist parties capture a large part of what is going on. My confidence rests on the quality of existing studies that my arguments draw on, as well as the abundance of empirical examples available to illustrate the theoretical points I make. I am aware though, that there are loose threads, and sometimes a superficial rendering of the insights of the various disciplinary fields which a model of democratic defence as normal politics necessarily incorporates. I do not claim that this book provides an empirical argument about the effectiveness of opposition to populist parties in contemporary Europe. More research is needed for this.

It would be desirable but beyond the scope of this research to couch work on the effects of IoPPs in a more substantial theory of voting behaviour or theories of party choice. Arguments about the constraints on illiberal and anti-democratic policies of populist parties in government need to be grounded in more complex theories of policymaking and a finer appreciation of what explains variation across political systems. A more sophisticated conception of transnational and multi-level governance in the EU would strengthen arguments about the effects of international IoPPs on domestic politics. We could learn a lot about persuasion with a deeper appreciation of social theory. A deeper engagement with political communication theory could enhance what is a rather superficial understanding of online forms of opposition to populist parties in this book.

One type of IoPP I do not touch on is policy and legislative responses, which includes new legislation, reforms, or public programmes. These may address problematic behaviour of populist parties (such as online hate speech) or longer-term programmes of civil education, changes in electoral rules, emergency legislation, or socio-economic policy reforms to address grievances raised by populist parties (reasonable or otherwise). I do not do so, because it is more demanding methodologically to specify whether such reforms are an initiative opposing populist parties, or whether they pursue more general policy goals or both. This is clearly a topic of interest and relevance which could be fruitfully taken up in future research.

I focus on a small set of goals and perverse effects pursued by populist parties, reflecting in part the state of our knowledge on the topic. There may be more goals, or perverse effects than those I focus on here. These include goals and unintended consequences not just affecting populist parties themselves, but broader consequences of populist mobilization such as polarization, trust in political institutions and fellow citizens, or changing conceptions of what a good democracy looks like. Another obvious next question concerns the interaction of goals and perverse effects over and above those shown in Figure C.1. In the book, I have focused on initiatives opposing populism independently. I did this to try to make it easier to pick up on the variety of effects the same initiative might produce, but also to simplify an already complex subject of study.

In short, I do not claim the last word on the set of initiatives opposing populist parties, the goals they pursue or unintended consequences, how they work, or their effectiveness. Rather, the book provides theories, concepts, hypotheses, and examples. It is an invitation to scrutinize, test, critique, and develop further what we already know about how and to what end those who disagree with populist parties oppose them.

APPENDICES

APPENDIX I

Quality of Democracy Scores (V-Dem) for Governments Led by Populist Parties in Europe (2000–2020)

Table A.1 below shows difference scores for Europe's populist-dominated governments between 2000 and 2020 for the V-Dem electoral democracy index (EDI) and liberal democracy index (LDI). The difference scores are calculated by subtracting country scores in the last year of a populist-dominated government from the country scores in the year before that government began. Data is shown for parties represented in European parliaments in 2020 that have at some point in the last two decades played a major role in governing cabinets. Major roles in government include holding the position of prime minister, leading a minority government, or being the largest party (or equal largest party) in a coalition government. A negative score indicates a decline in democratic quality. Where a populist party formed a new government within less than a year of being in opposition (e.g., GERB), V-Dem difference scores were calculated for old and new cabinets combined. The SVP, which participated in all but one Federal Council cabinets (2007–2008) since it was formed in 1971, was excluded from analysis. Where a government had not ended in 2020, V-Dem data from that year was used as a substitute for a party's last year in government.

Table A.1 V-Dem data on quality of democracy scores for governments led by populist parties in Europe (2000–2020)

Country	Party	Government	Opposition	V-Dem quality of democracy difference scores (%) (Score for populists' last year in government minus score for year before government formed) Electoral democracy index	V-Dem quality of democracy difference scores (%) Liberal democracy index
Bulgaria	Citizens for European Development of Bulgaria (GERB)	Borisov I: 2009–2013 Borisov II: 2014–2016 Borisov III: 2017–2021	Feb 2013–Nov 2014 Nov 2016–May 2017 May 2021–	−9	−14
Czechia	Action of Dissatisfied Citizens (ANO)	Babis I: December 2017–June 2018 Babis II: 2018–2021	Dec 2021–	−4	−6
Greece	Coalition of the Radical Left (SYRIZA)	Tsipras I: Jan 2015–Aug 2015 Tsipras II: 2015–2019 Tsipras III: Jan 2019–July 2019	8 July 2019–	−6	−8
Hungary	Hungarian Civic Alliance (Fidesz)	Orban II, III and IV May 2010–	—	−40	−41
Italy	Forza Italia (FI)	Berlusconi II and III: 2001–2006 Berlusconi IV: 2008–2011	2006–2008 Nov 2011–	1 −1	2 1
	Five Star Movement (5SM)	Conti I: 2018–2019 Conti II: 2019 – 2021 Draghi: 2021–2022	— — October 2022	−2	−1

Latvia	**Who Owns the State (KPV-LV)**	Karins I: Jan 2019–2022	—	-1
Lithuania	**Labour Party (DP) (9.8%)**	Brazauskas IV and V: 2004–2006	2006–2012 Oct 2016–	0
Poland	**Law and Justice (PiS)**	Marcinkiewicz I & II, Kaczynski: 2005–2007	2007–2015	-1
		Szydlo, Morawiecki I & II, Nov 2015–		-32
Slovakia	**Direction - Social Democracy (Smer)**	Fico I: 2006–2010	2010–2012	0
		Fico II, III, IV & Pellegrini: 2012–2020	March 2020–	-1
Slovenia	**Slovenian Democratic Party (SDS)**	Jansa I: 2004–2008	2008–2012	-1
		Jansa II: 2012–2013	2013–2020	0
		Jansa III: 2020–2022	June 2022–	-9
	List Marjan Šarec (LMŠ)	Sarec: 2018–2020	Jan 2020–2022	-13

(Second-to-last column values: -1, 0, -1, -25, 0, -2, -2, 0, -6, -1)

APPENDIX II

Moderation and Radicalization of Populist Party Ideological Positions

Moderation and radicalization of a populist party's ideological positions can be estimated using data on change in party policy positions over time (where available) in the Chapel Hill Expert Survey data 1999–2019. See Jolly, S., Bakker, S., Hooghe, L., Marks, G., Polk, J., Rovny, J., Steenbergen, M., & Vachudova, M.A., 2022. 'Chapel Hill Expert Survey Trend File, 1999–2019'. *Electoral Studies, 75. 102420.*

Data

Five items from the Chapel Hill Expert Survey were used to calculate change in ideological positions. Data on a party's 'overall ideology' draws on LRGEN, estimating the position of the party in terms of its overall ideological stance between the extreme left and extreme right. Data on 'socio-economic' positions draws on LRECON, estimating the position of the party in terms of its ideological stance on economic issues. Data on 'socio-cultural' positions draws on GALTAN, estimating the position of the party in terms of their views on 'libertarian' or 'postmaterialist' issues, which favour expanded personal freedoms, versus 'traditional' or 'authoritarian' views on political issues, which favour order, tradition, and stability and a role for government as a moral authority on social and cultural issues. Populist parties' positions on European integration draws on EU_POSITION, which estimates the 'overall orientation of the party leadership towards European integration'. Data on 'anti-elite' views is drawn from ANTIELITE_SALIENCE which estimates how important a party's 'anti-establishment and anti-elite rhetoric' are.

Measuring Moderation and Radicalization

With the exception of estimates of the overall orientation of party leadership towards European integration, which uses a seven-point scale, party positions are ranked an 11-point scale. Change in estimated party ideology for 'overall ideology', 'socio-economic', and 'socio-cultural' and 'European integration' are coded as *moderation* if it moved away from either high or low scores on the scale towards the mid-point, while a change was coded as *radicalization* where a party policy score moved closer to the high or low points on the scale away from the mid-point. By contrast, for anti-elitist discourse changes in policy scores were coded as *moderation* if they became less salient and as *radicalization* if they became more salient.

The magnitude of moderation and radicalization was calculated with reference to the following thresholds. *For parties subject to ostracism,* change in party policy position scores were coded as *no change* if there was a difference of less than 1 point *between the most extreme and least extreme policy position* held by the populist party over the whole period where data was available. Where the difference in policy positions changed from between 1.0 and 1.9 points, it is coded as *moderation/ radicalization*. Where the difference in policy positions changed by more than 2 points it is coded as *high moderation/high radicalization*.

For parties participating in governing, change in party position measured the difference in estimated party positions from (a) the data point closest to but before the year the party entered government, or where this was not available the first year of governing, and (b) the year closest to the last year of, but during, its participation in government, or where this was not available the year closest to its last governing year. Changes in policy positions were coded as *no change* if there was a difference of less than 1 point *between a party's stance just before, or upon entering government, and at or near the end of that governing period*. Where the difference in policy positions changed from between 1.0 and 1.9 points, it is coded as *moderation/ radicalization*. Where the difference in policy positions changed by more than 2 points it is *coded as high moderation/high radicalization*.

Additional Notes

Coding for Freedom Part of Austria's (FPÖ) participation in government between 2000 and 2005 was based on calculations from estimates of policy positions in 1999 before the government was constituted and data from 2006, one year after it had left government following a split forming the Alliance for the Future of Austria (BZÖ) (which stayed in government). Coding for FPÖ's participation in government between 2017 and 2019 was based on calculations from estimates of policy positions in 2014, two years before it entered government and the year it left government.

Coding for Finns Party's (PS) participation in government between 2015 was based on data from 2014, before it entered government and 2019, two years after it left government following a split forming a new party that would come to be called Blue Reform (SIN) (which stayed in government).

Coding for Citizens for European Development of Bulgaria (GERB) was based on calculations from estimates of policy positions in the first year of governing and data from the mid-point in its most recent period of governing.

Coding for the Czech Action of Dissatisfied Citizens (ANO) was based on data from estimates of policy positions in its first year of governing in a coalition government where it was the second-largest coalition partner and data from the mid-point in its most recent period of governing.

Coding for the second and third governments of the Slovakian Direction-Social Democracy (Direction-SMER) was based on calculations from estimates of policy positions in the last year of governing in the previous government and data one year after it left the government.

Coding for the second governments of Slovenian Democratic Party (SDS) was based on calculations from estimates of policy positions from data in the year after it left the government. Calculations for anti-elite salience are only available for 2014 and 2019, so these were the data points used to calculate differences in policy positions and code for moderation or radicalization.

APPENDIX III

Selected European Court of Human Rights Rulings against Fidesz (2010–2021) and Law and Justice (2015–2021)

Hungary	ECHR violation
Magyar Keresztény Mennonita Egyház and Others v Hungary, 8 April 2014 The 2011 Hungarian Law on the Church, which required certain religious minorities to reapply for lost status as registered churches, was incompatible with the State's duty of neutrality in religious matters.	Freedom of assembly and association (Article 11) Freedom of thought, conscience, and religion (Article 9)
Karácsony and Others v Hungary, 17 May 2016 Hungarian parliamentarians from opposition parties were fined for disrupting the work of parliament (showing billboards and using a megaphone) and did not have access to procedural safeguards allowing them to challenge the measures against them.	Freedom of expression (Article 10)
Baka v Hungary, 23 June 2016 Premature termination of mandate of András Baka, president of the Hungarian Supreme Court, following criticisms of government judicial reforms	Access to a tribunal (Article 6(1)) Freedom of expression (Article 10).
Erményi v Hungary, 22 November 2016 Premature termination of mandate of Lajos Erményi, vice-president of the Hungarian Supreme Court and forced retirement as president of Civil Law Division of the Supreme Court after lowering of retirement age for judges.	Respect for private life (Article 8)
Magyar Helsinki Bizottság v Hungary, 8 November 2016 Hungarian authorities' refusal to provide a human rights NGO with information relating to the public defenders system in Hungary had impaired the NGO's exercise of freedom to receive and impart information.	Freedom of expression (Article 10).
Király and Dömötör v Hungary, 17 January 2017 The police had failed to protect two men of Roma origin from racist abuse during an anti-Roma demonstration. Authorities' failure to investigate the incident properly raised concerns the public would think the State legitimized or tolerated organized intimidation of the Roma community.	Private and family life (Article 8)

Continued

Continued

Hungary	ECHR violation
Miracle Europe Kft v Hungary, 22 February 2017 An action for damages concerning a construction project was assigned to a court by the National Judicial Office using discretionary powers which meant the case was not heard by a 'tribunal established by law'.	Right to a fair hearing (Article 6(1))
Szurovecz v Hungary, 8 October 2019 Hungarian authorities had not given sufficiently good reasons to warrant denying a journalist access to refugee reception facilities to conduct research on living conditions. This access was a condition for press freedom.	Freedom of expression (Article 10)
Ilias and Ahmed v Hungary, 21 November 2019 Two asylum-seekers from Bangladesh had their applications for asylum rejected in Hungary and were removed to Serbia. Here they faced problematic asylum proceedings or were sent on further to Greece, where refugee camp conditions were incompatible with the Convention.	Prohibition of torture and inhuman and degrading treatment (Article 3).
Magyar Kétfarkú Kutya Párt v Hungary, 20 January 2020 The National Election Commission fined a Hungarian opposition party for developing an app anonymously publishing information about invalid ballots cast during the government's 2016 referendum on EU migration plans. The court ruled the fine violated the right to free expression on a matter of public interest.	Freedom of expression (Article 10)

Poland	ECHR violation
Solksa and Rybicka v Poland, 20 September 2018 The decision of Polish prosecuting authorities to exhume bodies of victims of the Polish Air Force plane crash in Smolensk in 2010 deprived families of the victims the protection of private and family life.	Privacy and family life (Article 8)
M.K and Others v Poland, 23 February 2020 Guards on the Polish-Belarus border repeatedly refused to admit asylum applicants into Poland. They had come from Chechnya and the refusal to accept applications denied people the ability to ask for international protection.	Prohibition of torture or inhuman or degrading treatment (Article 3) Prohibition of collective expulsion of aliens (Article 4 of Protocol No. 4) effective remedy (Article 13 among others) Individual petition (Article 34)
Broda and Bojara v Poland, 29 June 2021 Vice-presidents of the Kielce Regional Court, Mariusz Broda and Alina Bojara, were not able to legally challenge the decisions of the minister of justice which prematurely ended their term of office.	Right to access to a court (Article 6(1))

Poland	ECHR violation
Xero Flor W Polsce v Poland, 7 May 2021 A company which tried to get compensation from the State for damage to one of its products (turf) by animals was tried in the Constitutional Court, which the ECtHR ruled was not a 'tribunal established by law' because one of its judges had been appointed using unlawful procedures.	Right to a free trial (Article 6)
Reczkowicz v Poland, 27 July 2021 A judgment against a barrister in the Disciplinary Chamber of the Polish Supreme Court had not been tried in a 'tribunal established by law'. The Disciplinary Chamber lacked impartiality and independence because the procedure for appointing judges had been unduly influenced by the legislative and executive powers.	Right to a free trial (Article 6)

Source: European Court of Human Rights, *The ECHR and Hungary: Facts and Figures*, August 2021; European Court of Human Rights, *Poland: Press Country Profile*, September 2021.

APPENDIX IV

Selected EU Infringement Rulings on Values-Related Cases against Poland and Hungary (2012–2021)

Hungary		
Case	Alleged treaty violations	Result
Infringement proceedings C-286/12, Commission v Hungary (Judicial Retirement Age), 2 October 2012	Infringement of Directive 2000/78 on equal treatment in employment and occupation.	Legal provisions lowering retirement age for judges, prosecutors, and notaries from 70 to 62 violated EU rules on age discrimination.
Infringement proceedings C-288/12 Commission v Hungary, (independence data protection), 8 April 2014	Directive 95/46/EC on data protection.	A 2011 law permitting the premature termination of the Data Protection Commissioner's term of office violated EU law requiring the independence of Data Protection supervisory authorities.
Infringement proceedings C-66/18 Commission v Hungary (Lex CEU), 6 October 2020	General Agreement on Trade and Services (GATS), Directive 2006/123/EC on free movement of services. CFR, Article 13 on academic freedom, Article 14 (3) on freedom to found educational establishments, Article 16 on freedom to conduct a business.	A 2017 law on higher education required foreign universities in Hungary to have a physical campus in their home country and for Hungary and the home country to regulate the university's activities in an international treaty within six months. If no treaty was agreed, the foreign university would be forced to close. The Hungarian law was ruled incompatible with international and EU law on free movement of services, freedom of establishment, and various fundamental rights provisions. The Central European University had already moved large parts of its operations to Vienna.

Continued

Continued

Hungary

Case	Alleged treaty violations	Result
Infringement proceedings C-78/18 Commission v Hungary (NGOs), 18 June 2020	Article 63 TFEU on free movement of capital, CFR articles 7 on respect for private life, Article 8 on data protection and Article 12 on freedom of association.	A 2017 law on civil society organization transparency required them to register foreign donations with Hungarian authorities. Organizations would be required to indicate on webpages and publications that they received support from abroad. Despite CJEU ruling that the law violated EU law, Open Society Institute and other prominent NGOS left Hungary.
Infringement proceedings C-808/18 Commission v Hungary, (asylum) 17 December 2020	Directive 2013/32/EU on asylum procedures; Directive 2013/33/EU on asylum reception, Directive 2008/115/EC on asylum returns	2015 and 2017 laws on asylum restricting access to international protection procedures, unlawfully detaining applicants in transit zones and moving illegally staying third-country nationals to a border area without observing the guarantees surrounding a return procedure violated EU law.
Infringement proceedings, Case C-821/19 Commission v Hungary (Stop Soros), 16 November 2021	Directive 2013/32/EU on asylum procedures	2018 legal measures known as the 'Stop Soros Laws' amended rules on illegal immigration, adding new grounds for rejecting asylum applications and criminalizing activity carried out to help asylum seekers, violated EU law.
Pending infringement proceedings (anti-LGBTIQ laws) initiated, 15 July 2021	Includes, Article 2 TEU on EU values, Article 56 TFEU on free movement of services, Article 34 TFEU on free movement of goods, CFR Article 1 on human dignity, Article 7 on private and family life, Article 11 on freedom of expression and Article 21 on sexual orientation nondiscrimination, Directive 2010/13/EU on Audiovisual Media Services, Directive 2020/31/EC on E-commerce.	A 2021 law prohibited or limited access to content that promoted or portrayed so-called divergence from self-identity corresponding to sex at birth, sex change, or homosexuality for adults under 18. It required a disclaimer on a children's book with LGBTIQ content. The law prohibited the provision of services displaying this content, even if these services originated from other member states.

Poland

Case	Alleged treaty violations	Result
Infringement: C-619/18 Commission v Poland (Independence of the Supreme Court), 24 June 2019	Article 19(1) TEU on obligation for effective legal protection; CFR. Article 47 on right to effective remedy and a fair trial.	A 2017 Law on the Supreme Court which lowered the retirement age of judges violated the principle of the irremovability of judges. Discretionary powers given in the law to the Polish president to prolong the terms of Supreme Court judges infringed the principle of judicial independence.
Infringement: C-192/18 (Independence of Ordinary Courts), 5 November 2019	Article 157 TFEU on equal pay), Directive 2006/54 on gender equality in employment, Article 19(1) TEU on obligation for effective legal protection. CFR Article 47 on right to effective remedy and a fair trial.	Various judicial reforms in 2016 and 2017 lowered the retirement age for judges and public prosecutors, differentiating by gender (females 60 years, males 65 years) violated the principle of equal opportunities and equal treatment of men and women in employment. Discretionary powers given to the minister of justice to prolong the terms of retiring judges infringed the principle of the irremovability of judges and judicial independence.
Infringement proceeding C-791/19 Commission vs Poland (Independence of the Disciplinary Chamber of the Supreme Court) 15 July 2021. Commission and Belgium, Denmark, Netherlands, Finland, Sweden	Article 19(1) TEU on obligation for effective legal protection; and Article 267 TFEU on preliminary rulings.	A 2017 law established a new Disciplinary Chamber in the Supreme Court, with responsibility to hear disciplinary cases against judges. The Disciplinary Chamber was composed of judges of the National Council of the Judiciary, most of whose members were appointed by political authorities. The court ruled that these arrangements undermined the independence and impartiality of the judiciary and therefore could not guarantee effective legal protection in fields covered by EU law. National laws which exposed judges to disciplinary proceedings if they made preliminary rulings to the CJEU violated EU law.

Continued

Appendix IV

Continued

Poland

Case	Alleged treaty violations	Result
Infringement Proceeding C-204/21 Safeguarding independence of Polish judges), 5 June 2023.	Article 19(1) TEU on obligation for effective legal protection, Article 267 TFEU on preliminary rulings and principle of the primacy of EU law. Regulation 2016/679 on data protection. CFR Article 47 on right to effective remedy and a fair trial; Article 7 on private and family life and Article 8 on protection of personal data.	The so-called 'muzzle law' of December 2019 forbade Polish national courts from reviewing compliance with EU requirements that courts are independent and impartial tribunals previously established by law. This violated EU law. The law also illegally placed the examination of complaints and legal issues concerning the lack of independence of a court or judge under the exclusive jurisdiction of the Extraordinary Review and Public Affairs Chamber of the Supreme Court. Judges from other judicial bodies who made such decisions would be subject to proceedings in the Disciplinary Chamber of the Supreme Court, whose independence and impartiality were not guaranteed. Requirements for newly appointed judges to provide information, including membership of a political party, breached right to private life and data protection rules.

Note abbreviations: TEU: Treaty on European Union; TFEU: Treaty on the Functioning of the European Union; CFR: EU Charter of Fundamental Rights

References

Books and Articles

Abedi, A. (2002). Challenges to established parties: The effects of party system features on the electoral fortunes of anti-political-establishment parties. *European Journal of Political Research,* 41, 551–583.

Abou-Chadi, T. & Krause, W. (2020). The causal effect of radical right success on mainstream parties' policy positions: A regression discontinuity approach. *British Journal of Political Science,* 50, 829–847.

Ágh, A. (2021). The emergence of the Europeanized party systems in EAU: The turning point at the 2019 EP elections in Hungary. *Comparative Politics,* 14, 20–41.

Akkerman, T. (2021). The Netherlands. In: *Populism and New Patterns of Political Competition in Western Europe* (edited by D. Albertazzi & D. Vampa). Pp. 131–147. London: Routledge.

Akkerman, T., Lange, S. de, & Roodouijn, M. (eds) (2016). *Radical Right-Wing Populist Parties in Western Europe: Into the Mainstream?* Abingdon: Routledge.

Akkerman, T. & Lange, S.L. de. (2012). Radical right parties in office: Incumbency records and the electoral cost of governing. *Government and Opposition,* 47, 574–596.

Akkerman, T. & Rooduijn, M. (2015). Pariahs or partners? Inclusion and exclusion of radical right parties and the effects on their policy positions. *Political Studies,* 63, 1140–1157.

Albertazzi, D., Bonansinga, D., & Vampa, D. (2021). The Strategies of Party Competition: A Typology. In: *Populism and New Patterns of Political Competition in Western Europe* (edited by D. Albertazzi & D. Vampa) Pp. 50–72. London: Routledge.

Albertazzi, D., Giovannini, A., & Seddone, A. (2018). 'No regionalism please, we are Leghisti!' The transformation of the Italian Lega Nord under the leadership of Matteo Salvini. *Regional & Federal Studies,* 28, 645–671.

Albertazzi, D. & McDonnell, D. (2015). *Populists in Power.* London: Routledge.

Albertazzi, D. & Vampa, D. (eds) (2021). *Populism and New Patterns of Political Competition in Western Europe.* London: Routledge.

Alter, K.J. (2012). The Multiple Roles of International Courts and Tribunals. In: *Interdisciplinary Perspectives on International Law and International Relations* (edited by J.L. Dunoff & M.A. Pollack). Pp. 345–370. Cambridge: Cambridge University Press.

Amenta, E. (2005). Political Contexts, Challenger Strategies, and Mobilization: Explaining the Impact of the Townsend Plan. In: *Routing the Opposition: Social Movements, Public Policy, and Democracy* (edited by D.S. Meyer, V. Jenness, & H. Ingram). Pp. 29–64. Minneapolis, MI: University of Minnesota Press.

Amenta, E. & Caren, N. (2007). The Legislative, Organizational, and Beneficiary Consequences of State-Oriented Challengers. In: *The Blackwell Companion to Social Movements* (edited by D.A. Snow, S.A. Soule, & H. Kriesi). Pp. 461–488. Oxford: Blackwell.

Andrews, K.T. (2001). Social movements and policy implementation: The Mississippi civil rights movement and the war on poverty, 1965 to 1971. *American Sociological Review,* 66, 71–95.

Arató, K. (2020). Hungary. In: *The European Parliament Election of 2019 in East-Central Europe* (edited by V. Hloušek & P. Kaniok). Pp. 107–130. Cham: Springer International Publishing.

Art, D. (2007). Reacting to the radical right: Lessons from Germany and Austria. *Party Politics*, 13, 331–349.

Art, D. (2018). The AfD and the end of containment in Germany? *German Politics and Society*, 36, 76–86.

Arzheimer, K. & Carter, E. (2006). Political opportunity structures and right-wing extremist party success. *European Journal of Political Research*, 45, 419–443.

Aslanidis, P. (2016). Is populism an ideology? A refutation and a new perspective. *Political Studies*, 64, 88–104.

Backes, U. (2006). Limits of political freedom in democratic constitutional states: A comparative study on Germany, France and the USA. *Totalitarismus und Demokratie*, 3, 265–282.

Bale, T. (2003). Cinderella and her ugly sisters: The mainstream and extreme right in Europe's bipolarising party systems. *West European Politics*, 26, 67–90.

Bale, T. (2007). Are bans on political parties bound to turn out badly? A comparative investigation of three 'intolerant' democracies: Turkey, Spain, and Belgium. *Comparative European Politics*, 5, 141–157.

Bale, T., Green-Pedersen, C., & Krouwel, A. et al. (2008). If you can't beat them, join them? Explaining Social Democratic responses to the challenge from the populist radical right in Western Europe. *Political Studies*, 58, 410–426.

Bardi, L. & Mair, P. (2008). The parameters of party systems. *Party Politics*, 14, 147–166.

Barr, R. (2018). Populism ss a Political Strategy. In: *Routledge Handbook of Global Populism* (edited by C. de la Torre) Pp. 44–56. Abingdon: Routledge.

Batory, A. (2016). Defying the commission: Creative compliance and respect for the rule of law in the EU. *Public Administration*, 94, 685–699.

Behrens, P., Terry, N., & Jensen, O. (2019). Introduction. In: *Holocaust and Genocide Denial: A Contextual Perspective* (edited by P. Behrens, N. Terry, & O. Jensen). Pp. 1–6. London: Routledge.

Benford, R.D. & Snow, D.A. (2000). Framing processes and social movements: An overview and assessment. *Annual Review of Sociology*, 26, 611–639.

Bennett, L. & Segerberg, A. (2013). *The Logic of Connective Action: Digital Media and the LondonPersonalization of Contentious Politics*. Cambridge: Cambridge University Press.

Berge, B. von dem & Poguntke, T. (2013). The influence of Europarties on Central and Eastern European partner parties: A theoretical and analytical model. *European Political Science Review*, 5, 311–334.

Berman, S. (2008). Taming extremist parties: Lessons from Europe. *Journal of Democracy*, 19, 5–18.

Bermeo, N. (2016). On democratic backsliding. *Journal of Democracy*, 27, 5–19.

Bernhard, L., Biancalana, C., & Mazzoleni, O. (2021). Switzerland. In: *Populism and New Patterns of Political Competition in Western Europe* (edited by D. Albertazzi & D. Vampa) Pp. 148–167. London: Routledge.

Besselink, L. (2017). *The Bite, the Bark, and the Howl*. In: The Enforcement of EU Law and Values: Ensuring Member States' Compliance (edited by A Jakab & D Kochenov) Oxford: Oxford University Press.

Betz, H.-G. (1994). *Radical Right-Wing populism in Western Europe*. Basingstoke: Macmillan.

Betz, H.-G. (2002). Against globalization: Xenophobia, identity politics and a populism of exclusion in Western Europe. *Politique et sociétés*, 21, 9–28.

Betz, H.-G. (2016). The New Politics of Resentment. In: *The Populist Radical Party: A Reader* (edited by C. Mudde). Pp. 338–351. London: Taylor & Francis.

Bielinka-Kowalewska, K. (2017). #czarnyprotest: The Black protest for abortion rights in Poland. *New Politics*, 16, 53–60.

Blauberger, M. & Hüllen, V. van (2021). Conditionality of EU funds: An instrument to enforce EU fundamental values? *Journal of European Integration*, 43, 1–16.

Blauberger, M. & Kelemen, R.D. (2017). Can courts rescue national democracy? Judicial safeguards against democratic backsliding in the EU. *Journal of European Public Policy*, 24, 321–336.

Bleich, E. (2011). The rise of hate speech and hate crime laws in liberal democracies. *Journal of Ethnic and Migration Studies*, 37, 917–934.

Bligh, G. (2013). Defending democracy: A new understanding of the party-banning phenomenon. Vanderbilt Journal of Transnational Law, 46, 1321–1379.

Bojarski, Ł. (2021). Civil society organizations for and with the courts and judges—Struggle for the rule of law and judicial independence: The case of Poland 1976–2020. *German Law Journal*, 22, 1344–1384.

Boras, P. (2022). *The Final Countdown: The EU, Poland, and the Rule of Law*. European Council of Foreign Relations, ecfr.eu.

Boris, J. & Vári, G. (2015). The Road of the Hungarian Solidarity Movement. In: *The Hungarian Patient: Social Opposition to an Illiberal Democracy* (edited by P. Krasztev & J. Van Til). Pp. 181–206. Budapest: Central European University Press.

Bourne, A. (2012). Democratisation and the proscription of political parties. *European Constitutional Law Review*, 19, 1065–1085.

Bourne, A. (2018). *Democratic Dilemmas: Why Democracies Ban Parties*. London: Routledge.

Bourne, A. (2022). From militant democracy to normal politics? How European democracies respond to populist parties. *European Constitutional Law Review*, 18, 488–510.

Bourne, A. (2023). Initiatives opposing populist parties in Europe: Types, methods, and patterns. *Comparative European Politics*, https://doi.org/10.1057/s41295-023-00343-7.

Boykoff, J. (2007). Limiting dissent: The mechanisms of state repression in the USA. *Social Movement Studies*, 6, 281–310.

Braunthal, G. (1990). *Political Loyalty and Public Service in West Germany: The 1972 Decree against Radicals and its Consequences*. Amherst: University of Massachussetts Press.

Brems, E. (2006). Belgium: The Vlaams Blok political party convicted indirectly of racism. *International Journal of Constitutional Law*, 4, 702–711.

Brubaker, R. (2017). Why populism? *Theory and Society*, 46, 357–385.

Brug, W. van der, Fennema, M., & Tillie, J. (2005). Why some anti-immigrant parties fail and others succeed: A two-step model of aggregate electoral support. *Comparative Political Studies*, 38, 537–573.

Bugaric, B. (2016). Protecting Democrcy Inside the EU: On Article 7 TEU and the Hungarian Turn to Authoritarianism. In: *Reinforcing Rule of Law Oversight in the European Union* (edited by C. Closa & D. Kochenov). Pp. 82–101. Cambridge: Cambridge University Press.

Burstein, P. (1999). Social Movements and Public Policy. In: *How Social Movements Matter* (edited by M. Giugni, D. McAdam, & C. Tilly) Pp. 3–21. Minneapolis, MI: University of Minnesota Press.

Burstein, P., Einwohner, R., & Hollander, J. (1995). The Success of Political Movements: A Bargaining Perspective. In: *The Politics of Social Protest* (edited by C. Jenkins, B. Klandermans and J. Craig Jenkins). Pp. 275–295. London: UCL Press.

Burstein, P. & Linton, A. (2002). The impact of political parties, interest groups, and social movement organizations on public policy: Some recent evidence and theoretical concerns. *Social Forces*, 81, 380–408.

Bútorová, Z. & Bútora, M. (2019). The pendulum swing of Slovakia's democracy. *Social Research*, 86, 83–112.

Canovan, M. (1999). Trust the people! Populism and the two faces of democracy. *Political Studies*, XLVII, 2–16.

Canovan, M. (2002). Taking Politics to the People: Populism as the Ideology of Democracy. In: *Democracies and The Populist Challenge* (edited by Y. Mény & Y. Surel). London: Palgrave Macmillan.

Capoccia, G. (2001). Defending democracy: Strategies of reaction to political extremism in inter-war Europe. *European Journal of Political Research*, 39, 431–460.

Capoccia, G. (2005). *Defending Democracy: Reactions to Extremism in Interwar Europe*. Baltimore: Johns Hopkins University Press.

Capoccia, G. (2013). Militant democracy: The institutional bases of democratic self-preservation. *Annual Review of Law and Social Sciences*, 9, 207–226.

Caruso, L. & De Blasio, E. (2021). From the streets to the web: Communication and democratic participation in the case of the 'Sardines'. *Contemporary Italian Politics*, 13, 242–258.

Chiaramonte, A., De Sio, L. & Emanuele, V. (2020). Salvini's success and the collapse of the Five-star Movement: The European elections of 2019. *Contemporary Italian Politics*, 12, 140–154.

Closa, C. (2019). The politics of guarding the Treaties: Commission scrutiny of rule of law compliance. *Journal of European Public Policy*, 26, 696–716.

Closa, C. (2021). Institutional logics and the EU's limited sanctioning capacity under Article 7 TEU. *International Political Science Review*, 42, 501–515.

Cotta, M. (2020). The anti-establishment parties at the helm: From great hopes to failure and a limited resurrection. *Contemporary Italian Politics*, 12, 126–139.

Cress, D.M. & Snow, D.A. (2000). The outcomes of homeless mobilization: The influence of organization, disruption, political mediation, and framing. *American Journal of Sociology*, 105, 1063–1104.

Dahl, R. (2000). *On Democracy*. New Haven and London: Yale University Press.

Davenport, C. (2004). Repression and Mobilization: Insights from Political Science and Sociology. In: *Repression and Mobilization* (edited by C. Davenport, H. Johnston, & C. Mueller). Pp. vii–xli. Minneapolis and London: University of Minnesota Press.

Davenport, C. (2007). *State Repression and the Domestic Democratic Peace*. Cambridge: Cambridge University Press.

Deloy, C. (2011). *General Elections in Slovenia*. Foundation Robert Schuman.

de la Torre, Carlos (2019), *Routledge Handbook of Global Populism*, Oxon: Routledge.

Dézé, A. (2003). Between Adaptation, Differentiation and Distinction: Extreme Right-Wing Parties within Democratic Political Systems. In: *Western Democracies and the New Extreme Right Challenge* (edited by R. Eatwell & C. Mudde). Pp. 19–40. London: Routledge.

Diamond, L. (2015). Facing up to the democratic recession. *Journal of Democracy*, 26, 141–155.

Downs, A. (1957). *An Economic Theory of Democracy*. New York: Harper & Row.

Downs, W. (2001). Pariahs in their midst: Belgian and Norwegian parties react to extremist threats. *West European Politics*, 24, 23–42.

Downs, W. (2012). *Political Extremism in Democracies: Combatting Intolerance*. Basingstoke: Palgrave Macmillan.

Drezov, Kyril (2013). A neighbour in turmoil: Two waves of popular protest in 2013 Bulgaria. *Journal of Global Faultlines*, 1(2), 52–57.

Earl, J. (2003). Tanks, tear gas, and taxes: Toward a theory of movement repression. *Sociological Theory*, 21, 44–68.

Earl, J. (2011). Political repression: Iron fists, velvet gloves, and diffuse control. *Annual Review of Sociology*, 37, 261–284.

Earl, J. (2016). Protest Online: Theorizing the Consequences of Online Engagement. In: *The Consequences of Social Movements* (edited by L. Bosi, M. Giugni, & K. Uba). Pp. 363–400. Cambridge: Cambridge University Press.

Eatwell, R. (2000). The rebirth of the 'extreme right' in Western Europe? *Parliamentary Affairs*, 53, 407–425.

Eatwell, R. & Goodwin, M.J. (2018). *National Populism: The Revolt against Liberal Democracy*. London: Pelican.

Eberl, J. M, Huber, L.M & Plescia, C. (2020). A tale of firsts: the 2019 Austria snap election, *West European Politics*, 43, 1350–1363.

Edwards, B., McCarthy, J.D., & Mataic, D.R. (2018). The Resource Context of Social Movements. In: *The Wiley Blackwell Companion to Social Movements* (edited by D.A. Snow, S.A. Soule, H. Kriesi & H.J. McCammon). Pp. 79–97. Chichester: John Wiley.

Engesser, S., Ernst, N., Esser, F., & Büchel, F. (2017). Populism and social media: How politicians spread a fragmented ideology. *Information, Communication & Society*, 20, 1109–1126.

Enyedi, Z. (2016). Populist polarization and party system institutionalization: The role of party politics in de-democratization. *Problems of Post-Communism*, 63, 210–220.

Enyedi, Z. & Róna, D. (2018). Governmental and Oppositional Populism: Competition and Division of Labour. In: *Absorbing the Blow: Populist Parties in their Impact on Parties and Party Systems* (edited by S. Wolinetz & A. Zaslove). Pp. 251–272. London: Rowman & Littlefield.

Epstein, R.A. & Sedelmeier, U. (2008). Beyond conditionality: International institutions in postcommunist Europe after enlargement. *Journal of European Public Policy*, 15, 795–805.

Erk, J. (2005). From Vlaams Blok to Vlaams Belang: The Belgian far-right renames itself. *West European Politics*, 28, 493–502.

Evans, J. & Ivaldi, G. (2021). France: Party System Change and the Demise of the Post-Gaullist Right. In: *Riding the Populist Wave: Europe's Mainstream Right in Crisis* (edited by T. Bale & C. Rovira Kaltwasser). Pp. 113–140. Cambridge: Cambridge University Press.

Fallend, F. & Heinisch, R. (2016). Collaboration as successful strategy against right-wing populism? The case of the centre-right coalition in Austria, 2000–2007. *Democratization*, 23, 324–344.

Faraguna, P. (2011). Report on the Italian Constitutional Court's case law. *Journal for Constitutional Theory and Philosophy of Law*, 11, 127–138.

Ferrari, E. (2019). 'Free country, free internet': The symbolic power of technology in the Hungarian internet tax protests. *Media, Culture & Society*, 41, 70–85.

Ferree, M.M. (2005). Soft Repression: Ridicule, Stigma and Silencing in Gender-Based Movements. In: *Repression and Mobilization* (edited by C. Davenport, H. Johnston, & C. Mueller). Pp. 138–155. Minneapolis, MI: University of Minnesota Press.

Fieschi, C. (2019). *Populocracy: The Tyranny of Authenticity and the Rise of Populism*. Newcastle upon Tyne: Agenda Publishing.

Fink-Hafner, D. (2013). Slovenia. *European Journal of Political Research. Political Data Yearbook*, 52, 217–222.

Fink-Hafner, D. & Krasovec, A. (2014). Slovenia. *European Journal of Political Research. Political Data Yearbook*, 53, 281–286.

Finnemore, M. & Sikkink, K. (1998). International norm dynamics and political change. *International Organization*, 52, 887–917.

Fox, G. & Nolte, G. (2000). Intolerant Democracies. In: *Democratic Governance and International Law* (edited by G. Fox & B. Roth). Pp. 389–435. Cambridge: Cambridge University Press.

Fox Piven, F. & Cloward, R.A. (1979). *Poor People's Movements*. New York: Vintage. Penguin Random House.

Freeden, M. (2017). After the Brexit referendum: Revisiting populism as an ideology. *Journal of Political Ideologies*, 22, 1–11.

Friman, H.R. (2015). Introduction: Unpacking the Mobilization of Shame. In: *The Politics of Leverage in International Relations* (edited by H.R. Friman). Pp. 1–29. London: Palgrave Macmillan.

Galston, W. (2018). The populist challenge to liberal democracy. *Journal of Democracy*, 29, 5–19.

236　References

Galtung, J. (1967). On the effects of international economic sanctions, with examples from the case of Rhodesia. *World Politics*, 19, 378–416.
Gamson, W.A. (2007). Bystanders, Public Opinion, and the Media. In: *The Blackwell Companion to Social Movements* (edited by D.A. Snow, S.A. Soule, & H. Kriesi). Pp. 242–261. Oxford: Blackwell.
Gamson, W.A. & Meyer, D.S. (1996). Framing Political Opportunity. In: *Comparative Perspectives on Social Movements* (edited by D. McAdam, J.D. McCarthy, & M.N. Zald). Pp. 275–290. New York: Cambridge University Press.
Gerbaudo, P. (2018). *The Digital Party: Political Organisation and Online Democracy*. London: Pluto.
Givan, R.K., Roberts, K.M., & Soule, S.A. (2010). Introduction: The Dimensions of Diffusion. In: *The Diffusion of Social Movements* (edited by R. Kolin Givan, K.M. Roberts, & S.A. Soule). Pp. 1–16. Cambridge: Cambridge University Press.
Goffman, E. (1963). *Stigma: Notes on the Management of Spoiled Identity*. New York: Touchstone.
Goldner Lang, I. (2019). The rule of law, the force of law and the power of money in the EU. *Croatian Yearbook of European Law and Policy*, 15, 1–26.
Goldsmith, J.L. & Posner, E.A. (2005). *The Limits of International Law*. Oxford: Oxford University Press.
Goodin, R.E. (1996). Institutions and their Design. In: *Theory of Institutional Design* (edited by, R.E Goodin). Pp. 1–53. Cambridge: Cambridge University Press.
Gordon, D. (1987). Limits on extremist political parties: A comparison of Israeli jurisprudence with that of the United States and West Germany. *Hastings International and Comparative Law Review*, 10, 347–400.
Grabbe, H. (2001). How does Europeanization affect CEE governance? Conditionality, diffusion, and diversity. *Journal of European Public Policy*, 8, 1013–1031.
Grabbe, H. (2014). Six lessons of enlargement ten years on: The EU's transformative power in retrospect and prospect. *Journal of Common Market Studies*, 52, 40–56.
Greskovits, B. (2015). The hollowing and backsliding of democracy in East Central Europe. *Global Policy*, 6, 28–37.
Guasti, P. (2020). Populism in power and democracy: Democratic decay and resilience in the Czech Republic (2013–2020). *Politics and Governance*, 8, 473–484.
Guzman, A. (2008). *How International Law Works*. Oxford: Oxford University Press.
Gwiazda, A. (2021). Right-wing populism and feminist politics: The case of Law and Justice in Poland. *International Political Science Review*, 42, 580–595.
Hall, B. (2019). Gendering resistance to right-wing populism: Black protest and a new wave of feminist activism in Poland? *American Behavioral Scientist*, 63, 1497–1515.
Hall, P.A. & Taylor, R.C.R. (1996). Political science and the three new institutionalisms. *Political Studies*, 44, 936–957.
Hamdaoui, S. (2021a). Anti-populism during the Yellow Vest protests: From combatting the Rassemblement National to dealing with street populists. *British Journal of Political and International Relations*, 0, 1–18.
Hamdaoui, S. (2021b). A 'stylistic anti-populism': An analysis of the Sardine movement's opposition to Matteo Salvini in Italy. *Social Movement Studies*, 1–17.
Hardt, S. & Eliantonio, M. (2011). 'Thou shalt be saved' (from trial)? The ruling of the Italian Constitutional Court on Berlusconi's immunity law in a comparative perspective. *European Constitutional Law Review*, 7, 17–39.
Harteveld, E., Mendoza, P., & Rooduijn, M (2022). 'Affective polarization and the populist radical right: Creating the hating? *Government and Opposition*, 57, 703–727.
Haughton, T. (2011). Half full but also half empty: Conditionality, compliance and the quality of democracy in Central and Eastern Europe. *Political Studies Review*, 9, 323–333.

Haughton, T. (2014). Money, margins and the motors of politics: The EU and the development of party politics in Central and Eastern Europe. *Journal of Common Market Studies*, 52, 71–87.

Haughton, T. & Krasovec, A. (2014). Predictably unpredictable: The 2014 parliamentary elections in Slovenia. *European Parties Elections and Referendums Network.*, https://epern. wordpress.com/2014/07/17/predictably-unpredictable-the-2014-parliamentary-elections-in-slovenia/

Haughton, T. & Rybář, M. (2009). A tool in the toolbox: Assessing the impact of EU membership on party politics in Slovakia. *Journal of Communist Studies and Transition Politics*, 25, 540–563.

Hawkins, K.A. (2010). *Venezuela's Chavismo and Populism in Comparative Perspective*. Cambridge: Cambridge University Press.

Hawkins, K.A. (2018). The Ideational Approach. In: *Routledge Handbook of Global Populism* (edited by C. de la Torre). Pp. 57–72. Abingdon: Routledge.

Hawkins, K.A. & Rovira Kaltwasser, C. (2017). The ideational approach to populism. *Latin American Research Review*, 52, 513–528.

Heinisch, R. (2003). Success in opposition—failure in government: Explaining the performance of right-wing populist parties in public office. *West European Politics*, 26, 91–130.

Heinisch, R., Habersack, F., & Fallend, F. (2021). Austria. In: *Populism and New Patterns of Political Competition in Western Europe* (edited by D. Albertazzi & D. Vampa). Pp. 73–91. London: Routledge.

Heinisch, R. & Mazzoleni, O. (2017). Analysing and Explaining Populism: Bringing Frame, Actor and Context Back In. In: *Political Populism: A Handbook, International Studies on Populism* (edited by R. Heinisch, O. Mazzoleni, & C. Holtz-Bacha). Pp. 105–122. Baden-Baden: Nomos Verlagsgesellschaft.

Heinze, A.-S. & Weisskircher, M. (2021). No strong leaders needed? AfD party organisation between collective leadership, internal democracy, and 'movement-party' strategy. *Politics and Governance*, 9, 263–274.

Helfer, L.R. & Slaughter, A.-M. (1997). Toward a theory of effective supranational adjudication. *Yale Law Journal*, 107, 273–291.

Hellström, A. & Nilsson, T. (2010). 'We are the good guys': Ideological positioning of the nationalist party Sverigedemokraterna in contemporary Swedish politics. *Ethnicities*, 10, 55–76.

Huber, R.A. & Schimpf, C.H. (2017). On the distinct effects of left-wing and right-wing Populism on democratic quality. *Politics and Governance*, 5, 146–165.

Hutter, S., Kriesi, H., & Lorenzini, J. (2018). Social Movements in Interaction with Political Parties. In: *The Wiley Blackwell Companion to Social Movements* (edited by D.A. Snow, S.A. Soule, H. Kriesi, & H.J. McCammon). Pp. 322–337. Chichester: John Wiley.

Hutter, S. & Vliegenthart, R. (2018). Who responds to protest? Protest politics and party responsiveness in Western Europe. *Party Politics*, 24, 358–369.

Ignazi, P. (2003). *Extreme Right Parties in Western Europe*. Oxford: Oxford University Press.

Ilonszki, G. & Dudzińska, A. (2021). Opposition behaviour against the third wave of autocratisation: Hungary and Poland compared. *European Political Science*, 20, 603–616.

Invernizzi Accetti, C. & Zuckerman, I. (2017). What's Wrong with Militant Democracy? *Political Studies*, 65, 182–199.

Ivaldi, G. (2016). A New Course for the French Radical Right? The Front National and 'De-demonisation'. In: *Radical Right-Wing Populist Parties in Western Europe into the Mainstream?* (edited by T. Akkerman, S. de Lange, & M. Roodouijn). Pp. 225–246. London: Routledge.

Jacobs, L. & van Spanje, J. (2020). Prosecuted, yet popular? Hate speech prosecution of anti-immigrant politicians in the news and electoral support. *Comparative European Politics*, 18, 899–924.

Jagers, J. & Walgrave, S. (2007). Populism as political communication style: An empirical study of political parties' discourse in Belgium. *European Journal of Political Research*, 46, 319–345.

Jenne, E.K. & Mudde, C. (2012). Can outsiders help? *Journal of Democracy*, 23, 147–155.

Jolly, S., Bakker, S., Hooghe, L., Marks, G., Polk, J., Rovny, J., Steenbergen, M., & Vachudova, M.A., (2022). 'Chapel Hill Expert Survey Trend File, 1999–2019'. *Electoral Studies*, 75, 102420.

Juul Christiansen, F. (2016). The Danish People's Party: Combining Cooperation and Radical Positions. In: *Radical Right-Wing Populist Parties in Western Europe into the Mainstream?* (edited by T. Akkerman, S. de Lange, & M. Roodouijn). Pp. 94–112. London: Routledge.

Kaltwasser, C.R. & Taggart, P. (2016). Dealing with populists in government: A framework for analysis. *Democratization*, 23, 201–220.

Kaltwasser Rovira, C., Taggart, P., Espejo Ochoa, P., & Ostiguy, P. (2017). Populism: An Overview of the Concept and State of the Art. In: *The Oxford Handbook of Populism* (edited by C. Kaltwasser Rovira, P. Taggart, P. Espejo Ochoa, & P. Ostiguy). Pp. 1–26. Oxford: Oxford University Press.

Karolewski, I. P. (2016). Protest and participation in post-transformation Poland: The case of the Committee for the Defense of Democracy (KOD). *Communist and Post-Communist Studies*, 49, 255–267.

Keane, J. (2004). *Violence and Democracy*. Cambridge: Cambridge University Press.

Keck, M. E. & Sikkink, K. (1998). *Activists beyond Borders: Advocacy Networks in International Politics*. Ithaca, NY: Cornell University Press.

Kelemen, R. D. (2020). The European Union's authoritarian equilibrium. *Journal of European Public Policy*, 27, 481–499.

Keller, H. & Stone Sweet, A. (2016). *A Europe of Rights: The Impact of the ECHR on National Legal Systems*. Oxford: Oxford University Press.

Keohane, R. O. (1989). *International Institutions and State Power. Essays in International Relations Theory*. New York: Routledge.

Keohane, R. O. (1997) When does international law come home? *Houston Law Review*, 35, 699–713.

Keohane, R. O. (2002). Introduction: From Interdependence and Institutions to Globalization and Governance. In: *Power and Governance in a Partially Globalized World*. Pp. 1–23. New York: Routledge.

Keohane, R. O., Moravcsik, A., & Slaughter, A.-M. (2000). Legalized dispute resolution: Interstate and transnational. *International Organization*, 54, 457–488.

Keohane, R.O. & Nye, Jr., J.S. (1987). Power and interdependence revisited. *International Organization*, 41, 725–753.

Kim, S. (2021). *Discourse, Hegemony and Populism in the Visegrád Four*. London: Routledge.

Kirchheimer, O. (1961). *Political Justice: The Use of Legal Procedure for Political Ends*. Princeton: Princeton University Press.

Kirn, G. (2018). Maribor's Social Uprising in the European Crisis: From Antipolitics of People to Politicisation of Periphery's Surplus Population. In: *Social Movements in the Balkans: Rebellion and Protest from Maribor to Taksim* (edited by F. Bieber & D. Brentin) Pp. 30–47. London: Routledge.

Kirshner, A. (2014). *A Theory of Militant Democracy: The Ethics of Combatting Political Extremism*. New Haven, CT: Yale University Press.

Kitschelt, H. & McGann, A.J. (1997). *The Radical Wing in Western Europe: A Comparative Analysis*. Ann Arbor: University of Michigan Press.

Klamt, M. (2007). Militant Democracy and the Democratic Dilemma: Different Ways of Protecting Democratic institutions. In: *Explorations in Legal Cultures* (edited by F. Bruinsma & D. Nelken) Pp. 133–160. London: Reed Business.

Klandermans, B. (1984). Mobilization and participation: Social-psychological expansions of resource mobilization theory. *American Sociological Review*, 49, 583–600.

Kochenov, D. & Pech, L. (2016). Better late than never? On the European Commission's rule of law framework and its first activation: Commission's rule of law framework. *Journal of Common Market Studies*, 54, 1062–1074.

Kolarova, R. & Spirova, M. (2014). Bulgaria. *European Journal of Political Research. Political Data Yearbook*, 53, 45–56.

Kolb, F. (2007). *Protest and Opportunities. The Political Outcomes of Social Movements.* Chicago: Campus Verlag.

Kommers, D.P. (1997). *The Constitutional Jurisprudence of the Federal Republic of Germany.* 2nd edn. Durham: Duke University Press.

Koopmans, R. (2005). Repression and the Public Sphere: Discursive Opportunities for Repression against the Extreme Right in Germany in the 1990s. In: *Repression and Mobilization* (edited by C. Davenport, H. Johnston, & C. Mueller). Pp. 159–188. Minneapolis, MI: University of Minnesota Press.

Kosař, D., Petrov, J., & Šipulová, K. et al. (2020). *Domestic Judicial Treatment of European Court of Human Rights Case Law: Beyond Compliance.* 1st edn. London: Routledge.

Kosař, D. & Šipulová, K. (2018). The Strasbourg Court meets abusive constitutionalism: Baka v. Hungary and the rule of law. *Hague Journal on the Rule of Law*, 10, 83–110.

Kosiara-Pedersen, K. (2020). Stronger core, weaker fringes: The Danish general election 2019. *West European Politics*, 43, 1011–1022.

Krašovec, A. (2015). Slovenia. *European Journal of Political Research. Political Data Yearbook*, 54, 269–277.

Krause, W., Cohen, D., & Abou-Chadi, T. (2023) Does accommodation work? Mainstream party strategies and the success of radical right parties. *Political Science Research and Methods*, 11, 172–179.

Krause, W. & Giebler, H. (2020). Shifting welfare policy positions: The impact of radical right populist party success beyond migration politics. *Representation*, 56, 331–348.

Krekó, P. (2017). *Rethinking the Far Right in Hungary: Defeating Orbán is Impossible without Jobbik's Votes.* Friedrich Ebert Stiftung.

Krekó, P. & Juhász, A. (2018). *The Hungarian Far Right. Social Demand, Political Supply and International Context.* Stuttgart and Hanover: ibidem Press.

Kriesi, H. (2004). Political Context and Opportunity. In: *The Blackwell Companion of Social Movements* (edited by D.A. Snow, S.A. Soule, & H. Kriesi). Pp. 67–90. Oxford: Blackwell.

Kriesi, H., Grande, E., & Lachat, R. et al. (2005). Globalization and the transformation of the national political space: Six European countries compared. *European Journal of Political Research*, 45, 921–956.

Kriesi, H., Koopmans, R., Dyvendak, J.W., & Giugni, M. (1995). *New Social Movements in Western Europe: A Comparative Analysis.* London: UCL Press.

Kriesi, H. & Pappas, T.S. (2015). European Populism in the Shadow of the Great Recession. Colchester: ECPR Press.

Lacatus, C. & Sedelmeier, U. (2020). Does monitoring without enforcement make a difference? The European Union and anti-corruption policies in Bulgaria and Romania after accession. *Journal of European Public Policy*, 27, 1236–1255.

Laclau, E. (2005). *On Populist Reason.* London: Verso.

Lacny, J. (2021). The rule of law conditionality under Regulation No. 2092/2020: Is it all about the money? *Hague Journal on the Rule of Law*, 13, 79–105.

Láštic, E. (2019). Slovakia: Political developments and data in 2018. *European Journal of Political Research. Political Data Yearbook*, 58, 241–247.
Laver, M. & Schofield, N. (1998). *Multiparty Government: The Politics of Coalition in Europe.* Ann Arbor: University of Michigan Press.
Levite, A. & Tarrow, S. (1983). The legitimation of excluded parties in dominant party systems: A comparison of Israel and Italy. *Comparative Politics*, 15, 295–327.
Levitsky, S. & Loxton, J. (2013). Populism and competitive authoritarianism in the Andes. *Democratization*, 20, 107–136.
Levitsky, S. & Loxton, J. (2019). Populism and Competitive Authoritarianism in Latin America. In: *Routledge Handbook of Global Populism* (edited by C. de la Torre). Pp. 334–350. Abingdon: Routledge.
Levitsky, S. & Way, L.A. (2010). *Competitive Authoritarianism: Hybrid Regimes after the Cold War.* Cambridge: Cambridge University Press.
Levitsky, S. & Way, L. (2020). The new competitive authoritarianism. *Journal of Democracy*, 31, 51–65.
Levitsky, S. & Ziblatt, D. (2018). *How Democracies Die.* New York: Crown.
Lewis, P.G. (2008). Changes in the party politics of the new EU member states in Central Europe: Patterns of Europeanization and democratization. *Journal of Southern Europe and the Balkans*, 10, 151–165.
Lichbach, M.I. (1987). Deterrence or escalation? The puzzle of aggregate studies of repression and dissent. *Journal of Conflict Resolution*, 31, 266–297.
Locke, J. (1689). A letter concerning toleration.
Loewenstein, K. (1937). Militant democracy and fundamental rights II. *American Political Science Review*, 31, 638–658.
Lucardie, P., Akkerman, T., & Pauwels, T. (2021). It is Still a Long Way from Madou Square to Law Street: The Evolution of the Flemish Bloc. In: *Riding the Populist Wave: Europe's Mainstream Right in Crisis* (edited by T. Bale & C. Rovira Kaltwasser). Pp. 208–224. Cambridge: Cambridge University Press.
Lührmann, A. & Lindberg, S.I. (2019). A third wave of autocratization is here: What is new about it? *Democratization*, 26, 1095–1113.
Lührmann, A., Tannenberg, M., & Lindberg, S.I. (2018). Regimes of the World (RoW): Opening new avenues for the comparative study of political regimes. *Politics and Governance*, 6, 60–77.
Macklem, P. (2012). Guarding the perimeter: Militant democracy and religious freedom in Europe. *Constellations*, 19, 575–590.
Mair, P. (2002). Populist Democracy vs Party Democracy. In: *Democracies and the Populist Challenge* (edited by Y. Mény & Y. Surel). Pp. 81–98. London: Palgrave Macmillan.
Malkopoulou, A. (2019). Introduction: Militant Democracy and its Critics. In: *Militant Democracy and its Critics* (edited by A. Malkopoulou & A.S. Kirshner). Pp. 1–12. Edinburgh: Edinburgh University Press.
Malkopoulou, A. & Kirshner, A. (eds) (2019). *Militant Democracy and its Critics.* Edinburgh: Edinburgh University Press.
Malkopoulou, A. & Norman, L. (2018). Three models of democratic self-defence: Militant democracy and its alternatives. *Political Studes,* 66, 442–458.
March, J. & Olsen, J. (1996). Institutional perspectives on political institutions. *Governance: An International Journal of Policy and Administration*, 9, 247–264.
Martin, L. & Stevenson, R. (2001). Government formation in parliamentary democracies. *American Journal of Political Science*, 45, 33–50.
Marx Ferree, M. (2004). Soft Repression: Ridicule, Stigma and Silencing in Gender-Based Movements. In: *Repression and Mobilization* (edited by C. Davenport, H. Johnston & C. Mueller). Pp. 138–155. Minneapolis and London: University of Minnesota Press.

McAdam, D., Tarrow, S. & Tilly, C. (2001) *Dynamics of contention*. Cambridge: Cambridge University Press.
McCarthy, J.D. & McPhail, C. (2006). Protest Mobilization, Protest Repression and their Interaction. In: *Repression and Mobilization* (edited by C. Davenport, H. Johnston, & C. Mueller). Pp. 3–32. Minneapolis, MI: University of Minnesota Press.
McCarthy, J.D. & Zald, M.N. (2002). The Enduring Vitality of the Resource Mobilization Theory of Social Movements. In: *Handbook of Sociological Theory* (edited by J.H. Turner). Pp. 533–565. New York: Plenum Publishers.
McKinnon, C. (2006). *Toleration: A Critical Introduction*. London: Routledge.
McNally, D. (2016). Norms, corruption, and voting for Berlusconi: Corruption and voter support. *Politics & Policy*, 44, 976–1008.
Meguid, B.M. (2005). Competition between unequals: The role of mainstream party strategy in niche party success. *American Political Science Review*, 99, 347–359.
Meijers M. & Zaslove, A. (2020). *Populism and Political Parties Expert Survey 2018 (POPPA)*. https://doi.org/10.7910/DVN/8NEL7B, Harvard Dataverse.
Meijers, M.J., & Zaslove, A. (2021). Measuring populism in political parties: Appraisal of a new approach. *Comparative Political Studies*, 54, 372–377.
Meléndez, C. & Rovira Kaltwasser, C. (2021). Negative partisanship towards the populist radical right and democratic resilience in Western Europe. *Democratization*, 28, 949–969.
Mény, Y. & Surel, Y. (2002a). The Constitutive Ambiguity of Populism. In: *Democracies and the Populist Challenge* (edited by Y. Mény & Y. Surel). Pp. 1–21. London: Palgrave Macmillan.
Mény, Y. & Surel, Y. (eds) (2002b). *Democracies and the Populist Challenge*. London: Palgrave Macmillan.
Meret, S. (2021). Denmark. In: *Populism and New Patterns of Political Competition in Western Europe* (edited by D. Albertazzi & D. Vampa). Pp. 168–186. London: Routledge.
Merlingen, M., Mudde, C., & Sedelmeier, U. (2001). The right and the righteous? European norms, domestic politics and the sanctions against Austria. *Journal of Common Market Studies*, 39, 59–77.
Michael, G. & Minkenberg, M. (2007). A continuum for responding to the extreme right: A comparison between the United States and Germany. *Studies in Conflict and Terrorism*, 30, 1109–1123.
Minkenberg, M. (2003). The West European radical right as a collective actor: Modelling the impact of cultural and structural variables on party formation and movement mobilization. *Comparative European Politics*, 1, 149–170.
Miró, J. (2019). Beyond populism and institutionalism: Anti-populism and the management of austerity in Spain. *Constellations*, 26, 116–131.
Moffitt, B. (2016). *The Global Rise of Populism: Performance, Political Style and Representation*. Redwood City, CA: Stanford University Press.
Moffitt, B. (2018). The populism/anti-populism divide in Western Europe. *Democratic Theory*, 5, 1–16.
Molnár, V. (2016). Civil Society in an Illiberal Democracy. In: *Brave New Hungary: Mapping the 'System of National Cooperation'* (edited by J.M. Kovács & B. Trencsenyi). Pp. 51–72. Blue Ridge Summit, PA: Lexington Books.
Moore, W.H. (1998). Repression and dissent: Substitution, context and timing. *American Journal of Political Science*, 42, 851–873.
Moravcsik, A. (2012). Liberal Theories of International Law. In: *Interdisciplinary Perspectives on International Law and International Relations* (edited by J.L. Dunoff & M.A. Pollack). Pp. 83–118. Cambridge: Cambridge University Press.
Moravcsik, A. & Vachudova, M.A. (2003). National interests, state power, and EU enlargement. *East European Politics and Societies: and Cultures*, 17, 42–57.

Moschella, M. & Rhodes, M. (2020). Introduction. *Contemporary Italian Politics*, 12, 112–125.
Motak, D., Krotofil, J., & Wójciak, D. (2021). The battle for symbolic power: Kraków as a stage of renegotiation of the social position of the Catholic Church in Poland. *Religions*, 12, 594.
Mouffe, C. (2000). *The Democratic Paradox*. London: Verso.
Mouffe, C. (2018). *For a Left Populism*. La Vergne: Verso.
Mounk, Y. (2018). *The People vs. Democracy: Why Our Freedom is in Danger and How to Save It*. Cambridge: Harvard University Press.
Mudde, C. (2004). The populist zeitgeist. *Government and Opposition*, 39, 541–563.
Mudde, C. (2007). Populist Radical Right Parties in Europe. Cambridge: Cambridge University Press.
Mudde, C. & Rovira Kaltwasser, C. (2012). Populism and (Liberal) Democracy: A Framework for Analysis. In: *Populism in Europe and the Americas: Threat or Corrective for Democracy?* (edited by C. Mudde & C. Rovira Kaltwasser). Pp. 1–26. Cambridge: Cambridge University Press.
Mudde, C. & Rovira Kaltwasser, C. (2013). Exclusionary vs. inclusionary populism: Comparing contemporary Europe and Latin America. *Government and Opposition*, 48, 147–174.
Mudde, C. & Rovira Kaltwasser, C. (2017). *Populism: A Very Short Introduction*. Oxford: Oxford University Press.
Müller, J.-W. (2012). Militant Democracy. In: *The Oxford Handbook of Comparative Constitutional Law* (edited by M. Rosenfeld & A. Sajó). Pp. 1253–1269. Oxford: Oxford University Press.
Müller, J.-W. (2014a). The EU as a militant democracy, or: Are there limits to constitutional mutations within EU member states? *Revista de Estudios Políticos*, 22.
Müller, J.-W. (2014b). Europe's other democracy problem: The challenge of protecting democracy and the rule of law within EU member states. *Juncture*, 21, 151–157.
Müller, J.-W. (2016a). *What is Populism?* Philadelphia: University of Pennsylvania Press.
Müller, J.-W. (2016b). Protecting popular self-government from the people? New normative perspectives on militant democracy. *Annual Review of Political Science*, 19, 249–265.
Müller, W. & Strøm, K. (1999). *Policy Office or Votes?* Cambridge: Cambridge University Press.
Nguyen, T. (2022) The Hungary files: Untangling the political and economic knots, V*erfBlog*, 2022/12/08, https://verfassungsblog.de/the-hungary-files.
Niesen, P. (2002). Anti-extremism, negative republicanism, civil society: Three paradigms for banning political parties. *German Law Journal*, 3, 249–286.
Niesen, P. (2012). Banning the former ruling party. *Constellations*, 19, 540–561.
Norris, P. & Inglehart, R. (2019). *Cultural Backlash: Trump, Brexit, and Authoritarian Populism*. Cambridge: Cambridge University Press.
Nye, Jr., J.S. & Keohane, R.O. (1977). *Power and Interdependence: World Politics in Transition*. Boston: Little, Brown and Company.
Ostiguy, P. (2017). Populism: A Socio-Cultural Approach. In: *The Oxford Handbook of Populism* (edited by C. Kaltwasser Rovira, P. Taggart, P. Espejo Ochoa, & P. Ostiguy). Pp. 73–100. Oxford: Oxford University Press.
Pappas, T.S. (2019). *Populism and Liberal Democracy: A Comparative and Theoretical Analysis*. Oxford: Oxford University Press.
Pautz, H. (2021). Germany. In: *Populism and New Patterns of Political Competition in Western Europe* (edited by D. Albertazzi & D. Vampa). Pp. 112–130. London: Routledge.
Pauwels, T. (2011). Explaining the strange decline of the populist radical right Vlaams Belang in Belgium: The impact of permanent opposition. *Acta Politica*, 46, 60–82.
Pech, L. & Kochenov, D. (2021). Respect for the rule of law in the case law of the European Court of Justice: A casebook overview of key judgments since the Portuguese judges case. SIEPS Report Stockholm.

Pech, L. & Jaraczewski, J. (2023) Systemic Theat to the Rule of Law in Poland: Updated and new Article 7(1) TEU Recommendations. Democratic Institute Working Papers, 2023/02. Vienna: Central European University.

Pech, L. & Platon, S. (2018). *Rule of Law Backsliding in the EU: The Court of Justice to the Rescue? Some Thoughts on the ECJ Ruling in Associação Sindical dos Juízes Portugueses*. EU Law Analysis.

Pech, L., Wachowiec, P., & Mazur, D. (2021). Poland's rule of law breakdown: A five-year assessment of EU's (in)action. *Hague Journal on the Rule of Law*, 13, 1–43.

Pedahzur, A. (2004). The Defending Democracy and the Extreme Right: A Comparative Analysis. In: *Western Democracies and the New Extreme Right Challenge* (edited by R. Eatwell & C. Mudde). Pp. 108–132. London: Routledge.

Petócz, G. (2015). Milla: A Suspended Experiment. In: *The Hungarian Patient: Social Opposition to an Illiberal Democracy* (edited by P. Krasztev & J. Van Til). Pp. 207–229. Budapest: Central European University Press.

Petrov, J. (2020). The populist challenge to the European Court of Human Rights. *International Journal of Constitutional Law*, 18, 476–508.

Piccio, D.R. (2016). The Impact of Social Movements on Political Parties. In: *The Consequences of Social Movements* (edited by L. Bosi, M. Giugni, & K. Uba). Pp. 263–284. Cambridge: Cambridge University Press.

Pierson, P (2000). Increasing returns, path dependence, and the study of politics. *American Political Science Review*, 94, 251–267.

Pirro, A.L. & Taggart, P. (2018). The populist politics of Euroscepticism in times of crisis: A framework for analysis. *Politics*, 38, 253–262.

Póczik, S. & Sárik, E. (2019). Vigilante Militias and Activities against Roma and Migrants in Hungary. In: *Vigilantism against Migrants and Minorities*. (edited by Bjørgo, T. & Mareš, M.) Pp. 103–128. Milton: Routledge.

Popper, K. (1966). *The Open Society and its Enemies*. London: Routledge.

Porta, D. della (2008). Research on social movements and political violence. *Qualitative Sociology*, 31, 221–230.

Porta, D. della & Diani, M. (2006). *Social Movements: An Introduction*. Malden, Mass: Wiley-Blackwell.

Pospíšil, I. (2020). Activist Constitutional Court as Utility Tool for Correcting Politics: Structure, Composition and Case-law. In: *Czech Democracy in Crisis* (edited by A. Lorenz & H. Formánková). Pp. 133–155. Cham: Springer.

Pridham, G. (2006). Assessing democratic consolidation in Central & Eastern Europe: The European dimension. *Acta Politica*, 41, 342–369.

Pytlas, B. (2016). *Radical Right Parties in Central and Eastern Europe: Mainstream Party Competition and Electoral Fortune*. Abingdon: Routledge.

Radiukiewicz, A. (2019). Defenders of democracy at the protest. *Polish Sociological Review*, 355–370.

Ravik Jupskås, A. (2016). The Taming of the Shrew: How the Progress Party (Almost) Became Part of the Mainstream. In: *Radical Right-Wing Populist Parties in Western Europe: Into the Mainstream?* (edited by T. Akkerman, S. de Lange, & M. Roodouijn). Pp. 94–111. Abingdon: Routledge.

Rawls, J. (1971). *A Theory of Justice*. Oxford: Oxford University Press.

Rijpkema, B. (2018). *Militant Democracy: The Limits of Democratic Tolerance*. Abingdon: Routledge.

Ripoll Servent, A. (2019). The European Parliament after the 2019 elections: Testing the boundaries of the 'cordon sanitaire'. *Journal of Contemporary European Research*, 15, 331–342.

Risse, T. & Ropp, S.C. (2013). Introduction and Overview. In: *The Persistent Power of Human Rights* (edited by T. Risse, S.C. Ropp, & K. Sikkink). Pp. 3–25. Cambridge: Cambridge University Press.

Risse, T. & Sikkink, K. (1999). The Socialization of International Human Rights Norms into Domestic Practices: Introduction. In: *The Power of Human Rights* (edited by T. Risse, S.C. Ropp, & K. Sikkink). Pp. 1–38. Cambridge: Cambridge University Press.

Risse, T. & Sikkink, K. (2013). Conclusions. In: *The Persistent Power of Human Rights* (edited by T. Risse, S.C. Ropp, & K. Sikkink). Pp. 275–295. Cambridge: Cambridge University Press.

Risse-Kappen, T., Ropp, S., & Sikkink, K. (eds) (1999). *The Power of Human Rights: International Norms and Domestic Change*. Cambridge: Cambridge University Press.

Risse-Kappen, T., Ropp, S.C., & Sikkink, K. (eds) (2013) *The Persistent Power of Human Rights*. Cambridge: Cambridge University Press.

Roberts, K.M. (2019). Bipolar disorders: Varieties of capitalism and populist out-flanking on the left and right. *Polity*, 51, 641–653.

Rochon, T.R. (2018). *Culture Moves: Ideas, Activism, and Changing Values*. Princeton: Princeton University Press.

Rodrik, D. (2018). Populism and the Economics of Globalization. *Journal of International Business Policy*, 1, 12–33.

Roggeband, C. & Klandermans, B. (eds) (2017). *Handbook of Social Movements Across Disciplines. Handbooks of Sociology and Social Research*. Cham: Springer.

Rone, J. (2017). Left in Translation: The Curious Absence of Austerity Frames in the 2013 Bulgarian Protests. In: *Global Diffusion of Protest* (edited by D. della Porta). Pp. 137–166. Amsterdam University Press.

Rooduijn, M. (2019). State of the field: How to study populism and adjacent topics? A plea for both more and less focus. *European Journal of Political Research*, 58, 362–372.

Rooduijn, M., Kessel, S. van, & Froio, C. et al. (2019). The PopuList: An Overview of Populist, Far Right, Far Left and Eurosceptic Parties in Europe, https://popu-list.org/.

Rooduijn, M. & Pauwels, T. (2011). Measuring populism: Comparing two methods of content analysis. *West European Politics*, 34, 1272–1283.

Rosenblum, N.L. (2008). *On the Side of the Angels: An Appreciation of Parties and Partisanship*. Princeton: Princeton University Press.

Rovira Kaltwasser, C. (2019). Militant Democracy Versus Populism. In: *Militant Democracy and its Critics* (edited by A. Malkopoulou & A. Kirshner). Pp. 72–91. Edinburgh: Edinburgh University Press.

Rovira Kaltwasser, C. and Taggart, P. (2016). Dealing with populists in government: A framework for analysis, *Democratization*, 23(2), Pp. 201–220.

Rucht, D. (2013). Protest Movements and Their Media Usages. In: *Mediation and Protest Movements* (edited by B. Cammaerts, A. Matoni, & P. McCurdy). Pp. 249–268. Bristol: Intellect.

Rummens, S. (2020). Resolving the Paradox of Tolerance. In: *Militant Democacy and its Critics* (edited by A. Malkopoulou & A. Kirshner). Pp. 112–132. Edinburgh University Press.

Rummens, S. & Abts, K. (2010). Defending democracy: The concentric containment of political extremism. *Political Studes*, 58, 649–665.

Ruth-Lovell, S.P., Lührmann, A., & Grahn, S. (2019). Democracy and populism: Testing a contentious relationship. *SSRN Electronic Journal*.

Rydgren, J. (2005). Is extreme right-wing populism contagious? Explaining the emergence of a new party family. *European Journal of Political Research*, 44, 413–437.

Rydgren, J. (2007). The sociology of the radical right. *Annual Review of Sociology*, 33, 241–262.

Sadurski, W. (2004). Accession's democracy dividend: The impact of the EU enlargement upon democracy in the new member states of Central and Eastern Europe. *European Law Journal*, 10, 371–401.

Sadurski, W. (2010). Adding a bite to a bark? A Ssory of Article 7, the EU enlargement, and Jörg Haider. *Columbia Journal of European Law*, 16(3), 385–426.

Sadurski, W. (2019a). Polish constitutional tribunal under PiS: From an activist court to a paralysed tribunal, to a governmental enabler. *Hague Journal on the Rule of Law*, 11, 63–84.

Sadurski, W. (2019b). *Poland's Constitutional Breakdown*. Oxford: Oxford University Press.

Sajó, A. (2021). *Ruling by Cheating: Governance in Illiberal Democracy*. Cambridge: Cambridge University Press.

Salo, S. & Rydgren, J. (2021). *The Battle Over Working-Class Voters: How Social Democracy Has Responded to the Populist Radical Right in the Nordic Countries*. Abingdon: Taylor & Francis.

Sartori, G. (1976). *Parties and Party Systems: A Framework for Analysis*. Cambridge: Cambridge University Press.

Scanlon, T. (2003). *The Difficulty of Tolerance*. Cambridge: Cambridge University Press.

Schain, M.A. (2006). The extreme-right and immigration policymaking: Measuring direct and indirect effects. *West European Politics*, 29, 270–289.

Scheppele, K.L. (2013). The Rule of Law and the Frankenstate: Why Governance Checklists Do Not Work: Commentary. *Governance*, 26, 559–562.

Scheppele, K.L. (2018). Autocratic legalism. *University of Chicago Law Review*, 85, 545–585.

Scheppele, K.L., Kelemen, D. & Morijn, J. (2002). *The Good, the Bad and the Ugly: The Commission Proposes Freezing Funds to Hungary*, VerfBlog, 2022/12/01, https://verfassungsblog.de/the-good-the-bad-and-the-ugly-2/, https://doi.org/10.17176/20221202-001548-0.

Scheppele, K.L., Vladimirovich Kochenov, D., & Grabowska-Moroz, B. (2020). EU values are law, after all: Enforcing EU values through systemic infringement actions by the European Commission and the member states of the European Union. *Yearbook of European Law*, 39, 3–121.

Schimmelfennig, F. & Sedelmeier, U. (2004). Governance by conditionality: EU rule transfer to the candidate countries of Central and Eastern Europe. *Journal of European Public Policy*, 11, 661–679.

Schimmelfennig, F. & Sedelmeier, U. (2020). The Europeanization of Eastern Europe: The external incentives model revisited. *Journal of European Public Policy*, 27, 814–833.

Schlipphak, B. & Treib, O. (2017). Playing the blame game on Brussels: The domestic political effects of EU interventions against democratic backsliding. *Journal of European Public Policy*, 24, 352–365.

Schmidt, M. & Bogdanowicz, P. (2018). The infringement procedure in the rule of law crisis: How to make efective use of article 258 TFEU. *Common Market Law Review*, 55, 1061–1100.

Schmidt, V. (2008). Discursive institutionalism: The explanatory power of ideas and discourse. *Annual Review of Political Science*, 11, 303–326.

Schumpeter, J. (1947). *Capitalism, Socialism, and Democracy*. London: George Allen & Unwin.

Schwörer, J. & Fernández-García, B. (2021). Demonisation of political discourses? How mainstream parties talk about the populist radical right. *West European Politics*, 44, 1401–1424.

Sedelmeier, U. (2017). Political safeguards against democratic backsliding in the EU: The limits of material sanctions and the scope of social pressure. *Journal of European Public Policy*, 24, 337–351.

Shields, J. (2021). France. In: *Populism and New Patterns of Political Competition in Western Europe* (edited by D. Albertazzi & D. Vampa). Pp. 92–111. London: Routledge.

Sijstermans, J. (2021). The Vlaams Belang: A mass party of the 21st century. *Politics and Governance*, 9, 275–285.
Simmons, B.A. (2009). *Mobilizing for Human Rights: International Law in Domestic Politics.* Cambridge: Cambridge University Press.
Spendzharova, A.B. & Vachudova, M.A. (2012). Catching up? Consolidating liberal democracy in Bulgaria and Romania after EU accession. *West European Politics*, 35, 39–58.
Spirova, M. (2008). Europarties and party development in EU-candidate states: The case of Bulgaria. *Europe-Asia Studies,* 60, 791–808.
Spirova, M. & Sharenkova-Toshkova, R. (2021). Juggling friends and foes: Prime Minister Borissov's surprise survival in Bulgaria. *East European Politics*, 37, 432–447.
Startin, N. (2010). Where to for the radical right in the European Parliament? *Perspectives on European Politics and Society*, 11, 429–449.
Stavrakakis, Y. (2014). The return of 'the people': Populism and anti-populism in the shadow of the European crisis. *Constellations*, 21, 505–517.
Stavrakakis, Y. (2018). Paradoxes of polarization: Democracy's inherent division and the (anti-) populist challenge. *American Behavioral Scientist*, 62, 43–58.
Steinberg, R.H. (2012). Wanted – Dead or Alive. Realism in International Law. In: *Interdisciplinary Perspectives on International Law and International Relations.* Pp. 146–174. Cambridge: Cambridge University Press
Steinmo, S., Thelen, K., & Longstreth, F. (1992) *Structuring Politics: Historical Institutionalism in Comparative Analysis.* New York. Cambridge University Press.
Sunstein, C.R. (2017). *#Republic: Divided Democracy in the Age of Social Media.* Oxford: Princeton University Press.
Swank, D. & Betz, H.-G. (2003). Globalization, the welfare state and right-wing populism in Western Europe. *Socio-Economic Review,* 1, 215–245.
Szczerbiak, A. (2020) Poland. In: *The European Parliament Election of 2019 in East-Central Europe* (edited by V. Hloušek & Kaniok, P.) Pp. 179–199. Cham: Palgrave Macmillan
Taggart, P. (2002). Populism and the Pathology of Representative Politics. In: *Democracies and the Populist Challenge* (edited by Y. Mény & Y. Surel). Pp. 62–80. London: Palgrave Macmillan.
Tarrow, S. (2010). Dynamics of Diffusion: Mechanisms, Institutions, and Scale Shift. In: *The Diffusion of Social Movements* (edited by R.K. Givan, K.M. Roberts, & S.A. Soule). Pp. 204–220. Cambridge: Cambridge University Press.
Tarrow, S. (2011). *Power in Movement: Social Movements and Contentious Politics.* New York: Cambridge University Press.
Tarrow, S., McAdam, D., & Tilly, C. (2001). *Dynamics of Contention.* Cambridge: Cambridge University Press.
Tarrow, S. & Tilly, C. (2006). *Contentious Politics.* Oxford: Oxford University Press.
Taylor, V. & van Dyke, N. (2007). 'Get Up, Stand Up': Tactical Repertoires of Social Movements. In: *The Blackwell Companion to Social Movements* (edited by D.A. Snow, S.A. Soule, & H. Kriesi). Pp. 262–293. Oxford: Blackwell.
Thompson, A. (2012) Coercive Enforcement of International Law. In: *Interdisciplinary Perspectives on International Law and International Relations.* Pp. 146–174. Cambridge: Cambridge University Press.
Tilly, C. (2003). *The Politics of Collective Violence.* Cambridge: Cambridge University Press.
Tilly, C. (2004). Repression, Mobilization, and Explanation. In: *Repression and Mobilization* (edited by C. Davenport, H. Johnston, & C. Mueller). Pp. 211–226. Minneapolis and London: University of Minnesota Press.
Tsatsanis, E. (2021). Greece. In: *Populism and New Patterns of Political Competition in Western Europe* (edited by D. Albertazzi & D. Vampa). Pp. 231–249. Abingdon: Routledge.

Tyulkina, S. (2015). *Militant Democracy: Undemocratic Political Parties and Beyond*. London: Routledge.

Tyulkina, S. (2019). Militant Democracy as an Inherent Democratic Quality. In: *Militant Democracy and its Critics* (edited by A. Malkopoulou & A. Kirshner). Pp. 207–225. Edinburgh: Edinburgh University Press.

Uitz, R. (2020). Funding illiberal democracy: The case for credible budgetary conditionality in the EU. *SSRN Electronic Journal*.

V-Dem Institute (2021). Autocratization turns viral, Democracy Report 2020. University of Gothenburg.

Vágó, G. (2019). Hot winter in Hungary: Protest against the 'slave laws'. *Heinrich Böll Stiftung*, 12 March.

Vachudova, A.M. (2005). *Europe Undivided: Democracy, Leverage, and Integration after Communism*. Oxford: Oxford University Press.

Vachudova, M.A. (2008). Tempered by the EU? Political parties and party systems before and after accession. *Journal of European Public Policy*, 15, 861–879.

Vampa, D. (2017). Matteo Salvini's Northern League in 2016. *Italian Politics*, 32, 32–50.

Vampa, D. (2021). The United Kingdom. In: *Populism and New Patterns of Political Competition in Western Europe* (edited by D. Albertazzi & D. Vampa). Pp. 206–230. London: Routledge.

Vampa, D. & Albertazzi, D. (2021). Conclusion. In: *Populism and New Patterns of Political Competition in Western Europe* (edited by D. Albertazzi & D. Vampa). Pp. 206–230. London: Routledge.

Van der Brug, W., Fennema, M., & Tillie, J. (2005). Why some anti-immigrant parties fail and others succeed: A two-step model of aggregate electoral support. *Comparative Political Studies*, 38, 537–573.

Van Donselaar, J. (2017). Patterns of Response to the Extreme Right in Western Europe. In: *The Populist Radical Right: A Reader* (edited by C. Mudde). Pp. 543–557. London: Routledge.

Van Heerden, S.C. & Brug, W. van der. (2017). Demonisation and electoral support for populist radical right parties: A temporary effect. *Electoral Studies*, 47, 36–45.

Van Kessel, S. (2014). The populist cat-dog: Applying the concept of populism to contemporary European party systems. *Journal of Political Ideologies*, 19, 99–118.

Van Spanje, J. (2011). Keeping the rascals in: Anti-political-establishment parties and their cost of governing in established democracies. *European Journal of Political Research*, 50, 609–635.

Van Spanje, J. (2018). *Controlling the Electoral Marketplace. How Established Parties Ward Off Competition*. Springer.

Van Spanje, J. & Azrout, R. (2019). Tainted love: How stigmatization of a political party in news media reduces its electoral support. *International Journal of Public Opinion Research*, 31, 283–308.

Van Spanje, J. & van der Brug, W. (2007). The party as pariah: The exclusion of anti-Immigration parties and its effect on their ideological positions. *West European Politics*, 30, 1022–1040.

Van Spanje, J. & van der Brug, W. (2009). Being intolerant of the intolerant. The exclusion of Western European anti-immigration parties and its consequences for party choice. *Acta Politica*, 44, 353–384.

Van Spanje, J. & Vreese, C. de (2015). The good, the bad and the voter: The impact of hate speech prosecution of a politician on electoral support for his party. *Party Politics*, 21, 115–130.

Van Spanje, J. & Weber, T. (2019). Does ostracism affect party support? Comparative lessons and experimental evidence. *Party Politics*, 25, 745–758.

Varga, M. (2014). Hungary's 'anti-capitalist' far right: Jobbik and the Hungarian Guard. *Nationalities Papers*, 42, 791–807.

Várnagy, R. (2020). Hungary: Political developments and data in 2019. *European Journal of Political Research. Political Data Yearbook*, 59, 175–181.

Vedung, E. (2012). Six Models of Evaluation. In: *Routledge Handbook of Public Policy* (edited by E. Araral, S. Fritzen, M. Howlett, M. Ramesh, & Xun Wu). Pp. 387–400. London: Routledge.

Verbeek, B. & Zaslove, A. (2016). Italy: A case of mutating populism? *Democratization*, 23, 304–323.

Vittori, D. & Morlino, L. (2021). Populism and Democracy in Europe. In: *Populism and New Patterns of Political Competition in Western Europe* (edited by D. Albertazzi & D. Vampa). Pp. 19–49. Abingdon: Routledge.

Waldron, J. (1981). A right to do wrong. *Ethics*, 92, 21–39.

Weyland, K. (2017). Populism: A Political-Strategic Approach. In: *Oxford Handbook of Populism* (edited by P. Taggart, P. Ostiguy, C. Kaltwasser Rovira, & P. Espejo Ochoa). Pp. 48–72. Oxford: Oxford University Press.

Weyland, K. (2001). Clarifying a contested concept: Populism in the study of Latin American politics. *Comparative Politics*, 34, 1, 1–22.

Widfeldt, A. (2016). *Extreme Right Parties in Scandinavia*. Pp. 174–233. London: Routledge.

Wistrich, R. (2012). *Holocaust Denial: The Politics of Perfidy*. Berlin: De Gruyter.

World Press Freedom Index (2021). Reporters without borders.

Yotova, D. (2020). Bulgaria's anti-corruption protests explained—and why they matter for the EU. *European Council on Foreign Relations*, 28 July.

Zaslove, A. (2012). The populist radical right in government: The structure and agency of success and failure. *Comparative European Politics*, 10, 421–448.

Ziblatt, D. & Levitsky, S. (2018). *How Democracies Die*. New York: Crown.

Zielonka, J. (2018). *Counter-Revolution: Liberal Europe in Retreat*. Oxford: Oxford University Press.

Zontea, A. (2015). The Hungarian Student Network: A Counterculture in the Making. In: *The Hungarian Patient: Social Opposition to an Illiberal Democracy* (edited by P. Krasztev & J. van Til). Pp. 263–289. Budapest: Central European University Press.

Zulianello, M. (2019). *Anti-System Parties: From Parliamentary Breakthrough to Government*. Abingdon: Routledge.

Zulianello, M. (2020). Varieties of populist parties and party systems in Europe: From state-of-the-art to the application of a novel classification scheme to 66 parties in 33 countries. *Government and Opposition*, 55, 327–347.

Zulianello, M. (2021). The league of Matteo Salvini: Fostering and exporting a modern mass-party grounded on 'phygital' activism. *Politics and Governance*, 9, 228–239.

Zúquete, J.P. (2007). *Missionary Politics in Contemporary Europe*. Syracuse: Syracuse University Press.

Official Documents

Bundesamt für Verfassungsschutz (BfV) (2021). Defence of the Constitution, https://www.verfassungsschutz.de/DE/verfassungsschutz/auftrag/verfassung-schuetzen/verfassung-schuetzen_artikel.html, retrieved 30 November 2021.

Council of the European Union (2022a). Rule of law conditionality mechanism: Council decides to suspend €6.3 billion given only partial remedial action by Hungary. Press release. 12 December.

Council of the European Union (2022b). NextGenerationEU: Memberstates approve national plan of Hungary. Press release. 12 December.
Court of Justice of the EU (2021). Press Release no. 159/21.
Durao Barrosso, J.M. (2012). State of the Union Address by the President of the European Commission.
European Commission (2017). Proposal for a COUNCIL DECISION on the determination of a clear risk of a serious breach by the Republic of Poland of the rule of law COM 2017/0835 final.
European Commission (2021). Press release. Independence of Polish Judges: Commission asks European Court of Justice for financial penalties against Poland on the activity of the Disciplinary Chamber.
European Court of Human Rights (2021a). Press release. Newly created chamber of the Polish Supreme Court was in breach of the Convention (Reczkowicz v. Poland application no. 43447/19) 22 July.
European Court of Human Rights (2021b). *The ECHR and Hungary: Facts and Figures*, August 2021.
European Court of Human Rights (2021c). *Poland: Press Country Profile*, September 2021
European Parliament (2018). The situation in Hungary, European Parliament resolution of 12 September 2018 on a proposal calling for the council to determine, pursuant to Article 7(1) on the Treaty on European Union, the existence of a clear risk of a serious breach by Hungary of the values on which the Union is founded (No. P8_TA (2018)0340). European Parliament.
European Parliament (2021). Plenary session 19/10/2021. Available at: https://www.europarl.europa.eu/plenary/pl/vod.html?mode=unit&vodLanguage=PL&playerStartTime=20211019-09:23:06&playerEndTime=20211019-09:48:35#
Federal Minister of the Interior (2020). Brief summary 2020 Report on the Protection of the Constitution, Facts and Trends.

List of Cases

Judgment of the ECtHR of 8 April 2014. Magyar Keresztény Mennonita Egyház and Others v Hungary. Application no. 21623/13.
Judgment of the ECtHR of 17 May 2016. Karácsony and Others v Hungary. Application 42461/13.
Judgment of the ECtHR of 17 May 2016. Karácsony and Others v Hungary. Application 42461/13.
Judgment of the ECtHR of 23 June 2016. Baka v Hungary. Application no. 20261/12.
Judgment of the ECtHR of 8 November 2016. Magyar Helsinki Bizottság v Hungary. Application no. 18030/11.
Judgment of the ECtHR of 22 November 2016. Erményi v Hungary. Application no. 22254/14
Judgment of the ECtHR of 17 January 2017. Király and Dömötör v Hungary. Application 1085/13.
Judgment of the ECtHR of 22 February 2017. Miracle Europe Kft v Hungary. Application no. 57774/13.
Judgment of the ECtHR of 20 September 2018. Solksa and Rybicka v Poland. Applications no. 30491/17 and 31083/17.
Judgment of the ECtHR of 8 October 2019. Szurovecz v Hungary. Application no. 15428/16.
Judgment of the ECtHR of 21 November 2019. Ilias and Ahmed v Hungary. Application No. 47287/15.

Judgment of the ECtHR of 20 January 2020. Magyar Kétfarkú Kutya Párt v Hungary. Application no. 201/17.
Judgment of the ECtHR of 23 February 2020. M.K. and Others v Poland. Applications no. 40503/17, 42902/17 and 43643/17.
Judgment of the ECtHR of 7 May 2021. Xero Flor W Polsce v Poland. Application no. 4907/18.
Judgment of the ECtHR of 29 June 2021. Broda and Bojara v Poland. Applications no. 26691/18 and 27367/18.
Judgment of the ECtHR of 27 July 2021. Reczkowicz v Poland. Application no. 43447/19.
Judgment of the CJEU (First Chamber) of 8 November 2012. Commission v Hungary. Case 286/12 ECLI:EU:C:2012:687.
Judgment of the CJEU (Grand Chamber) of 8 April 2014. Commission v Hungary. Case C-288/12 ECLI:EU:C:2014:237.
Judgment of the CJEU (Grand Chamber) of 27 February 2018. Associacão Sindical dos Juizes Portugueses v Tribonal de Contas. Case C-64/16 ECLI:EU:C:2018:117.
Judgment of the CJEU (Grand Chamber) of 24 June 2019. Commission v Poland. Case C-618/18 ECLI:EU:C:2019:531.
Judgment of the CJEU (Grand Chamber) of 5 November 2019. Commission v Poland. Joined Cases C-192/18, C-624/18 and C-625/18 ECLI:EU:C:2019:924.
Judgment of the CJEU (Grand Chamber) of 19 November 2019. A.K. and Others v Sąd Najwyższy, CP v Sąd Najwyższy and DO v Sąd Najwyższyv. Joined Cases C-585/18 and C-563/18 ECLI:EU:C:2019:982.
Judgment of the CJEU (Grand Chamber) of 18 June 2020. Commission v Hungary. Case 78/18 ECLI:EU:C:2020:476.
Judgment of the CJEU (Grand Chamber) of 6 October 2020. Commission v Hungary. Case C-66/18 ECLI:EU:C:2020:792.
Judgment of the CJEU (Grand Chamber) of 17 December 2020. Commmission v Hungary. Case C-808/18 ECLI:EU:C:2020:1029.
Judgment of the CJEU (Grand Chamber) of 2 March 2021. A.B. and Others v Krajowa Rada Sądownictwa and Others. Case C-824/18 ECLI:EU:C:2021:153.
Judgment of the CJEU (Grand Chamber) of 20 April 2021. Repubblika v li-Prim Ministru. Case C-896/19 EU:C:2021:31.
Judgment of the CJEU (Grand Chamber) of 18 May 2021. Asociaţia 'Forumul Judecătorilor din România' and Others v Inspecţia Judiciară and Others. Joined Cases C-83/19, C-127/19, C-195/19, C-291/19, C-355/19 and C-397/19 ECLI:EU:C:2021:393.
Judgment of the CJEU (Grand Chamber) of 15 July 2021. Commission v Poland. Case C-791/19 ECLI:EU:C:2021:596.
Judgment of the CJEU (Grand Chamber) of 18 November 2021. Commission v Hungary. Case C-821/19 ECLI:EU:C:2021:930.

Newspaper Articles and Internet Publications

Bayer, L. (2021). EU power to cut funds over rule-of-law concerns is legal, top EU court adviser says. Politico.eu, 2 December.
BBC News. (2014). The many trials of Silvio Berlusconi explained, 9 May.
BBC News. (2020). Geert Wilders: Dutch far-right leader cleared of inciting hatred, 4 September.
BBC News (2021). Austrian ex-far-right leader Strache guilty of corruption, 27 August.
Brezar, A. (2020). Will Janez Janša take Slovenia down the same populist road as Hungary? Euronews, 28 October.

Brzozowski, A. (2018). 'Sad day' as Poland banned from EU judicial body. Euractiv.com, 18 September.
Brzozowski, A. (2019) France and German pile pressure on Poland and Hungary over rule of law, Euractiv.com, 10 April.
Bucik, M. (2013). Slovenia in turmoil. OpenDemocracy, 4 February. https://www.opendemocracy.net/en/slovenia-in-turmoil/
De La Baume, M. and Heath, R. (2018). Parliament denounces Hungarian illiberalism. Politico.eu, September 11.
De La Baume, M. and Herszenhorn, D.M. (2018). Orbán clashes with European Parliament critics. Politico.eu, 11 September.
Deutsche Welle. (2017). Italy's Umberto Bossi jained, Deutsche Welle, 7 October.
Deutsche Welle (2019). EU's Jean-Claude Juncker slams Viktor Orbán over Soros migrant poster, 19 Febuary.
Deutsche Welle. (2020). Germany's AfD faces heav fine for illegal campaign financing, 9 January.
Diehl, J., Müller, A.-K., Siemens, A., & Wiedmann-Schmidt, W. (2021). German officials seek to turn up the heat on the AfD. Spiegel International, 5 March.
Dimitrov, M. (2018). Borissov downplays Bulgaria's support for Hungary. Balkan Insight, 20 September.
Dimitrov, M., Vladisavljevic, A., & Luca, A.M. (2018). Hungary's Orban finds Balkan allies against censure vote. Balkan Insight, September 12.
Dunai, M. (2020). *Hungary ruling in Roma segregation case 'unfair': PM Orban*, Reuters, 15 May.
Dzhambazova, B. (2020). Riot police and protesters clash in Bulgaria as corruption crisis deepens. *Politico*, 2 September.
Eder, F. and von der Burchard, H. (2021) 'A shame': Von der Leyen vows EU will fight Hungary's anti-LBGTQ+ law, Politico.eu, 23 June.
Ejchart-Dubois, M. (2021). The jokes have ended. Verfassungsblog: On matters constitutional, verfassungsblog.de, 17 September.
Euractiv (2017). EU opens sanctions procedure against Hungary, Poland and Czech Republic over refugees. Euroactiv.com, 13 June.
Euroactiv (2020). Poland slams EU Soviet-style blackmailing on rule of law. Euractiv.com, 14 October.
Euronews (2021a). Pandora papers: Financial secrets of world leaders revealed in data leak., 15 October.
Euronews (2021b). Centre-right parties sign coalition deal to form a new Czech government., 9 November.
France24. (2019) Judge rules Berlusconi 'co-responsible' in bribery case., 5 October.
Gijs, C. (2022). Poland 'not there yet' in backtracking on judicia reforms to get EU cash. Politico.eu. 5 April.
Global Freedom of Expression (2021). Alternative für Deutschland (AfD) v Federal Office for the Protection of the Constitution of Germany. retrieved 20 February 2022.
Guardian. (2012). Jean-Marie Le Pen convicted of contesting crimes against humanity, 16 February.
Guardian. (2016). Jean-Marie Le Pen fined again for dismissing Holocaust as 'detail', 6 April.
Henley, J. (2021). Hungary: Anti-Orbán alliance leads ruling party in 2022 election poll. *Guardian*, 28 October.
Herszenhorn, D., Bayer, L., and De La Baume, M. (2021) Warsaw and Brussels wage no-win battle over rule of law, 19 October.

Hungarian Civil Libertis Union (2017). Court agrees with HCLU: Hungarian Police discriminated against Roma, 1 March, https://www.liberties.eu/en/stories/hungarian-police-discriminated-roma/11548

Hutt, D. (2021). Six takeaways from the Czech Republic's historic election. Euronews, 13 October.

Jaraczewski, J. (2021). Gazing into the abyss. Verfassungsblog: On matters constitutional. Verfassungsblog.de, 12 October.

Kosc, W. (2021). Polish regions beat a retreat on anti-LGBTQ+ resolutions. Politico.eu, 28 September.

Michalopoulos, Sarantis (2017), Orban attacks the European Court of Human Rights, Euractiv.com, 30 March.

Mortkowitz, S. (2021). Pandora papers imperil tough reelection campaign for Babis. Politico.eu, 4 October.

Politico.eu. (2018). EU court orders Marine Le Pen to repay European Parliament €300,000, 19 June.

Preussen, W. (2023). Czech presidential candidate Babiš acquitted of agri subsidies fraud charges. Politico.eu, 9 January.

Oliver, C. (2020). How Bulgaria became the EU's mafia state. Politico.eu, September 9.

Oliver, C., Burchard, H. von der, & Baume, M. de la (2020). Borissov faces showdown as EU concerns mount over Bulgaria. Politico.eu, 9 September.

Repubblica. (2019). 'Fondi Lega la Cassazione prescrive la truffa di Bossi e Belsito', 6 August

Stephens, J. (2020). Constitutional Court upholds 'Lex Babis' law on ministerial conflicts of interest. Brno Daily, 18 February.

Slovenian Times. (2015). Patria Scandal: From Plans to Equip Army to Verdicts and Retrial, 25 April.

Tamma, P. (2017). Brussels triggers unprecedented action against Poland. Euroactiv.com, 20 December.

Varga, J. (2021) Parliament and the rule of law: An elephant in a china shop, Euractiv.com, 14 June.

Wanat, Z. (2020). Polish towns pay a steep price for anti-LGBTQ+ views. Politico.eu, August 3.

Wanat, Z. (2021a). Polish region sticks with anti-LGBTQ+ resolution despite threat of losing EU cash. Politico.eu, 19 August.

Wanat, Z. (2021c) Poland's 'Russian roulette' with the EU, Politico.eu. 21 October.

Wanat, Z. (2021d) Poland hit with record €1M daily fine in EU rule-of-law dispute, Politico.eu. 27 October.

Wanat, Z. & Tamma, P. (2021). Brussels ups the ante in rule-of-law dispute with Poland'. Politico.eu, 7 September.

Yle.fi. (2012). Supreme Court orders Halla-aho to pay for hate speech, Yle.fi, 8 June

Yle.fi. (2011). Hirvisaari convicted of hate speech, yle.fi, 12 December.

Zalan, E. (2021). EU Commission tight-lipped on Hungary recovery-plan decision. EU Observer, 1 October.

Index

For the benefit of digital users, indexed terms that span two pages (e.g., 52–53) may, on occasion, appear on only one of those pages.

Action of Dissatisfied Citizens (ANO), 26t, 31f, 39f, 86t, 89–90, 113–114, 181
Adversarialism, 62, 103–104, 111, 131–132, 144, 159, 168, 171–172, 177
Alternative for Germany (AfD), 26t, 30, 31f, 75–76, 78–79f, 116–120, 183–184
Anti-populism, 14–15, 177
Article 7 Treaty on European Union, 146, 186
Austrian Freedom Party (FPÖ), 26t, 31f, 85, 86t, 89–91, 95–96, 117–118, 123, 146, 155

Checks and balances, 58–59, 100–103, 108, 112–115, 124–125
Citizens for European Development of Bulgaria (GERB), 26t, 30, 31f, 39f, 39–40, 86t, 90, 160–161, 181
Coalition of the Radical Left (SYRIZA), 26t, 31f, 39f, 177–179
Coercive Confrontation, 56, 144, 159, 168, 171–172, 177
Cooperation, 28–29, 26t, 61, 71–72, 74, 75–76, 85, 97
Cooptation, 61, 70–71, 74, 75–76, 82, 96–97
Counter discourses (sovereignty and populist), 158–159, 176–177, 190–192
Court of Justice of the European Union (CJEU), 113, 115, 124
Curbing anti-democratic and illiberal policies, 199, 208f

Danish People's Party (DF), 26t, 31f, 76–77, 85, 86t, 89–91, 95
Democratic backsliding, 16–17, 35, 46, 103, 147–149, 169, 174, 176–177, 186
Democratic Defence, 2, 7–8, 45–46, 55
  Grievance Model, 8–10
  Normal Politics Model, 10
Direction – Social Democracy (SMER), 26t, 31f, 83–84, 90, 161, 180–181

Disruption, 144–146, 159

Effectiveness, definition, 19f, 196, 207, 208f
Enforcement, 100, 108
European Commission, 125–127, 147–148, 154, 186
European Court of Human Rights, 102, 124
European Parliament, 187–188, 190–191
European Union, 138–141, 172–173, 175

Fidesz (Hungarian Civic Alliance), 7–8, 26t, 30, 31f, 39f, 39–40, 84, 86t, 90, 114, 115, 124, 125–126, 128–134, 147–152, 155–159, 162, 175–176, 186
Finns Party (PS), 26t, 31f, 86t, 91, 95–96, 117–118, 183
Five Star Movement, 26t, 31f, 39f, 86t, 91–92, 95, 113
Flemish Interest (VB), 78–80, 79f, 83–84, 117–118, 123, 184–185
Forbearance, 60
Forward Italy (FI), 26t, 30, 31f, 39f, 86t, 90, 114–115, 117–118, 124
Framing, 166–170

(In)tolerance, 13–14, 49

Judicial controls, 59, 100–104, 108, 115–119, 125–127

Law and Justice (PiS), 7–8, 26t, 30, 31f, 39f, 39–40, 83–84, 86t, 90, 113, 114, 125, 126, 128–132, 134, 147–154, 157–159, 162, 175–176, 181–182, 186
League, 26t, 31f, 86t, 89–91, 95, 113–115, 117–118, 122–123, 177–178, 184–185
Leverage, 17, 138, 173

Militant democracy, 5–8, 44–46, 49–50, 53–54
Moderation, 14–15, 72, 80, 84, 92–95, 93t, 94t, 107, 118–124, 142–144, 156–157, 171, 185–186, 203, 208f

Movement for Better Hungary (Jobbik), 26t, 31f, 84, 117, 120, 156–157

National Rally (formerly National Front), 26t, 31f, 78–79f, 84–85, 121–122, 133–134, 184–185
Norwegian Progress Party, 26t, 95

Office for the Protection of the Constitution (BfV) (Germany), 116–117, 119–120
Oppositional Politics, 62–104, 112–115
Ordinarly legal controls and pedagogy, 58
Ostracism, 55, 70–71, 74, 75–76, 92–97

Podemos, 26t, 31f, 86t, 95–96, 177–179
Political conditionaliy, 140–142, 146
Party for Freedom (PVV), 26t, 30, 31f, 76–77, 86t, 117–118, 120–121, 133–134, 179–180
Populism
  Definitions, 1–3, 21, 22
  and democracy, 1–2, 12–13, 15, 21–22, 32, 39f, 39–40
  Explanations, 8–9
  Extremism, 6–7, 46
  and illiberalism, 34
Public and political persuasion, 17–18, 59–60, 62, 168, 171–172, 176, 177, 186
Public opinion, 168–169

Radicalization, 15, 72, 80, 84, 92–95, 93t, 94t, 107, 171–172, 206

Repression, 100–101, 104
Resources, 14–15, 75, 85, 95–96, 104, 105, 111, 116, 118–124, 127, 158, 171–172, 175–176, 179–180, 183–185, 202, 205, 208f
Rights-restrictions, 53, 100–104, 115–117, 140–144, 146
Rule of law budget conditionality in the EU, 146
Rule of Law Framework, 186–187

Sanctions, 140–142, 146
Shaming, 17–18, 172, 186
Slovenian Democratic Party (SDD), 26t, 31f, 39f, 112–113, 117–118, 122, 159–160
Strategic choice, 16
Stigmatization, 17–18, 170–172, 183–186
Sweden Democrats, 26t, 31f, 78–79, 81t, 185–186
Swiss People's Party (SVP), 26t, 31f, 86, 90–91, 95–96

United Kingdom Independence Party (UKIP), 83–84

Votes for populist parties, 14–15, 25–29, 26t, 70, 75–76, 82–84, 86t, 89–92, 104–108, 111–113, 118–124, 127, 142–144, 154–155, 159, 168–172, 175–177, 179–181, 183–185, 200, 204, 208f
Vox, 26t, 31f